Cambridge Studies in Management

12

Safety at work: the limits of self-regulation

Cambridge Studies in Management

Formerly Management and Industrial Relations series

Editors

WILLIAM BROWN, *University of Cambridge*
ANTHONY HOPWOOD, *London School of Economics*
and PAUL WILLMAN, *London Business School*

The series focuses on the human and organisational aspects of management. It covers the areas of organisation theory and behaviour, strategy and business policy, the organisational and social aspects of accounting, personnel and human resource management, industrial relations and industrial sociology.

The series aims for high standards of scholarship and seeks to publish the best among original theoretical and empirical research; innovative contributions to advancing understanding in the area; books which synthesize and/or review the best of current research, and aim to make the work published in specialist journals more widely accessible; and texts for upper-level undergraduates, for graduates and for vocational courses such as MBA programmes. Edited collections may be accepted where they maintain a high and consistent standard and are on a coherent, clearly defined, and relevant theme.

The books are intended for an international audience among specialists in universities and business schools, undergraduate, graduate and MBA students, and also for a wider readership among business practitioners and trade unionists.

Safety at work:
the limits of
self-regulation

SANDRA DAWSON

PAUL WILLMAN

ALAN CLINTON

MARTIN BAMFORD

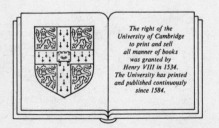

The right of the
University of Cambridge
to print and sell
all manner of books
was granted by
Henry VIII in 1534.
The University has printed
and published continuously
since 1584.

CAMBRIDGE UNIVERSITY PRESS

Cambridge
New York   New Rochelle   Melbourne   Sydney

Published by the Press Syndicate of the University of Cambridge
The Pitt Building, Trumpington Street, Cambridge CB2 1RP
32 East 57th Street, New York, NY 10022, USA
10 Stamford Road, Oakleigh, Melbourne 3166, Australia

First published 1988

Printed in Great Britain at the University Press, Cambridge

British Library cataloguing in publication data
Safety at work: the limits of self-regulation.
1. Great Britain. Industrial health and
industrial safety. Law. Health and safety
at work etc. Act 1974 – Critical studies
I. Dawson, Sandra
344.104′465

Library of Congress cataloguing in publication data
Dawson, Sandra
Safety at work: the limits of self-regulation / Sandra Dawson ...
[et al.].
p.   cm. – (Cambridge studies in management)
Bibliography.
ISBN 0–521–35497–8
1. Industrial safety – Great Britain.   I. Title.   II. Series.
HD7262.5.G7D38 1988
363.1′1′0941 – dc19   88-9573

ISBN 0 521 35497 8

Contents

Contents

Contents

Figures

Tables

List of tables

List of tables

Abbreviations

APAU	Accident Prevention Advisory Unit
ACAS	Advisory Conciliation and Arbitration Service
ASTMS	Association of Scientific Technical & Managerial Staffs
AUEW	Amalgamated Union of Engineering Workers
BFU	Bakers, Food & Allied Workers Union
CBI	Confederation of British Industry
CIA	Chemical Industries Association
CIMAH	Control of Industrial Major Accident Hazards (Regulations) 1984
CISHEC	Chemical Industry Safety & Health Council
COIT	Central Office of Industrial Tribunals
CONIAC	Construction Industry Advisory Committee
COSHH	Control of Substances Hazardous to Health (Regulations)
CSO	Central Statistical Office
DE	Department of Employment
DHSS	Department of Health and Social Security
DLO	Direct Labour Organisation
EAT	Employment Appeal Tribunal
EETPU	Electrical, Electronic, Telecommunication and Plumbing Union
EHO	Environmental Health Officer
EPA	Employment Protection Act, 1975
EP(C)A	Employment Protection (Consolidation) Act, 1978
FCG	Field Consultant Groups (HSE)
FTAT	Furniture, Timber and Allied Trades Union
GMBATU	General, Municipal, Boilermakers and Allied Trade Union
HASAWA	Health and Safety at Work etc. Act 1974
HELA	Health and Safety Executive Liaison with Local Authorities

List of abbreviations

HMFI	Her Majesty's Factory Inspectorate
HSC	Health and Safety Commission
HSE	Health and Safety Executive
HSIB	Health and Safety Information Bulletin
IAC	Industry Advisory Committee
ILO	International Labour Organisation
IPCS	Institute of Professional Civil Servants
IRLR	Industrial Relations Law Report
LTA	Lost Time Accident
MLH	Minimum List Heading
MSC	Manpower Services Commission
NADOR	Notification of Accidents and Dangerous Occurrences Regulations, 1980
NALGO	National and Local Government Officers Association
NCB	National Coal Board
NEDC	National Economic Development Council
NIG	National Industry Group of HSE
NII	Nuclear Installations Inspectorate
NJAC	National Joint Advisory Committee on Health & Safety in the Chemical Industry
OEL	Occupational Exposure Limits
OSHA	Occupational Safety and Health Administration (in USA)
OSRPA	Offices, Shops and Railway Premises Act, 1956
PPITB	Printing and Publishing Industrial Training Board
PSI	Policy Studies Institute
RIDDOR	Reporting of Injuries, Diseases and Dangerous Occurrences Regulations, 1985
SAC	Subject Advisory Committee
SIC	Standard Industrial Classification
SRC/SERC	Science Research Council, renamed Science and Engineering Research Council
SRSCR	Safety Representatives and Safety Committees Regulations, 1977
SSRC/ESRC	Social Science Research Council, renamed Economic and Social Research Council
TGWU	Transport and General Workers' Union
TUC	Trades Union Congress
TULRA	Trade Union and Labour Relations Act, 1974
TLV	Threshold Limit Value
UCATT	Union of Construction, Allied Trades and Technicians
USDAW	Union of Shop, Distributive and Allied Workers

Acknowledgements

Research into health and safety at work at Imperial College was initiated with considerable help from Professor Dorothy Wedderburn who has retained an interest in our work. The research was supported by two grants: the first from the Joint Committee of the SERC and ESRC, the second from the ESRC. The authors would like to thank the Research Councils for their support and everyone involved in the chemical, construction and retail industries who gave so generously of their time and interest to the study. Employees of the HSE have also been very helpful at various stages of the research. We would particularly like to thank Dr Adrian Cohen at the HSE for his interest in our work and his colleagues for their help in correcting factual inaccuracies and providing statistical information. We also met with members of the Centre for Sociolegal Studies at Wolfson College, Oxford, on several occasions to discuss our mutual interests in the regulation of safety at work.

The authors would like to acknowledge the contributions of David Stevens and Philip Poynter to the work which is reported in Chapters 4 and 7. They are also grateful for the advice and comments on the first draft of the manuscript which they received from employees of the Health and Safety Executive, David Gee and Professors W. Brown, R. Hepple and R. Martin. The responsibility for the text, notwithstanding these helpful contributions, lies, of course, entirely with the authors.

Several kind and long suffering people working at Imperial College have helped in the typing and processing of the text. We are grateful to them all, and especially to Patricia Burge who took the book from one revision to another without complaint.

SANDRA DAWSON, PAUL WILLMAN

Preface

The purpose of this book is to examine the nature and effect of one of the major pieces of social legislation of recent decades – the Health and Safety at Work Act of 1974. It aims to place the Act against the background of the various discussions that brought it about, notably the *Report on Safety and Health at Work* produced in 1972 by a committee chaired by Lord Robens, and the general political and legislative context of the time. It examines the committee's ideas of self regulation and workforce involvement which were so influential in the drafting of the 1974 Act and the associated Safety Representatives and Safety Committee Regulations (1977), and discusses their development and viability in the context of the later 1970s and 1980s.

The Act was intended to be a radical departure from previous efforts to reduce the incidence of death, injury and disease arising from employment. It sought to prevent accidents and to consolidate a diversified set of laws and enforcement methods through the development of general powers and duties. Instead of simply punishing employers or workers who did not observe external rules, its aim was to encourage improved safety standards by stimulating the development of mechanisms for the self regulation of safety within minimum statutory requirements. The principal responsibility for safety, and the legal obligation, was firmly placed upon employers, employees, suppliers and other people involved in the supply of goods and services through work.

The legislation has now been in operation for over a decade. Although it has not been immune to criticism, this particular piece of legislation, unlike many other statutes on labour law passed during the 1970s, has not been a major subject for party political debate and it has not changed with each change of government. There is thus the opportunity to study the impact of a relatively stable framework of safety law across an economically and politically turbulent period. Even though the changes created by the legislation were less fundamental than was sometimes promised, and had particular internal contradictions which reflected the history of the period in which they were introduced, they undoubtedly had a significant impact.

In the six years following the 1974 Act, fewer people were killed and injured at work, both in absolute terms and relative to workforce size, industrial activity and other measures. This improvement can to a great extent be attributed to the Act and to all the associated regulations, discussions, and institutions at every level that followed it. However there is strong evidence that this trend did not continue past 1981. More people were being killed or seriously injured in the manufacturing and construction industries by the middle of the 1980s than at the beginning of the decade. The toll of serious injury seems to be getting worse in both relative and absolute terms.

Some of these developments can be attributed to economic recession or to changes in industrial structure. Even so, they make it necessary to reconsider the principles established over a decade ago to see whether they still work in the political and legal atmosphere of the late 1980s. Past improvements are not being sustained, and this must merit the careful consideration of anyone concerned to make workplaces as safe and healthy as possible. This concern is the centrepiece of the research reported in this volume.

Research in industrial safety began in Imperial College in 1979 when Sandra Dawson, David Stevens and Philip Poynter, supported by funds from the Joint Committee of the (then) SSRC and SRC, conducted a study of the development and operation of health and safety policies and practices in the chemical industry. This work led to the development of a model of how to construct and manage an effective health and safety programme and, of equal importance, to an understanding of some of the reasons why such a programme was often not achieved in practice. The findings of this earlier research are summarised in Chapter 4 and its contribution to the model of effective self regulation is covered in Chapter 7. The second research group, consisting of the authors of this book, carried out its research between 1982 and 1985, funded by the Monitoring of Labour Legislation Panel of the (then) SSRC. The panel was particularly concerned that the research should focus on the effects both of the 1974 Act and 1977 Safety Representatives and Safety Committee Regulations and should pay due regard to the experience of small and weakly unionised establishments. In this way it complemented the earlier work which was biased towards larger enterprises and those with fairly strong union presence. An additional concern of the second project was to take account of the impact of changing economic circumstances, particularly recession, on safety provision.

This book reports on the findings of these research projects. It is divided into three main parts. The first part is concerned with the development of

Preface

the legislation itself, with available methods for assessing its impact and with the trends which can be deduced from nationally available data. Chapter 1, on the legislation, examines the context of the legislation in terms of previous attempts to safeguard health and safety at work as well as the more general context of labour law. It shows how the legislation aimed to encapsulate the principles of self regulation in a set of general legal rules and new institutions. The need for agreement between employers and workers was accepted on all sides, but there was dispute about workforce representation solely through trade unions. This was the issue which at the time caused the greatest controversy. Our researches indicate, however, that, as it turned out, this matter eventually assumed a lesser significance.

Chapter 2 deals with accident statistics. It discusses the difficulties of their use because of changes and ambiguities in their collection and the definition of categories. These difficulties mean that one must be cautious in drawing conclusions on trends. However, the figures on the incidence of the combined rate for major and fatal accidents in construction and manufacturing leave little doubt that whilst the period immediately surrounding and following the passing of the Act coincided with a downward trend in the numbers of people being killed and injured at work, the period since 1980 has been associated with a rising trend of serious injury at work. The incidence of major and fatal accidents combined in manufacturing has increased by some 31 % in the period 1980–85, and that for construction over the same period by 45 %.

Chapter 3 deals with a second indicator of the impact of the legislation: the development of local institutions which were either formally established or else implied by the HASAWA and the SRSCR. It examines the findings of other research and deals in general with the response to requirements for written safety policies and arrangements for workforce improvement. It looks at the formal mechanisms which have developed since the Act, in terms of safety policies, safety specialists, safety representatives and safety committees. None of these institutions have, it seems, necessarily worked in quite the ways envisaged by those who set them up in 1974.

The second part of the book focuses on the findings of the Imperial College research on developments in three selected industries with particular emphasis on changes at the level of the firm and establishment. Chapter 4 deals with chemicals, Chapter 5 with construction and Chapter 6 with retail. In each chapter the development and industrial structure of each sector is discussed. This is followed by an examination of case studies of enterprises and establishments in order to examine the response to legislative requirements in terms of policies, organisation, arrangements and activities. The earlier study of developments in the chemical and related industries was biased towards larger establishments with strong trade union presence. The findings indicate that safety policies do not in themselves determine management practice – or even safety standards. Problems from the point of view of safety specialists are identified and it is shown that in practice it is not easy to separate negotiation about industrial relations matters from safety issues. Generally speaking, standards improved in the chemicals industry following the 1974 Act and the horrifying disaster at Flixborough at the same time. For reasons set out in the chapter, it is possible to see why such improvements may not have been sustained.

In the later studies of construction and retail, the research team was mindful of the concerns of the Monitoring Labour Legislation Panel outlined above, and thus covered high risk and low risk industrial sectors, each with a high proportion of small and weakly unionised establishments. The study of the safety conditions and practices in the building industry was undertaken at a time when the Site Safe 83 campaign was intended to bring about safety improvements but manifestly failed to do so. This chapter attempts to explain the failure, discussing the particular problems of management control associated with an expansion of subcontracting, and a significant increase in the proportion of construction work undertaken by very small firms and the self-employed. Given these trends, it is hardly surprising that little or nothing of the employee involvement envisaged in the 1970s was found and there was a good deal of evidence of poor safety practice typified perhaps by the refusal to wear hard hats even when it appeared essential to do so.

In the less hazardous retail shops we found fewer problems in terms of management control but much less awareness of any of the safety problems which nevertheless exist. There was some franchising in parts of the retail trade, but generally speaking, there was a trend to more centralised and clear cut management structures. This was reflected in the safety policies and clear lines of responsibility in some of the larger retail chains. However, the researchers found unsafe practices, particularly where management responsibilities were not made clear. There were some safety specialists whose role was often obscure and very few safety representatives and safety committees of the sort envisaged in the legislation of the mid 1970s.

The research also revealed differences in the manner and impact of external inspection and enforcement. Unlike chemicals and construction which fall within the purview of the Factory Inspectorate, retail outlets are subject to safety inspection and enforcement from Environmental Health Officers employed by local authorities, who carry out these responsibilities alongside their duties in respect of public health and hygiene. As a result, they tend to be somewhat more visible to employees, managers and senior executives.

Preface

Chapter 7 brings together the findings of the case studies and sets out some conclusions on the major constituents of effective self regulation at local level. It shows that effective self regulation requires people at work to be actively involved in the identification of hazards, the prescription and implementation of controls which will, at a minimum, meet statutory requirements, and the (often neglected) maintenance and monitoring of standards and activities. Three elements are shown to be crucial: knowledge, capacity and motivation. The important contributions of safety specialists and workforce representatives are discussed but above all the role and accomplishments of senior executives and line managers in matters of health and safety are identified as crucial. The discussion leads to the identification of conditions associated with small firm size, subcontracting, part-time and temporary employment and low levels of union membership which *prima facie* limit the extent to which one can reasonably presume that self regulation at local level will flourish.

The third part of the book focuses on developments at the national level. The Robens Committee of Inquiry had sought evidence both from employers and trade unions as well as from government. This spirit of tripartism became embodied in the Health and Safety Commission and its Advisory Committees which have representatives from employers, trade unions and government. Given that tripartism has tended to weaken in other areas, the response of such bodies to changing economic and political circumstances is seen to be of particular interest. These developments are the subject matter for Chapter 8. It discusses the functioning of the Health and Safety Commission, described by one commentator as 'the most corporatist body in Britain', with its role in providing a framework for the regulations that underpin safe working practice. It discusses the development of Joint Industrial Committees, with particular reference to a body covering the construction industry. At national level, both the CBI and TUC have remained relatively content with the organisation and achievements of the HSC although concern has been expressed about the length of time taken to produce regulations and codes of practice, proposals to use cost-benefit analysis as a basis for policy development, and the depletion of resources available to the HSC and HSE. The chapter concludes with a discussion of recent trends in HSC policy and their likely impact on local developments.

Analysis at national level is continued in Chapter 9 with a discussion of inspection and enforcement. Particular emphasis is given to the Factory Inspectorate who have responsibility for chemicals and construction and to Environmental Health Officers in local authorities who have responsibility for enforcing and inspecting workplace health and safety in retail. Self regulation implies external enforcement as a last resort. Nonetheless, the

Preface

advisory activities of the inspectorates as well as their enforcement practices remain important influences on the development of self regulatory institutions at industrial and workplace levels. Consideration is given to the evolution of the Factory Inspectorate and to the long held view that Inspectors should be educators who only use sanctions to a limited extent. A contrast is drawn with the rather different tradition of the Environmental Health Officers. The chapter discusses the establishment of the Health and Safety Executive following the 1974 Act, and efforts which have been made to centralise and standardise enforcement procedures. The activities of the Inspectors under the 1974 Act are noted, together with changes in their procedures during the 1980s, and significant reductions in their numbers. The concluding section of this chapter discusses the implications of different views about regulation and compliance for activities concerned with health and safety at work.

This outline of the book indicates an emphasis on some areas at the expense of others. We have been concerned almost exclusively with safety rather than with occupational health. Available evidence however suggests that the scale of the problem of death and serious incapacity arising from occupational disease is far greater than that resulting from accidents at work. For example, the HSC provisionally reported 889 deaths from prescribed industrial diseases in 1983, compared with 443 fatal accidents in the manufacturing services and construction industries for the same year. Evidence from Fox and Adelstein (1978) and from papers prepared by the GMBATU as part of the consultation process in the development of the COSHH regulations suggest that this is an underestimate and that there may be as many as 8000 deaths a year attributable to occupational disease (GMBATU, 1987: 5, 53). In the context of these figures this book, with its focus on the incidence and prevention of accidents at work, is only concerned with a fraction of the problem. Nonetheless, we consider that much of the more general discussion of self regulation and our conclusions and recommendations have relevance across the board of workplace safety and health.

Our approach has been partial in other respects. We have taken the legislation as our starting point and even here we have largely ignored individual responses to legislation in favour of a discussion of institutions. Finally, most of our empirical material implies a bias towards more recent events: in studying the construction and retail industries we have sought less to reconstruct the safety history of the period since 1974 than to describe how events stood at the end of it. Our justification for this is not simply methodological; as subsequent chapters will show, we argue that recent events pose severe problems for the operation of safety legislation which have policy implications.

These issues and problems are the subject of the concluding Chapter 10, which deals directly with the implications of our research for identifying the limits of self regulation. We seek to explain how the legislative changes of the 1980s, though leaving the 1974 Act and its associated institutions intact, have nevertheless altered the atmosphere in which it is enforced. The limited role of specialists, the lack of workforce involvement, the poor safety record in the small firms sector, all of these phenomena discovered during our researches, are part of the changed climate of the 1980s. Our argument is that these changes are associated with the increase in the combined rate of serious accidents and deaths since 1981.

The book concludes by asserting that it is necessary to look again at the efficacy of self regulation since its limitations are becoming clear. After a period in the mid to late 1970s in which the UK performance in health and safety at work improved, there is now in the mid to late 1980s strong evidence that employees in manufacturing or construction are more likely to be killed or seriously injured at work. In the spirit of advocating a new look at self regulation and enforcement policies, we conclude by putting forward a number of policy recommendations with a view to reviving discussions about how once again to reduce accidents and to improve safety and health at work.

PART 1

The legislation: background and impact

Chapter 1 discusses the details of the 1974 Health and Safety at Work Act and the 1977 Safety Representatives and Safety Committee Regulations. They are considered in the context created by developments in labour law during the 1960s and previous attempts to use legislation as a basis for reducing the toll of death and serious injury at work. Consideration is then given to assessing the impact of this legislation. Two sets of indicators are discussed. The first, trends in accident statistics, is the subject of Chapter 2. The second, the growth of local institutions in terms of safety policies, management organisation, specialists, safety representatives and safety committees, is the focus for Chapter 3. The discussion in each of these chapters urges caution in reaching conclusions about the impact of the 1974 Act and 1977 SRSCR. Nonetheless, however cautious a commentary, one is led to the conclusion that whereas the legislation was associated with significant positive developments until the turn of the decade in 1980, the period from 1981 until 1985 (the most recent figures available to the authors) is characterised by what, in terms of trends in some indicators, is a 'levelling off' and what, in terms of trends in others, is an actual reversal. It appears that health and safety provision for some employees is getting significantly worse once again.

1

The development of health and safety legislation

The 1974 Health and Safety at Work Act introduced a number of important changes. It sought to provide for the health and safety of all workers through the standard of 'reasonable practicability'. This principle was to overlay the many specific statutes and regulations which had provided inconsistent and in some cases non-existent provisions for the health, safety and welfare of the working population. The Act set out a number of general duties for employers, employees and suppliers with the aim of reducing risk and preventing accidents. This has been contrasted with the emphasis often implicit in previous legislation on providing compensation according to the measure of injury (Rideout 1979: 337). The 1974 Act also sought to reform the organisation and practice of external enforcement by securing greater unity between various sorts of inspectors and the extension of their powers.[1]

The most remarkable innovation was the attempt to use statute as a basis for fostering a particular attitude to the improvement of safety at work. This attitude is often described as the 'Robens philosophy', taking its name from the Chairman of the Committee of Inquiry on Safety and Health at Work, which reported in 1972. The philosophy rested upon two assumptions. First, that the function of health and safety law was to provide a regulatory framework within which those in industry could themselves undertake responsibility for safety at work. This is the doctrine of *self regulation*. The second, to some extent a corollary, was that there should be means for *workforce involvement* in health and safety; that is, safety should be the responsibility not only of employers and senior management, but also of employees who themselves experienced risks at work. Together, these principles ensured that the success of the Act would depend in part on the reactions of employers and employees in individual firms and establishments. It is therefore necessary to consider the Act and the subsequent Safety Representatives and Safety Committees Regulations

3

in the context both of industrial organisations (as we do in subsequent chapters) and of developments in labour law, to which we now turn.

The context of labour law

The HASAWA, innovative as it was, was debated and ultimately enacted within a changing legislative background. Although the Robens approach to self regulation was based to some extent on the assumption that the community of interest existing over safety issues would insulate safety legislation from changes in the mainstream of labour law, in practice the content of the statute was influenced by wider developments.

Until the 1960s, the lack of regulatory labour legislation in Britain was seen primarily as a tribute to the voluntarist tradition or, more precisely, as a preference for collective bargaining over legal enactment. There was of course a considerable volume of statute law covering certain aspects of employment. Parliament had, for example, demonstrated a persistent, if sporadic, legislative interest in matters concerning the payment of wages and industrial safety, but protection by statute was limited in both scope and application. Minimum wage legislation was designed to protect those workers not covered by collective bargaining arrangements, occupational safety statutes were aimed at remedying a single ascertained evil, and even the protections offered by the Truck Acts were not extended to non-manual workers. Moreover, in areas where the impact was more general, the rights granted were either negative, in terms of freedom from a particular practice, or in the form of duties placed upon the employer (Wedderburn 1971: 143–78). In the 1950s then the law sought to support a system of 'collectivist laissez faire' (Kahn-Freund 1959: 224) characterised by a reliance on voluntary mechanisms and the abstention of the law from detailed regulation.

From the 1960s however, governments concerned with the performance of the economy had been increasingly concerned to legislate in the area. As Clark and Wedderburn put it:

> the combination of low or even negative growth rates, the erosion of Britain's manufacturing base, and the steady increase in unemployment, has led governments to intervene in areas which they have traditionally [outside wartime] left largely to self regulation. The increasing politicization of industrial relations may be seen as an almost direct consequence of these social and economic changes.
>
> In this context it is not surprising that much of labour law has also changed (1983: 129).

4

These changes involved not only the different priorities of Labour and Conservative governments, but also the interaction of parliamentary statute and judicial decision, particularly in defining the lawful ambit of industrial conflict (Wedderburn 1980). Following Lewis (1983) and Clark and Wedderburn (1983) four phases can be distinguished. The first, in the late 1960s, saw the Labour government reject any voluntary solution to the perceived problem of 'disorderly' industrial relations, and, in the document *In Place of Strife* (1969) propose legislation to outlaw unofficial strikes. The second phase, which followed the failure of this approach, saw the Conservative government seek to impose a new framework with the 1971 Industrial Relations Act in which the law was to be the major instrument of industrial relations reform. The Act made collective agreements legally enforceable, introduced a set of civil liabilities known as 'unfair industrial practices' and created an enforcing body, the National Industrial Relations Court.

The third phase, which again followed a policy failure and the downfall of the government which proposed it, became known as the Social Contract. The incoming Labour government repealed the 1971 Act, restored the traditional immunities for strike action, and, in passing the 1975 Employment Protection Act, 'reshaped the institutional framework of collective labour law' (Lewis 1983: 373). New collective and individual rights, and 'intermediate' rights to individuals as union members were complemented by new institutions such as the Advisory, Conciliation and Arbitration Service, and the Central Arbitration Committee. Together with statutes on sex and race discrimination, the 1975 Act provided new rights for employees and a more solid foundation for union organisation.

Once more, this legislative package failed to outlive the government which installed it and, since 1979, successive Conservative governments have created a fourth phase. Restrictions on the immunity for strike action have been introduced, individual employment rights reduced and trade union structure and government reformed through a series of statutory requirements. Clark and Wedderburn argue that the beliefs behind this fourth phase are that:

> trade unions are a distortion of the market relation between
> employer and employee, and trade union aspirations to
> regulate jobs and labour markets, even by way of joint
> regulation, are incompatible with individual liberty (1983: 135).

Davies and Freedland go further, seeing the legislative changes as part of a wider commitment to market regulation, and the removal of obstacles to free market operation (1983: 17–19).

Discussion of the HASAW Act began in the first phase, the Act itself was formulated in the second and passed in the third. The Safety Representatives and Safety Committee Regulations were both formulated and passed in the third phase. The combination of the Act and SRSCR currently operates in the fourth. Throughout these changes, health and safety legislation has been part of, rather than insulated from, the currents of legislative change. In order to understand this, we must look more closely at the expanding body of labour legislation since the 1960s which prompted one writer to speak of the 'ever increasing legal regulation of industrial relations in the 1970's' (Lewis 1976: 15).

The nature of the expansion itself can be understood by utilising Kahn-Freund's (1972) distinction between the auxiliary, regulatory and restrictive functions of the law. The auxiliary function supports the autonomous system of collective bargaining by providing norms and sanctions to stimulate the bargaining process itself and provides for the encouragement and extension of trade union activity and collective bargaining. The regulatory function introduces statutory minimum terms or procedures into employment contracts, primarily to protect the employee. The restrictive function provides the rules of the game, the Queensberry rules of what is allowed and what is forbidden in the conduct of industrial hostilities; in short, they restrict the lawful ambit of industrial conflict.

On the basis of this distinction, it is evident that the volume of regulatory legislation began to expand in the 1960s and that of auxiliary legislation rather later, from 1974. The 1970s also saw the growth of a hybrid type of 'intermediate' right (Wedderburn 1980) which attached to individuals in employment by reason of trade union membership.

A new approach in the use and scope of regulatory legislation was evident in the 1963 Contracts of Employment Act and the 1965 Redundancy Payments Act. This legislation established a series of generalised positive rights and, for the first time, used

> the law as an instrument for creating standards to be observed
> by employers and workers individually and for increasing
> individual rights and obligations (Kahn-Freund 1972: 49).

This period of regulatory reform continued in the establishment of remedies for unfair dismissal, maternity rights, rights to guaranteed payments, rights to freedom from sexual and racial discrimination, and to pensions. Wedderburn (1980: 84) has noted that this legislation acknowledged, 'in its structure, the primacy of voluntary collective bargaining'. Thus, collectively agreed terms or procedures supplant statutory rights both in the eyes of the 'appropriate Minister' (EP(C)A s18) or of the Secretary of State in the case of dismissal (EP(C)A s65). Collective bargaining may always improve upon statutory rights. Moreover, while

> in other countries a similar expansion of employment
> protection rights often consolidates a set of norms already
> achieved by collective bargaining, in Britain it has largely been
> introduced to reach the parts of the system which voluntary
> bargaining could not effectively reach (Wedderburn 1980: 83).

This expressed the intuitive understanding of the operation of labour law current amongst practitioners. Moreover, the operation of the law relating to unfair dismissal suggests support for the need to expand employment protection through legislation. In 1976, 35% of tribunal respondents had a labour force of less than 50. Weakly organised industries were highly represented: 16.6% of applications were from distributive trades, 16.0% from miscellaneous services and 13.9% from construction (Department of Employment *Gazette* 1977: 214–15). Moreover, evidence from the same period implies that the probability of dismissal in small firms was even higher than this bias would imply. Daniel and Stilgoe (1978: 82) discovered a higher incidence of dismissal in smaller plants, together with a lower probability that the dismissal would result in a complaint. The success of the provisions in generating protection or redress may have been limited. Such small firms are less likely to be unionised (Bain and Elsheikh 1980) and in fact the percentage of applicants represented by trade unions has remained low and stable for several years: in 1979, 15.7% were so represented at conciliation stage and 14.6% at tribunals (Hawes and Smith 1981). Dickens *et al.* summarise the position:

> The characteristics of industrial tribunal applicants are thus
> determined by the differential likelihood of dismissal, the
> differential eligibility of dismissed workers according to the
> legal provisions and by a certain amount of self selection. The
> typical tribunal applicant, as revealed by our survey, is a male,
> manual worker, not in membership of a union, who has been
> dismissed after relatively short service by a small employer in
> the private sector (1985: 35).

The most rapid expansion of the 'floor of rights' in 1974 and 1975 coincided with the beginning of auxiliary legislation designed to assist collective bargaining. Such measures had in the past been limited to supplementing collective bargaining where its effect was weak. As far back as 1909 the Trade Boards Act had established a system of institutions designed to secure a legally enforceable minimum wage in certain industries. Later regulation of such bodies was established by the Wages Council Acts of 1959 and 1979. Under the latter statute, some three

7

million workers were covered by about 40 wages councils. Subsequently, the scope and operation of the wages council system has been altered.[2] Another means of limited intervention in working conditions was in the form of the Fair Wages Clause passed by the House of Commons in 1894, and on a number of occasions subsequently. The efforts to enforce trade union standards were widespread in public authorities but spasmodic in effect until their major modifications by the Conservative government in 1983. Such legislation never extended in any case to a legal right to bargain or a right to organise.

These limits were transcended with the passing of the Employment Protection Act (EPA) in 1975 and the consolidation of most of its provisions in the Employment Protection (Consolidation) Act (EP(C)A) in 1978. The EPA put the Advisory Conciliation and Arbitration Service on a statutory footing (s1). The recognition procedure (EPA ss11–16) and schedule 11 of the Act were designed to assist weakly organised unions to achieve negotiating rights and to 'mop up' pockets of low pay. Moreover, the disclosure provisions (EPA ss17–21) could be used by unions in weak positions 'impeded' from bargaining by lack of information (Gospel and Willman 1981).

The same statute developed a set of what Wedderburn (1980) has called 'intermediate individual rights' or rights which were contingent on trade union membership. These included rights to be free from the threat of dismissal or other disciplinary action by reason of trade union membership and rights to time off for trade union activity (EPA ss53, 57–8). This followed the removal of certain restrictions on the right to take collective action and the provision of certain auxiliary resources for trade unions (Trade Union and Labour Relations Act (TULRA) 1974, and Amendment 1976; EPA ss11–16, 17–21, sch 11). These rights generally related directly to trade union activity (EPA ss53–62), but in some other cases, for example advance notification of redundancy (EPA s99), recognised unions acquired the right to consult on behalf of those for whom they were recognised.

Although intermediate rights were individual in their operation, they were essentially collective in their origins, apparently encouraging and legitimising the spread of collective organisation. As such, their enactment blurred the distinction between individual and collective labour law (Lewis 1979) and, in Clark and Wedderburn's view, may have hastened a move away from voluntarism (1983: 188). Their development was a major innovation, and represented the 'construction of a collective right to associate out of the bricks of a set of individual employment rights' (Wedderburn 1976). In short, then, whereas the period before the Social Contract was characterised by an expansion of the general floor of rights, the Social Contract period itself from 1974 to 1979 involved the extension of rights to employees, to employees as members of trade unions and to trade unions as bargaining agents.

This legislative background is of particular relevance to the legislation on health and safety at work. The 1974 Act and the 1977 SRSCR in fact combine regulatory law and intermediate rights. In order to understand how this came about, and the consequences for the operation of safety legislation, it is necessary to review the progress of safety legislation during the last two decades.

The origins of the 1974 Act

Throughout the 1960s, there emerged in the face of a rising industrial accident rate and rapid changes in industrial processes and materials, a widespread demand for a new legislative initiative in the area of health and safety at work. Despite gradual extensions in the coverage of protective provisions throughout the nineteenth and twentieth centuries, safety legislation remained firmly rooted in what Hepple (1983: 405–8) has termed the 'Factories Acts Model'.

This model was characterised by its fragmentation and by the absence of workforce involvement. Fragmentation was rooted in the gradual extension of regulatory coverage through a struggle between employers and proponents of laissez-faire on the one hand and trade unions and reform groups on the other, conducted both inside and outside parliament. The tendency was for the passage of Acts involving detailed regulation of specific manufacturing processes and, even after consolidation in the Factories and Workshops Act of 1878, there remained a disparate and complex series of statutes and statutory instruments still reflected in the 1961 Factories Act.

The lack of workforce involvement arose from the Factories Act tradition of imposing specific duties on employers so that 'workers participation in the safety effort [was seen] as solely a matter of discipline at the workplace' (Howells 1974: 89). There were exceptions. For example as early as 1872 the Coal Mines Regulation Act established the right to appoint workmen inspectors in the mines. In 1927 there was a proposal from the Factory Inspectorate for compulsory safety committees in iron and steel, heavy engineering and shipbuilding under section 29 of the Workmen's Compensation Act 1923, but it was never implemented (Djang 1942: 110). Following the examples of statutory consultative machinery in the Nationalisation Acts, the Employment (Inspection and Safety Organisation) Bill of 1953 suggested mechanisms for the industry-wide election of safety representatives; it failed to reach the statute books. The dominant model remained that of the Factories Acts.

9

Opposition to workforce involvement in safety matters came from employers worried about infringements on managerial prerogative. However, lukewarm union support was also important, and this was based in the wider preference for legal abstention. As Hepple notes:

> The reason for the selective use of the 'method of legal enactment' as a means of worker protection, even when trade unions were in a position to demand comprehensive statutory regulation in the period after 1914, must be found in the pragmatic approach of the trade unions. As Kahn-Freund [1968: 4] explained, protective legislation cautiously expanded was seen as no more than a supplement to collective bargaining, useful in areas such as health safety and welfare where practical experience taught that negotiations and enforcement by union representatives were ineffective. For those who were strongly unionised minimum standards could be achieved without the help of legislation (Hepple 1983: 408).

By the time a Labour government was re-elected in 1966, the primacy of this voluntary solution was under attack. The TUC itself, for so long a staunch supporter of the voluntary principle, was demanding statutory support for workplace safety committees. It was in this atmosphere that the government eventually established a Committee of Inquiry chaired by Lord Robens and proposed legislative action in the form of the Employed Persons (Health and Safety) Bill. The loss of the 1970 general election prevented the Labour government from securing passage of the Bill. However, the incoming Conservative administration welcomed the Robens Committee's Report when it was published in 1972.

The Robens Report

The heart of the Robens Report, and the analysis from which its proposals for legislative change emerge, runs as follows:

> The primary responsibility for doing something about the present levels of occupational accidents and disease lies with those who create the risk and those who work with them ... Our present system encourages rather too much reliance on state regulation and rather too little on responsibility and voluntary self generating effort... There is a role for government action. But those roles should be predominantly concerned with influencing attitudes and creating a framework for better health and safety organization and action by industry itself (1972a: 7).

The proposals for legislative change thus emphasised not only the development of statutory rights and duties for both employers and employees, but also the development of institutions which would enable minimum standards to be improved upon.

The Report's approach to the role of law in health and safety was one of its more controversial aspects. First, it argued that reliance on a considerable volume of legislation fostered the attitude that health and safety was a matter for external regulation; at that time, nine main statutes were supported by some 500 statutory instruments (Hepple 1983:406). The Report notes:

> The existence of such a mass of law has an unfortunate and all pervading psychological effect. People are heavily conditioned to think of health and safety at work as in the first and most important instance a matter of detailed rules imposed by external agencies (Robens 1972a: 7).

The Report suggested that the primary role of the law should be to encourage workplace self regulation. The punitive approach was to be reserved for those workplaces which persistently and flagrantly refused to comply. The existing approach was also criticised for fostering two additional problems, the obsolescence of statutory standards and the fragmentation of jurisdiction. These matters were the consequence of rapid technical change and the *ad hoc* development of administrative structures. Taken together they effectively excluded a sizeable minority of workplaces and employees from statutory protection and actually hindered the Inspectorate's regulation by encouraging focus upon compliance with detailed regulations rather than 'the total picture' (Robens 1972a: 41).

The idea of self regulation was vital, since in it lay the resolution of the central paradox of the Report: that standards were to be improved by movement away from detailed regulations. Given the overall theme of this book – the viability and limits of self regulation – it is important to establish what this term meant for the Committee, both at national and local levels. At national level it was never seen in terms of the absence of legal standards and external enforcement; rather it was envisaged that the development of tripartite institutions together with enabling legislation would facilitate the involvement of representatives of employers, workers and other interested parties in the establishment of enforceable standards and the development of enforcement policy. At local level – in the workplace – self regulation was seen to involve the encouragement of systems which would create local motivation and capacity to act amongst employers, managers and workers so that minimum statutory requirements would be met and possibly improved upon. It was in this context that external enforcement of

11

standards was to be seen as mainly applying to recalcitrants who continued flagrantly to fail to achieve expected standards.

The idea of workforce involvement lay at the heart of self regulation. Whilst the Report saw the promotion of health and safety at work as an essential function of good management, it acknowledged it could not simply rely on managerial prerogative because 'real progress is impossible without the full cooperation and commitment of all employees' (Robens 1972a: 18). The duty of 'due care' which was to fall on employees, in parallel to the employer's duty to provide a safe workplace, was seen as insufficient in itself to secure such workforce involvement, and the Committee deliberated on the nature of the appropriate mechanisms.

Noting the widespread use of joint safety committees, the Committee still felt that safety representatives 'empowered to carry out inspections . . . [and] have access to and contacts with government and local authority safety inspectors' were more important. Such representatives could be 'elected through trade unions or work groups where appropriate' (Robens 1972a: 19–21). However, the Committee saw no 'legitimate scope for collective bargaining' on the subject of health and safety, a view obviously stemming from its belief that

> there is a greater natural identity of interest between 'the two sides' in relation to health and safety problems than in most other matters (1972a: 21).

Clearly then, the role of employees and their representatives was to engage in consultation with employers and to assist in the formulation and observance of safety provisions enacted and initiated through managerial structures. Self regulation was envisaged as a matter of employee observance of workplace discipline imposed by management, but mutually agreed by joint consultation. This unitary approach is also reflected in the Report's eventual retreat from statutory provisions for employee involvement and its proposal for 'a statutory duty to consult' founded on the belief that

> a statutory provision requiring the appointment of safety representatives and safety committees might be rather too rigid and, more importantly, too narrow in concept (Robens 1972a: 22).

The Conservative government responded to the Report by framing legislation which closely followed its proposals but, since the government fell before the Bill reached the statute books, it was the incoming Labour administration which eventually enacted the provisions.

The Health and Safety at Work etc. Act, 1974

The Act sought to establish a unity of approach through the establishment of a 'single standard of care, that of reasonable practicability' (Rideout 1979: 340). In these terms it brought the existing common law duty of 'care' into statute law. But in practice this is a highly variable standard. The Act did not repeal all of the previous specialised provisions covering particular industries or operations (HASAWA, 1974, Schedules 1 and 10). Thus legal standards continued to vary greatly depending on other Acts and Regulations. For example standards for noise levels in the woodworking industry are still very different to those elsewhere. The Act extended coverage of health and safety at work provisions to some seven or eight million employees in the so called 'new entrant' establishments, which had previously not been covered by legislation in this area. Nonetheless some establishments under government control, like the Ministry of Defence public health laboratories, the national health and prison services, were still exempt from the statutory requirements of the HASAWA through the provision of crown immunity.

The standard of reasonable practicability pervades sections 2–9 of the Act, which deal with the sets of general duties imposed on the various parties. The second section focuses on the general duties of the employer, who is to ensure, within the limits of reasonable practicability, a safe and healthy workplace (s2(1), 2(2)); to prepare a written statement of 'his general policy with respect to the health and safety at work of his employees' (s2(3)), and to bring it, or any revision of it, to the attention of all of his employees; to allow for the appointment of safety representatives and consultation with them (s2(4)–(6)); and to set up safety committees (s2(7)).

Sections 3–5 extend a number of similar duties to the self-employed and those in control of or concerned with premises. Section 6 requires suppliers, manufacturers, designers or importers of articles to be used at work to ensure their safety – again 'as far as is reasonably practicable'. The duty extends to the appropriate testing of equipment and to the making available of necessary information. Similar duties are imposed on suppliers of substances (s6(4)).[3]

Section 7 imposes the duty of reasonable care on employees. It is the duty of every employee while at work to take reasonable care for his or her own safety and for that of other persons who may be affected by his or her acts or omissions. There is also a duty (s7(b)) to cooperate with the employer to enable the employer to comply with his or her own statutory duties. Furthermore, there is a general duty laid on everybody not to interfere with or misuse anything provided in pursuance of any statutory duty connected with health safety and welfare (s8).

13

Sections 10–42 deal with the Health and Safety Commission and the operation of the Inspectorate. The Commission is to be tripartite, and within the overall control of the Secretary of State. Sections 10–14 define the powers of the two bodies. Section 15 empowers the Secretary of State to make statutory instruments and imposes a duty upon the Commission to consult affected parties. Section 16 allows for the issuing of codes of practice. Subsequent sections deal with the Inspectorate and its powers. An Inspector may enter at any time and any place when it is considered that the Act will apply (s20). He or she is empowered to issue improvement notices, requiring remedial action within a specified time period, or prohibition notices requiring partial or total cessation of operations if remedial action is not taken (ss21–6). Within certain restrictions, the Commission can serve a notice on any person compelling them to reveal information as required (ss27–8). Section 33 deals with offences and penalties. The former involve failure to discharge duties, obstruction of the Inspectorate and falsification. Penalties are largely in the form of fines, but there is provision for imprisonment for certain convictions.

In terms of its impact upon the workplace, the Act can be seen as a piece of enabling legislation through which those directly involved as employers, employees, suppliers etc. would be encouraged, within nationally enforced standards, to develop the forms of organisation and types of activities which they considered to be most appropriate to secure the safety and health of those at work. In this sense the Act was concerned to encourage self regulation.

In Kahn-Freund's (1972) terms the Act is a species of regulatory legislation. It enshrines the common law right to a safe system of work in statute and thereby facilitates the enforcement of this right by the Inspectorate. Unlike the earlier legislation, the Act recognises that health and safety cannot be confined to specific regulation of certain techniques or processes, or rest on the common law. However, the standard of 'reasonable practicability' differs from standards of absolute liability contained in some sections of the Factories Acts. The general definition of the term is given in the judgement in Edwards v. National Coal Board.

> 'Reasonably practicable' is a narrower term than 'physically possible' and seems to me to imply that a computation must be made by the owner in which the *quantum* of risk is placed on one scale and the sacrifice involved in the measures necessary for averting the risk (whether in money, time or trouble) is placed on the other and that, if it be shown that there is a gross disproportion between them – the risk being

insignificant in relation to the sacrifice – the defendants
discharge the onus on them (Quoted in Rideout 1979: 340).

The last sentence is significant. The HASAWA (s40) lays the burden of
proof of reasonable practicability in any proceedings, for an offence under
any of the relevant statutory provisions, on the defendant. In other words,
'once it is proved that a person has failed to prevent the existence of an
unsafe situation, the burden of proof will shift to that person to show that
he could not have taken suitable steps to eliminate that danger' (Howells
and Barrett 1982: 20).

The most important point to make about 'reasonable practicability' is
that it implies, following the direction of Edwards v. NCB, some form of
cost-benefit analysis.[4] The standard of safety in the Act invites
consideration of the expense and trouble involved in the avoidance of risk,
and although the courts may be stringent in the application of the standard,
some variance around it may be expected. As Rideout noted:

> It is the policy of the Health and Safety Executive to seek to
> establish, as it were, a minimum standard. Those who claim
> that they cannot reasonably attain this standard should be
> regarded as unfit to engage in the activity. However, more
> affluent employers will be expected, on a subjective application
> of reasonable practicability, to achieve a higher standard than
> the minimum (1979: 341).

There cannot, therefore, be a single enforced standard particularly as the
HASAWA did not repeal the Factories Act nor the Offices, Shops and
Railway Premises Act, nor did it dispense with the dozens of regulations for
particular trades and activities enacted under the Factories Act. In fact, its
schedule of repeals was short, consisting of minor amendments to various
statutes not primarily concerned in themselves with health and safety at
work (HASAWA, Schedule 10). It remains the case that many of the
prosecutions taken by the various Inspectorates since the passage of the
Act relate to failures to observe specific Factories Act duties, rather than
failures to observe the general duty of reasonable care. We shall discuss this
in more detail in Chapter 9.

Moreover, the sections of the 1974 Act dealing with enforcement, while
standardising the powers of Inspectorates, made no provision for the
unification of the Inspectorates themselves. The Secretary of State was
empowered to decide on the division of labour between various
Inspectorates – particularly between local authority and HSE Inspectors –
and to remove 'any uncertainty as to what are by virtue of this subsection

their respective responsibilites for the enforcement of these provisions'
(s18(2)b).

The Act did not, therefore, unify and simplify the structure of safety
regulation as Robens envisaged. Perhaps more importantly, the concept of
self regulation at the core of the Robens approach was modified
substantially in the Act's provisions for employee involvement. Since
Robens had been concerned to involve employees through consultation
rather than involving trade unions through collective bargaining, the
Committee's Report had recommended the involvement of representatives
of all employees in health and safety rather than just those of unionised
employees. The incoming Labour administration included a provision in
the Bill outlining a procedure for the appointment of union representatives
only. Analytically therefore this was, as Clark and Wedderburn remark, an
'auxiliary' legal provision (1983: 186). However, a House of Lords
amendment, providing also for employee representatives, was included in
the Act as section 2(5). This was based on the premise that consultation
through representatives was a right available to all employees, not just
those in trade unions.

For approximately the first year of the Act's operation, this remained the
position. However, with the election of a majority Labour government in
October 1974, the possibility arose of returning to the formulation of the
original Bill. In 1975, section 116 of the Employment Protection Act
repealed section 2(5), leaving the right to appoint safety representatives
only with recognised trade unions.

Clark and Wedderburn's contention that this is an auxiliary provision is
not based solely upon its location within a statute primarily concerned with
the extension of collective bargaining. On the assumption – clearly that of
the Act – that safety representatives could exert positive influence upon
safety at work, trade union membership could come to be associated with
safer workplaces and could expand accordingly. However, this approach
implied the provision of statutory rights for such representatives: where
these rights attach only to trade union appointees, they were 'intermediate'
in nature. This was at odds with the Robens philosophy, and subsequently
the SRSCR was to move the law even further away from it.

The Safety Representatives and Safety Committees Regulations 1977

With the passage of the Regulations (SRSCR), safety legislation began to
sit even more obviously in the auxiliary camp. Approved in 1977 and
operative from 1978, the Regulations extended intermediate rights and
auxiliary provisions to safety representatives as agents of trade unions.
Recognised trade unions alone may appoint safety representatives,

although there is no requirement that the representative be a union member (SRSCR 3(a)).

The fourth section of the Regulations details specific functions for safety representatives:

4(1) In addition to his function under section 2(4) of the 1974 Act to represent the employees in consultation with the employer under section 2(6) of the 1974 Act (which requires every employer to consult safety representatives with a view to the making and maintenance of arrangements which will enable him and his employees to cooperate effectively in promoting and developing measures to ensure the health and safety at work of the employees and in checking the effectiveness of such measures), each safety representative shall have the following functions:

(a) to investigate potential hazards and dangerous occurrences at the workplace (whether or not they are drawn to his attention by the employees he represents) and to examine the causes of accidents at the workplace;

(b) to investigate complaints by any employee he represents relating to that employee's health, safety or welfare at work;

(c) to make representations to the employer on matters arising out of sub-paragraphs (a) and (b) above;

(d) to make representations to the employer on general matters affecting the health, safety or welfare at work of the employees at the workplace;

(e) to carry out inspections in accordance with Regulations 5, 6 and 7 below;

(f) to represent the employees he was appointed to represent in consultations at the workplace with inspectors of the Health and Safety Executive and of any other enforcing authority;

(g) to receive information from inspectors in accordance with section 28(8) of the 1974 Act; and

(h) to attend meetings of safety committees where he attends in his capacity as a safety representative in connection with any of the above functions;

but without prejudice to sections 7 and 8 of the 1974 Act, no function given to a safety representative by this paragraph shall be construed as imposing any duty on him.

(2) An employer shall permit a safety representative to take

such time off with pay during the employee's working hours as shall be necessary for the purposes of:

(a) performing his functions under section 2(4) of the 1974 Act and paragraph (1)(a) to (h) above;

(b) undergoing such training in aspects of those functions as may be reasonable in all the circumstances having regard to any relevant provisions of a code of practice relating to time off for training approved for the time being by the Health and Safety Commission under section 16 of the 1974 Act. (SRSCR 4)

The fifth and sixth sections of the Regulations detail the representatives' rights to inspect the workplace on a routine basis every three months, as well as specifically when there has been a substantial change in conditions of work or new information has been published by the HSC or HSE or following notifiable accidents, occurrences and diseases. The seventh section provides safety representatives with the right to inspect documents and to receive relevant information from employers.

The ninth section deals with safety committees and, following section 2(7) of the HASAWA, requires employers to establish a safety committee within three months of a written request to do so, from at least two safety representatives. No specific powers or duties were given to safety committees by the Regulations.

The intermediate rights given to safety representatives in these Regulations took a familiar form. The wording of section 4(2) of the Regulations on time off for safety representatives parallels that of section 57(4) and 57(5) of the 1975 Employment Protection Act for trade union representatives. The provisions for recourse to industrial tribunals for enforcement (s11) are also substantially those of the EPA (s60).

Furthermore, the provisions on disclosure of information in the Regulations (s7) are similar to sections 17–19 of the 1975 EPA. There are two principal differences. The first is that, in this context, there is no requirement for the union to prove that it has been materially impeded, whether in collective bargaining or otherwise, by the absence of information. The second is that section 7(2) of the Regulations, covering restrictions on the general duty to employers to disclose information, omits section 18(1)(c) of the 1974 Act, preventing disclosure of information communicated in confidence. This is presumably intended to encourage the disclosure of information which may have originated with suppliers of equipment. Enforcement of failure to disclose information under the Regulations remains unclear, although 'The Commission believe that disagreements must be settled through the normal machinery for the resolution of industrial relations problems' (SRSCR: Preface).

The Regulations were the subject of some criticism, particularly from employers. The CBI was concerned to limit the circumstances under which trade unions could appoint safety representatives. In fact, the very link between union recognition and safety representatives was deplored (Barrett 1977: 176).

The legal background is important here, since it illustrates the extent to which safety legislation was caught up in the wider currents of labour law. The principle of workforce involvement as espoused by Robens did not distinguish in any important sense between unionised and non-unionised workplaces. However, such a distinction emerged in labour law in the 1970s. The Industrial Relations Act 1971 and subsequently the Employment Protection Act 1975 can both be said to contain auxiliary recognition provisions (ss45–7 of the 1971 Act and ss11–16 of the 1975 Act), in keeping with the historical preference within labour law for the encouragement of collective bargaining. The 1975 Act in addition gave certain rights to recognised trade unions – for example to information – and to individuals as members of trade unions – for example to time off for trade union activity.

The 1977 Regulations added to these rights, by giving unions the sole right to appoint safety representatives and by giving those representatives many of the rights given to trade union representatives under the 1975 Act. The backdrop of this was the overall commitment to the encouragement of collective bargaining, and union recognition and the rights associated with it as the preferred means of regulating relations between employers and employees.

One current problem for the operation of the Regulations is that since 1980 there has been no statutory route to union recognition and, indeed, the overall commitment to collective bargaining has waned in the face of a greater commitment to market regulation. Section 19(b) of the 1980 Employment Act repealed the (by then inoperative) recognition provisions originally introduced in the 1975 Act. Other measures in the 1980 and 1982 Employment Acts (such as the prohibitions on union recognition requirements and on pressure to impose such requirements in ss13–14 of the 1982 Act) further attenuate the commitment in law to extend collective bargaining, although the remit to ACAS, set out in section 1(2) of the 1975 Act, which includes the commitment, remains. The coverage of safety representatives is thus restricted to a set of unionised workplaces, since there remains no facility for the appointment of representatives with statutory powers in any other context. The expansion of union recognition, and thus of safety representative coverage, has been made more difficult.

In short, the history of workforce involvement from Robens to the SRSCR reveals the close relationship between safety legislation and labour legislation more generally. The net result of this close involvement is that the universal applicability of a single framework for workforce involvement is jeopardised.

Trade union involvement

An important issue in the development of legislation on safety has been the attitude of the trade unions towards legislative proposals. Throughout the post-war period, trade union attempts to improve protection against injury or ill health at work took three forms; pursuit of financial compensation for risk or injury, pressure for 'Factories Act' type detailed legislation and its effective enforcement, and the development of voluntary consultative or bargaining machinery at plant or industrial level. The idea of a natural harmony of interest was secondary to a concern to regulate employer behaviour, and the idea of legislative support for workforce involvement was secondary to the development of voluntary mechanisms. By the 1960s however there were signs of change.

For example, the TUC passed a motion in 1964 calling for the Factories Act to be extended to provide for the election of safety delegates and the establishment of safety committees. In evidence to Robens the TUC argued that

> Effective safety organisation must have the full support and confidence of work people and their unions and this can only be obtained by joint consultation at every stage in the working out and implementation of safety policy (Robens 1972b: 672).

By the mid 1970s, the TUC emphasis had shifted from consultation to bargaining. In the context of the debate on industrial democracy, the TUC argued that

> Unions should continue to press for joint control over non-wage areas and work organisation through the extension of collective bargaining: as part of the approach to extending industrial democracy this is indispensable (TUC 1974: 314).

Increasingly the preferred model involved a primary commitment to voluntary collective bargaining, bolstered by legislation: legal rights were seen as an addition to bargaining, not as a substitute. In the area of safety, the TUC argument became increasingly focused on the need to use collective organisations and direct negotiation with employers as a basis for trade union action to improve safety at work. In the event, this view prevailed over that of the CBI, who argued that there was still an identity of interests between employers and employed, thus that collective bargaining and direct negotiation were inappropriate.

The heat generated by these arguments over section 2(4) and 2(5) of the Act and the SRSCR has to some extent been dissipated by experience. In their respective evidence to the House of Commons Employment Committee (1982), the TUC and CBI chose to echo previous arguments, but both expressed the view that the legislation had been something of a success. Nevertheless the form of workforce involvement embodied in the SRSCR raises several important questions concerning the structure of the legislation. It is a mixture of universal and intermediate restricted rights which rely on auxiliary legislative props. This raises general questions of equity, and also of the usefulness of auxiliary legislation.

The logic of Robens and of the Act was that a universal general standard of care should be promoted: worker involvement was one mechanism for this promotion. Yet to the extent that the legislation itself presents the possibility of uneven standards of involvement, it may thus promote uneven application. This is particularly likely given the point outlined above – that other statutory rights appear to have been most useful to those working in non-unionised firms without the benefit of collective organisation. Rights to safety representation are restricted to those represented by recognised trade unions.

Although the present legislative climate is out of sympathy with the view, it is possible to argue that, because individuals should not benefit without any effort on their part, certain economic benefits ought only to accrue to dues-paying trade union members. It is also possible to argue that rights be granted to individuals to promote the public policy goal of collective bargaining though, again, this has more application to a previous phase of labour legislation than it does to the present context in 1987. However, it is difficult in equity to argue that uneven standards of safety protection should be generated on the basis of union membership unless it can also be argued that this raises standards overall.

Trade unionists might respond to these points in a number of ways. An important strand in the case for trade union appointed safety representatives is the view that individuals require collective support in order to perform the function adequately. This argument, that non-union representatives would be less effective, would also extend to the case where union and non-union appointees sit on the same safety committees, although in this case the argument is rather that union appointed representatives themselves may find their power diluted. More cynically, one can also argue that opposition to non-union representation stems in part from the concern to include safety issues among the incentives for trade union recruitment.

The second question concerns the usefulness of the 'intermediate' rights. Some of them do not appear to yield the advantages expected by some trade unionists. The example of rights to disclosure of information may be quoted. Sections 17–19 of the Employment Protection Act 1975 require employers to disclose to representatives of recognised trade unions information without which trade union representatives would be 'to a material extent impeded' in carrying out collective bargaining and 'which it would be in accordance with good industrial relations practice' to disclose. Employers need not disclose any information the disclosure of which would be against the interests of national security, or which would involve contravention of any other enactment. They need not disclose confidential information, or that relating to a specific individual without consent, or any information, the disclosure of which would cause substantial injury to their business, or any information they have obtained for the purposes of bringing any legal action. Finally, they need not disclose any document, and need not incur expenses in information provision 'out of reasonable proportion' to the value of the information in collective bargaining.

The evidence is that these provisions have not given access to large amounts of information. Gospel and Willman (1981) show that use of the provisions declined in the late 1970s and that the most likely recipients of new information were likely to be weakly organised white collar unions in search of information routinely disclosed elsewhere, for example concerning job evaluation schemes or relative pay.

These provisions are, however, the model for those on disclosure in section 7 of the SRSCR. The safety representative is entitled to certain information, and there is no requirement to show material impediment in bargaining, but the exclusions on the employer's duty are otherwise identical, save on the final issue of cost of production.

Although the absence of restrictions on disclosure of information in the SRSC Regulations appear to offer the prospect of more success, it is important to note that there appear to be problems in relation to this and other aspects of safety organisation. It is notable that not a single case has reached the Central Arbitration Committee, for example, on collective safety issues. The Factory Inspectorate themselves issue notices and serve prosecutions under the heading of 'safety organisation'. However, in 1979 only 1.8% of notices and 5.9% of prosecutions fell under this heading, and over half of the latter were concerned with 'training and instruction' (Chief Inspectors Report 1979). As Lewis has noted:

In legal theory the duty to consult over industrial safety could have been enforced by the Health and Safety Executive through improvement notices and criminal prosecutions. In practice, the Executive would not as a matter of policy use its legal powers to enforce industrial relations procedures, and consequently there was (and is) no legal enforcement at all, except for contravention of a recognised safety representatives right to paid time off, which may be referred to an industrial tribunal (Lewis 1983: 376).[5]

This is an important gap, since neither the Act nor the Regulations define the operation of employee involvement in any detail. The number of safety representatives, their method of appointment, the mechanisms for notifying and carrying out inspections and the provision of facilities for safety representatives are all left to discussions between trade unions and employers.[6] Moreover, although the Act and Regulations impose duties on employees and employers, and give trade unions certain rights, the latter are under no obligation to activate the system of participation laid down in the Regulations.

Many individual rights can be enforced through the tribunal system. It is held to be an implied term of all employment contracts that the employer will take reasonable care and act reasonably in the investigation of safety complaints; failure to do so may give rise to successful constructive dismissal claims.[7] Moreover, employees dismissed for safety reasons may find remedies through the tribunal system. The qualifying period for unfair dismissal claims for employees is normally two years' continuous service, but if the reason for dismissal is a requirement of one of the statutory safety provisions listed in schedule 1 (EP(C)A 1978), then the qualifying period is reduced to four weeks (EP(C)A s64(2)). Only 15 such provisions are listed at schedule 1.

Tribunals have generally held dismissal of employees for tampering with safety equipment, ignoring safety procedures and refusing to wear safety clothing to be fair.[8] Similarly, dismissal of employees who have caused accidents through unsafe behaviour has been held as fair.[9] However, employers have, in safety as in other dismissals, a general duty to show that they acted reasonably; where unsafe work is the result of inadequate training, where the refused safety equipment is itself inadequate, or where rules of natural justice are ignored, then dismissal may be unfair.[10]

Individual employees have the right to refuse to work unsafe equipment or in unsafe conditions, particularly if an infringement of the law is involved.[11] In such cases, the views of managers on what constitutes safe or unsafe working are not necessarily paramount. In one case, an employee's refusal to do a repair by welding since he thought it unsafe resulted in his dismissal. In considering the case, the tribunal pointed out that the employee knew more about welding than his employer did.[12]

Employees may thus use the tribunal system to help assure safety standards. However, the defects of the system of dismissal compensation affect safety dismissals too, and the amount of protection offered is accordingly generally limited to the receipt of some compensation for job loss. Many employees may prefer the risk of an unsafe working practice to that of the tribunal system. More importantly, the enforcement of regulatory provisions in this way will not of itself promote workforce involvement in safety at work.

Conclusion

Health and safety legislation consists of regulatory provisions as terms in employment contracts, sets of general duties, mainly imposed on the employer, and rights for trade unions and trade unionists which parallel the auxiliary provisions of the Employment Protection Act.

Given the importance of auxiliary legislation throughout the 1970s, the Robens' view of workforce involvement based on a unitary view of safety provision, which excluded it, appears strange. Robens apparently operated with a view of collective bargaining as a zero-sum game in which health and safety matters would be traded off against other issues where the two were seen as incompatible. Nevertheless, given the importance of collective bargaining as the prime mechanism for joint regulation in the UK, its exclusion from the realm of health and safety was curious and always unlikely to be maintained.

Notwithstanding these difficulties and contradictions, there is no doubt that, together with the foundation of national institutions, the legislation was concerned to enable the development of local institutions of self regulation in order to secure improved standards of health and safety at work. In turning from an analysis of the legislation itself to an assessment of its impact, the book focuses on two sets of indicators: accident statistics and the growth of local and national institutions created or encouraged by the 1974 Act and SRSCR. The task of impact assessment is not easy, not least because of the difficulties involved in attributing changes in any one indicator to the impact of legislation as opposed to other factors. There is even evidence of an interactive effect between our two sets of indicators. The establishment of safety committees, itself an institutional development, has been shown to be associated with a greater willingness to report accidents and consequently can be associated with rising trends in accident statistics. We now turn to a discussion of matters germane to this and other issues of assessment.

2

Assessing the impact: official statistics on accident rates

Since the Robens Committee had been concerned about the rise in officially notified accidents in the 1960s, one obvious indicator of the success of any enactment in this area would be an immediate and consequential decline in the level of industrial accidents. Potentially, official statistics are of considerable importance in the assessment of the effectiveness of legislation. However, the existence of legislation is not the only, nor even necessarily the most important influence on the reported level of accidents. Yet the attribution of any reduction in the notified accident rate to the effects of legislation assumes all other factors constant. Since such factors must include technology of manufacture, sectoral distribution of industrial activity, training and skill levels among the labour force as well as the size of the employed population, *ceteris paribus* assumptions are unlikely to be sensible for any time-series analysis. The relationship between the notified accident rate and the existence of legislation is thus relatively complex.

This aside, two other difficulties arise in discussing official statistics on accident rates. The first is that there appears to be substantial but uneven under-reporting which varies between industrial sectors and over time. The second concerns changes in the definition of the categories of reportable accidents which will enter the statistics. There is no single, complete series covering accidents at work since the passage of the Act. This chapter discusses these problems and then, within the limitations identified, assesses the underlying trend in accident rates.

The conclusion is that the five year period after the Act was characterised by a significant decline in the rate of serious and fatal accidents at work but that this trend has not continued into the 1980s. Indeed, in manufacturing and construction, the period 1980–85 has been characterised by a significant rise in the combined rate of major and fatal accidents at work at least in manufacturing and construction.

26

The collection of statistics

There have been provisions for direct reporting of what are known as lost time accidents, i.e. those requiring more than three days' absence from work, to the appropriate authority since 1923. However, for many years the basis of collection was affected by the legislative fragmentation which afflicted the entire health and safety area before 1974. For example, after 1963, accidents could be reported under the following statutes: Explosives Act (1875), Regulation of Railways and Railway Employment (Prevention of Accidents) Acts (1871, 1900, 1975), Mines and Quarries Act (1954), Agriculture (Safety, Health and Welfare Provisions) Act 1956, Factories Act (1961) and the Offices, Shops and Railway Premises Act (OSRPA) (1963). Neither the procedures for reporting nor the requirement to report were uniform across these different statutes. Furthermore, detailed analysis of accident rates was hampered by the lack of correspondence between the scope of enactments and the 1968 Standard Industrial Classification (SIC): particular problems, for example, arose in connection with the OSRP Act (HSC/1, 1978). Moreover, the possibility of dual counting of an accident under two different statutes could not be excluded.

The reporting provisions of the Factories Act and OSRP Act had the widest applicability, and were identical. Under both statutes, an accident was notifiable if
(a) it caused loss of life to a person employed in premises subject to the Factories Act or OSRP Act;
(b) it disabled any such person for more than three days from earning full wages at the work at which he was employed.
The former provides the definition of a fatal accident at work, the latter the accepted definition of a lost time accident at work.

Whereas these various statutes became part of the more extensive umbrella of safety legislation in 1974, regulations on the reporting of accidents provided for in the HASAWA did not become operative until 1981. Thus, for a seven year period no information was available on the seven to eight million people employed in the so-called 'new entrant' establishments who were covered by safety legislation for the first time in 1974. This exacerbated an existing problem of under-reporting under previous statutes.

The purpose of data collection had for some time been related to the needs of Inspectors in deciding whether or not to inspect. Thus there was the requirement to report 'three day' accidents, even though much of this information would eventually become available through the Department of Health and Social Security as accident victims completed claims for industrial injury benefit. Inspectors required the information more rapidly in order to decide which sites or workplaces to visit. However, according to a study conducted by the HSE, comparison of the direct returns with those eventually emerging from the DHSS suggests substantial under-reporting of the order of 25% in manufacturing and of 50% in the construction industry.[1]

The problem of under-reporting has always existed. Robens felt that the available statistics in 1972 were of little use either for monitoring or hazard identification purposes. Various authors have sought to make estimates either of the number or cost of unreported accidents which suggest under reporting of the order of one-fifth to three-fifths (Barth and Hunt 1980; Morgan and Davies 1981). The HSE itself suggested that only 25% of accidents in offices and shops were included in its 1977 report. Others have suggested that the limited legal duty to investigate and report is made worse by the failure of those responsible to report all accidents covered by the requirements (Kinnersley 1973; Carson 1982).

A remedy for the defects in the reporting requirements themselves was sought in the eventual establishment of reporting regulations under the 1974 Act. However, such regulations were not made until 1980, and they were not to survive for long. The Notification of Accidents and Dangerous Occurrences Regulations (NADOR, 1980) were a major departure in several respects. First, they extended coverage of reporting requirements to the 'new entrants' under the 1974 Act: voluntary reporting of 'new entrant' data had been incorporated in statistics from 1978 onwards, but the coverage was uneven and the data were not regarded as reliable. Secondly, they introduced a comprehensive list of 'major' injuries for which immediate notification was required and an extended list of dangerous occurrences which for reporting purposes were ranked equal to the major injuries: this categorisation differs from the previous 'serious injury' classification. This provision reflected the view widely held among safety professionals that for accident prevention purposes there is no reason to distinguish between those dangerous occurrences which cause injury and those which do not (HSIB 117, 1985: 4). Thirdly, NADOR introduced the requirement to report injuries to people other than direct employees, thus effectively widening the duty to report fatal accidents. A 'responsible person' was to report the accident, thus raising some problems about the locus of the duty to report where the injured party was other than a direct employee (HSE/9, 1986: 28).

However, the major change was the removal of the requirement directly to report lost time accidents. Whereas NADOR required the reporting of 'any fatality, major injury or dangerous occurrence' directly to the appropriate authority by employers, and a written report within seven days, other injuries involving more than three days' absence were notified through the DHSS. The employer was simply to enter the details of the accident in the accident record and complete the industry injury claims form when necessary. Such information arrived with the Inspectorate approximately three weeks after the incident. This was a relatively poor system for the reporting of such accidents but, once more, collection of data was related primarily to inspection decisions, and thus information concerning the more serious incidents was required more rapidly.

This system of lost time accident reporting through the DHSS created more serious problems when the Social Security and Housing Benefit Act (1982) introduced, with effect from April 1983, the self certification of absence from work for a period of up to seven days. Thus the 'three day absence' criterion was rendered difficult to operate. More importantly, the Act changed the arrangements for claiming industrial injury benefit. With effect from 6 April 1983, most employees injured at work could claim statutory sick pay (SSP) from their employer for the first eight weeks' of incapacity. Claims to the DHSS thus reduced; claims would only be met, for example, if an employee were not paid SSP by his or her employer or if the injury lasted over eight weeks.

It is difficult to separate out the effect of improved reporting under NADOR from any underlying changes in the accident rate, but it would seem that some improvement in reporting took place. The total accident figure for 1980 was approximately 275 000 (see Table 2.1). In 1981, under NADOR, approximately 435 000 accidents were reported (see Table 2.4). It seems highly unlikely that this rise could be accounted for by a change of this magnitude in the accident rate, even with the compulsory inclusion of 'new entrant' data, particularly since the fatal rate fell across the two years. However, subsequent changes in the system of industrial injury benefit led to 'an 80 % reduction in the flow of information under NADOR' (HSC/3, 1983), and made the system inoperable. In the first quarter of 1983, 91 000 notifications of 'over 3 day injuries' were notified to the HSE by the DHSS. In each of the succeeding quarters, the total was less than 25 000. The HSE concluded that these residual indirect reports were 'of no use as indicators of trends in occupational health and safety' (HSE/8, 1984: 44). The series of non-fatal accidents is thus seriously interrupted twice in the period since 1980; 1 January 1981 and 6 May 1983.

The series of fatal accidents is affected by the NADOR extension of the duty to report in 1981, but it and the series of 'major' accidents since 1981 are probably reasonably reliable indicators of the underlying population; this population is, under NADOR, less than 3 % of the total of reported industrial injuries.

A third change in the basis for collecting accident statistics resulted from the introduction of the Reporting of Injuries, Diseases, and Dangerous

Occurrences Regulations (RIDDOR) in 1986. RIDDOR reintroduced, with some changes to the definition and list of immediately notifiable injuries, the basic NADOR framework. However, there are several improvements. One new element is the extension in scope of reporting requirements to cover the self-employed and young people training for employment. A second is the reintroduction of direct reporting of lost time injury accidents, thereby re-establishing the three day rule. However, perhaps the most radical change is in the introduction of a basic system of industrial disease reporting. Employers will be under a duty to report cases of the 42 industrial diseases listed in a schedule to the regulations provided that the employee concerned is also working in one of the high risk occupations also listed in the schedule. Basic disagreement over the feasibility of industrial disease reporting in fact delayed replacement of NADOR by RIDDOR for a period of two years (HSIB 117, 1985: 3).

Implementation of RIDDOR will, in the opinion of the HSE, establish a more satisfactory system of accident reporting than that following the decline of NADOR. However, it is likely that there will be less complete reporting than under NADOR; there is thus yet another discontinuity in the basis of collection of statistics. Hence for those concerned to assess trends in industrial accidents over the period since the Act, it remains impossible to acquire a reliable and valid series of all notifiable accidents. Accidents reported under particular statutes, such as the OSRP Act and the Factories Act may be monitored from enactment to the establishment of NADOR on 1 January 1981. Similar series may be compiled for appropriate periods for mines and quarries. The effect of the HASAWA cannot be monitored prior to NADOR from the statistics since the extension of coverage of legislation was not paralleled by extension of the requirement to report. Presumably, the series on fatal accidents and, since 1981, on fatal and major accidents has greater validity, but as we shall see, movements in this series are not paralleled by movements in the general accident rate. This is unfortunately likely to continue in the future, since the RIDDOR approach to lost time accidents is unlikely to generate data comparable to the NADOR figures. With these rather severe reservations in mind, we turn to an analysis of the available data.

Trends in accident statistics to 1980

Table 2.1 presents national figures on fatal and non-fatal accidents reported to HSC enforcement authorities up to NADOR. Despite the addition of accidents reported under additional statutes and on a voluntary basis into the series across the period, there was a clear downward trend in overall numbers for both fatal and non-fatal accidents. This trend is

Table 2.1 *Total accidents reported to HSC enforcement authorities: 1971–80*

	Fatal	Non-fatal (thousands)	Working population (millions)^c
1971	776	378.0	21.8
1972	668	350.5	22.3
1973	765	371.5	22.3
1974	651	337.6	22.3
1975	620	328.5	22.1
1976	584^a	325.0^a	22.0
1977	524	327.3	22.1
1978	622^b	345.3^b	22.4
1979	615	321.1	22.3
1980	579	274.8	21.2

^{a} Figures from 1976 include accidents reported under Mineral Workings (Offshore Installation) Acts.
^{b} Figures from 1978 include accidents not yet compulsorily reportable from 'new entrants' to health and safety legislation coverage. If these 'new entrants' are excluded, then the figures are:

	Fatal	Non-fatal
1978	499	328.4
1979	492	299.6
1980	440	253.7

^{c} Employees in Employment, December each year adjusted, GB.
Source: Health and Safety Statistics 1975, 1976, 1977, 1978/9, 1980 DE Gazette.

particularly marked after 1973, and from 1978 onwards. In fact, if one excludes the new entrant figures which appear from 1978 onwards, then, as the table notes indicate, the picture is one of more or less continuous decline in the number of industrial accidents across the decade.

A downward trend in accident numbers may conceal static or rising incidence rates and be a function of, amongst other things, falling numbers employed. The figures on working population in column 3 of Table 2.1 illustrate that this is an unlikely explanation at least up to 1980. Alternately, it might be the case that a change in the sectoral mix of industrial activity towards low risk and away from high risk activities accounts for the overall fall. During the period, for example, two of the very high risk industries, construction and mining, experienced falls in

31

employment, thus exposing fewer employees to the dangers inherent in these activities.[2] General shifts away from manufacturing into generally lower risk service activity would similarly lower the overall accident rate even where incidence rates for specific sectors were rising.

One thus needs to look at incidence rates themselves. Table 2.2 presents incidence rates for the high risk sectors already mentioned, and for manufacturing as a whole. Across the decade, all three sets of figures show a marked decline in the fatal accident rate. Mines and quarries also shows a substantial decline in the total accident rate; the anomalous years are 1972 and 1974, where accident rates may have fallen due to strike activity and thus the lower overall exposure to risk. From the passage of HASAWA until 1980, the fall is continuous. The other two sets of figures on total accidents do not show such a substantial fall, although in both there is a tendency for rates to fall after the passage of the SRSCR in 1978. The effect of the Regulations is unclear, but the fall is of interest since, as we shall discuss in more detail below, one expected consequence of the introduction of safety institutions is a rise in the reported rate due to reporting effects.

No similar pattern is exhibited in the series of accidents reported under the OSRP Act. Although fatalities fell across the decade, Table 2.3 indicates a slight rise over the period in total reported accidents: no incidence rates can be calculated for this area as a whole, since there is no corresponding SIC or MLH (Minimum List Heading) category. However, incidence rates *can* be calculated for non-fatal accidents reported in retailing (MLH 820, 821) which reveal a slight rise during the limited period of data available. This rise is of some interest since the data cover the period from the passage of the Act up to the establishment of NAROR. Again, several hypotheses present themselves. The two MLHs are characterised by falling overall employment and a growing percentage of part time employment which may imply looser management control systems and a lower quality of labour (Robertson, Biggs and Goodchild 1982). Alternately, Distribution (SIC XXIII) is a sector in which union density increased slightly in the decade up to 1979 and this may have affected reporting rates. The OSRPA data probably suffer from even greater under-reporting problems than the other series. Many of the establishments covered by the Act were – and are – subject to local authority inspection and enforcement by Environmental Health Officers (EHOs). For the period under consideration, prior to NADOR, the accident and enforcement data of EHOs were compiled only on a voluntary basis. Even in 1981, some 10–20 % of the 461 local authorities submitted no returns (HSE/8, 1984:29). It is possible that the small variations in the total accident rate overall are simply due to variations in reporting.

These sorts of broad suppositions generally illustrate the inherent

Table 2.2 *Accident incidence rates – selected industries: 1971–80 (all enforcing authorities)*

| | Factories Acts[a] | | | | Mines and quarries | |
| | Construction | | Manufacturing | | Coal Mines | |
	Fatal (per 100 000)	Total (per 100)	Fatal (per 100 000)	Total (per 100)	Fatal (per 100 000)	Total (per 100)
1971	19.6	3.6	4.3	3.5	24.2	26.1
1972	18.7	3.7	3.9	3.5	22.1	20.5
1973	21.6	3.5	4.2	3.7	29.6	24.6
1974	16.0	3.3	4.5	3.5	18.7	19.3
1975	17.7	3.5	3.7	3.6	24.7	10.9
1976	15.3	3.5	3.4	3.5	19.6	10.0
1977	13.1	3.3	3.4	3.6	15.8	19.5
1978	12.2	3.4	3.1	3.6	25.4	18.9
1979	11.8	3.1	2.9	3.3	18.9	16.8
1980	13.0	3.0	2.7	2.9	17.3	15.2

[a] Excludes 'other industries' category and thus the possibility of dual counting with the Railway Inspectorate under OSRP Act.
Source: Health and Safety Statistics 1975, 1976, 1977, 1978/9, 1980.

ambiguity of the series once one accepts some unreliability and variance in the reporting mechanisms. There have been several attempts to explain the observed patterns of industrial accidents in econometric terms using measures of individual worker behaviour (skill, age, level of overtime working) as well as those relating to characteristics of the employing plant (size, payment system, capacity utilisation) but none has sought to get to grips with the impact of legislation itself. (See for example Steele 1974; Edwards and Scullion 1982; Beaumont 1983).

The HSE has tried to analyse the relationship between accident rates and the pattern of enforcement activity. Using multiple regression techniques, and data for 1980 and 1981, they explained 80 % of the variance of accident rates in a sample of 120 manufacturing MLHs in 1981 by a set of selected independent variables. This set consisted of current visit frequency (of Inspectors), accident rates in the preceding year (a proxy for risk), current level of compliance, establishment size, the proportion of male, manual and newly hired workers, the average overtime level and the ratio of current year to preceding year's employment level (HSE/18, 1985: 4–7). There are

Table 2.3 *Accidents reported to local authorities under the OSRP Act: 1971–80*

	Overall			Retailing		
	Non-fatal (thousands)	Fatal	Non-fatal accident rate (per 100)[b]	Non-fatal (thousands)	Fatal
1971	16.4	35	—	—	—
1972	18.1	15	—	—	—
1973	17.7	15	—	—	—
1974	16.7	20	—	5.9	5
1975	17.2	16	0.32	6.1	5
1976	18.4	20	0.35	6.5	3
1977	19.2	34[a]	0.38	7.1	5
1978	17.7	15	0.41	7.7	3
1979	18.9	27	0.43	8.2	5
1980	18.3	17	0.44	8.0	5

[a] Includes accidents reported to the Railways Inspectorate, since 1 June 1977.
[b] Calculated by dividing non-fatal accident rate by employment in MLHs 820, 821. September each year.
Source: Health and Safety Executive Reports 1975, 1976, 1977, 1978/9, 1980. DE Gazette

some problems with this approach, in particular with the selection of variables. The activities of the Inspectorates cannot reasonably be taken as a proxy for the impact of an Act which is self regulatory in intent. Moreover, within the set of independent variables, those relating to compliance activity were not statistically significant. The impact of the Act up to 1980 thus remains difficult to assess in this rigorous fashion.

Problems of attribution notwithstanding, one can nevertheless draw the conclusion that the period from the passage of the Act up to the establishment of NADOR was one during which the level of total reported accidents continued its long-established historical trend of decline. Moreover, this decline was not solely a fortuitous consequence of a shift in the level or mix of economic activity, rather it represented a decline in observed incidence rates – at least across manufacturing. The introduction of NADOR truncates the series, except for fatal accidents, but there are signs that during 1981–82, this trend for all reported injuries continued.

The NADOR returns 1981–82

'Full' NADOR figures are available only for 1981–82. They show that fatal accidents have continued to decline in number but that, across the comparable years 1981–82, the incidence rates for fatal and major injuries has tended to increase: this is true both for all industries and for the manufacturing SICs alone. The incidence rates for all injuries on the other hand continued to fall (see Table 2.4). A particularly disturbing feature of the change in incidence rates across the two years 1981–82 was that the risk of fatal or serious injury rose in a number of SIC categories which were already high risk, for example, mining, coal and petroleum products, bricks and pottery, timber and construction (SICs II, IV, XVI, XVII and XX)[3] (Table 2.5). In all, 13 of the 17 manufacturing SICs reported a rise in the incidence rate for all reported accidents across the two year period, even though the incidence rate for all injuries in manufacturing as a whole declined slightly.

It is difficult to interpret such a short series, particularly since the trend on fatal and major accidents appears to differ from that on total accidents. The HSE noted that there was a reduction in the number of occupational injuries reported in 1982 in comparison to 1981 and that this 'reduction continues the ... long term downward trend in the total of reported injuries' (HSE/8, 1984: 2). In retrospect, given the subsequent trend on fatal and major accidents, it must be noted that this may have obscured a considerable change in accident trends during this period.

Returns since the suspension of NADOR 1983–85

With the interruption of the NADOR arrangements for lost time accident reporting, it was only possible to discuss the trend on major and fatal accidents, for which the requirement for direct reporting continued. This series, depicted in Tables 2.4 and 2.5, is thus continuous since 1980. The picture since 1980 contrasts quite markedly with the decade before. Overall, the fatal and major rate for all industries has not declined; indeed it rose from 1981 to 1983 and again in 1985. In manufacturing, only two of the 17 SICs showed improved incidence records for the combined rate of total and major injuries. In some, such as metal manufacture (VI), textiles (XIII), leather (XIV) and bricks (XVI) there was considerable deterioration. Outside manufacturing, most SICs experienced a decline in incidence, with the notable exception of construction, where there was an absolute increase in the number of fatal and major accidents and a large increase in the incidence rate. Indeed, without the relatively low figure for mining and quarrying – presumably related to low levels of activity during the miners' strike – the figures for 1984 might show an even more consistent picture of deterioration.

In reviewing these statistics, the HSE remark that the long-term decline in fatal accidents in industry has

> continued from the turn of the century to the inception of the HSE in 1974 and on to the early 1980's, after which there would seem to be some levelling out (HSE/9, 1986: 31).

This levelling has occurred at a lower level than the accident rate prior to the Act – for example the HSE estimate a current incidence rate for fatal accidents of 2.1 per 100 000 (in 1984), compared with 5.6 in 1965. Nevertheless, the Inspectorate sees cause for some concern in the incidence rates for major and fatal accidents combined particularly in manufacturing and construction (HSE/9, 1986: 31). The Chief Inspector of Factories commented in his Report for 1985 that 'the upward trend in major injuries in manufacturing generally noted over the last three years appears not to have been reversed' (HSE/6, 1986: 4).

Whatever the problems in explaining this deteriorating position, it is reasonable to suggest that it is unlikely to be a reporting effect. Fatal and major accidents probably suffer from less under-reporting, for obvious reasons, than less serious ones. Moreover, for the period covered by Table 2.5, there are no important extensions of reporting (the table focuses on employees only). Nor is there any reason to believe that the reporting of these categories of accident within sectors has improved. The deterioration is more pronounced in some sectors than others, but most manufacturing SICs appear to be affected.

In manufacturing, incidence rates for fatal and major accidents combined rise from 70.8 in 1981 to 92.6 in 1985, the rate of increase for 1981–85 being 31%. A greater rise is evident in construction, from 164 in 1981 to 238.4 in 1985 with a rate of increase, 1981–85, of 45%. Overall, the rise in incidence rate in all industries for fatal and major accidents combined from 1981 to 1985 is from 60.3 to 65.3. This lower rate of increase for 'all industries' undoubtedly reflects a national shift in employment from manufacturing into service industries, which generally have lower accident rates.

The figures for fatal and major injuries to the self-employed and other non-employees for the period 1981–85 show an increase of 26% (Table 2.6). This rise probably reflects in part growing understanding of the need to report such injuries under NADOR. However, given the increase in self-employment and loose forms of subcontracting in construction and other industries which will be the subject of further comment in subsequent chapters, this clear trend is unlikely simply to reflect a reporting effect.

Table 2.4 *Injuries to employees reported under NADOR 1981–85; incidence rates per 100 000 (all enforcing authorities) given in brackets*

	1981	1982	1983	1984	1985
All industries					
Fatal	449	468	443	437	404
	(2.1)	(2.3)	(2.1)	(2.1)	(1.9)
Fatal and major	12 764	12 743	12 890	12 931	13 587
	(60.3)	(62.1)	(62.4)	(62.2)	(65.3)
All injuries	434 792	389 781	*a*	*a*	*a*
	(2050)	(1900)			
Manufacturing					
Fatal	109	127	111	125	108
	(1.8)	(2.3)	(2.0)	(2.3)	(2.0)
Fatal and major	4218	4193	4349	4774	4932
	(70.8)	(74.6)	(79.3)	(88.2)	(92.6)
All injuries	151 966	133 409	*a*	*a*	*a*
	(2550)	(2370)			
Construction					
Fatal	106	100	118	100	107
	(9.7)	(9.9)	(11.4)	(9.8)	(10.9)
Fatal and major	1796	2050	2294	2388	2351
	(164)	(204)	(220.7)	(234.4)	(238.4)
All injuries	45 868	41 112	*a*	*a*	*a*
	(4190)	(4070)			

a Series interrupted with changes in direct reporting of 'three day' accidents.
Source: Table 1 Health and Safety Commission Report 1985/86
Table 1.2 HSE statistics 1983 (HSE/9)
Tables 1.1A & 1.1B Health and Safety Statistics 1981/82 (HSE/8)

The limitations of the data must be borne in mind. The period of NADOR reporting for all accidents was brief, but it did show that the series of fatal and major accidents on the one hand and lost time accidents on the other could move in different directions in the short term. The overall accident record for all injuries might not show the same deterioration for the period 1981–85. The data are, however, unavailable.

Overall, then, changes in the reporting provisions create problems for attempts to assess the general trend of accidents at work since the passage of the Act in 1974. Three distinct series are available; those on fatalities and lost time accidents under the Factories Acts and OSRPA running up to

Table 2.5 Injuries to employees reported to enforcement authorities by industry: 1981–84

Order no.	Standard Industrial Classification	Number of injuries 1981			1982			1983			1984[p]			Fatal and major injuries incidence rates[a] (per 100 000 employees) 1981	1982	1983	1984[d]
		Fatal	Major	Fatal and major	Fatal	Major	Fatal and major	Fatal	Major	Fatal and major	Fatal	Major	Fatal and major				
I	Agriculture, forestry and fishing	31	165	196	27	147	174	29	200	229	29	268	297	55.4	49.1	65.8	86.9
II	Mining and quarrying[b]	61	1026	1087	70	1044	1114	46	1005	1051	52	480	532	324.6	343.7	330.7	178.7
III	Food, drink and tobacco	8	495	503	10	530	540	23	523	546	8	570	578	80.4	89.9	92.0	99.0
IV	Coal and petroleum products	3	41	44	3	50	53	1	44	45	1	34	35	153.3	211.2	150.5	121.1
V	Chemicals and allied industries	7	324	331	6	345	351	10	373	383	5	370	375	82.0	91.4	105.7	104.2
VI	Metal manufacture	19	539	558	27	470	497	13	483	496	28	500	528	174.7	171.4	183.5	204.2
VII	Mechanical engineering	10	401	471	18	457	475	16	476	492	15	540	555	61.2	66.2	68.1	77.6
VIII	Instrument engineering		33	33	–	31	31	–	34	34	1	40	41	24.8	23.9	26.4	30.6
IX	Electrical engineering	1	167	168	8	180	188	3	227	230	5	236	241	24.8	29.2	34.9	35.9
X	Shipbuilding and marine engineering	13	192	205	8	148	156	4	114	118	9	106	115	142.2	112.0	91.3	101.1
XI	Vehicles	5	334	339	5	267	272	8	293	301	3	299	302	56.4	49.7	57.1	60.0
XII	Metal goods not elsewhere specified	11	374	385	10	396	406	3	386	389	9	443	452	86.1	96.1	99.3	113.7
XIII	Textiles	6	176	182	6	198	204	5	210	215	3	219	222	57.3	68.5	74.9	80.9
XIV	Leather, leather goods and fur	–	15	15	–	26	26	–	16	16	1	29	30	50.7	91.9	53.9	104.5
XV	Clothing and footwear	2	51	53	1	35	36	5	47	52	–	60	60	19.7	14.0	20.9	24.8

XVI Bricks, pottery, glass, cement, etc.	5	198	203	229	240	4	227	231	13	269	282	94.8	118.9	120.8	150.3
XVII Timber, furniture, etc.	6	260	266	290	296	6	337	343	13	358	371	123.2	145.2	166.4	180.5
XVIII Paper, printing and publishing	4	275	279	269	275	6	255	261	5	294	299	54.7	56.0	54.3	61.8
XIX Other manufacturing industries	9	174	183	145	147	4	193	197	4	239	243	73.1	62.4	87.2	109.5
III—XIX: All manufacturing industries	109	4109	4218	4066	4193	111	4238	4349	123	4606	4729	70.8	74.6	79.3	87.4
XX Construction	106	1690	1796	1950	2050	118	2176	2294	100	2269	2369	164.0	204.0	220.7	232.6
XXI Gas, electricity and water	7	181	188	169	184	6	163	169	12	176	188	55.6	55.8	52.4	59.5
XXII Transport and communication	46	564	610	523	573	40	559	599	44	501	545	43.1	42.3	44.7	41.2
XXIII Distributive trades	10	242	252	219	229	12	195	207	4	220	224	9.3	8.6	7.5	7.8
XXIV Insurance, banking, finance and business services	—	14	14	9	12	—	19	19	—	18	18	1.1	0.9	1.4	1.3
XXV Professional and scientific services	6	1322	1328	1103	1107	7	1019	1026	5	1024	1029	36.4	30.3	27.3	27.1
XXVI Miscellaneous services	12	538	550	516	532	11	494	505	18	523	541	22.1	21.8	19.9	20.6
XXVII Public administration and defence	15	1166	1181	1051	1065	15	1197	1212	13	1107	1120	78.0	71.3	87.7	81.6
Unclassified[c]	46	1298	1344	1478	1510	48	1182	1240	32	1054	1086	—			
Total: all industries	449	12315	12764	12275	12743	443	12447	12890	432	12246	12678	60.3	62.1	62.4	60.9

[a] The rate is based on estimates of employees in employment. In particular note that SICs IV and XIV have workforces under 50 000. SIC XX (Construction) has a particularly mobile workforce.

[b] Includes figures for the oil and gas industry collected under the Mineral Workings (Offshore Installations) Act 1971. These are published in the Dept. of Energy's Report *Development of Oil and Gas Resources of the United Kingdom 1984*.

[c] Mainly injuries reported to local authorities. These local authority figures are based on around 400 voluntary returns to the HSE in 1981 and 1982, and around 370 in 1983 and 1984p, out of a possible total of 461 local authorities. For local authority returns any fatal injuries to non-employees are included with fatal injuries to employees; any major injuries to the self-employed are included with major injuries to employees.

[d] Final figures may include minor modifications to take account of changes in reporting arrangement for YTS trainees.

Source: Table 2.1A, HSE/9, 1986.

Table 2.6 *Injuries to self-employed and other non-employees, reported to HSC/HSE enforcement authorities: 1981–85*

Year	Fatal	Major	Major and fatal combined
1981	129	5701	5830
1982	132	5745	5877
1983	152	6445	6597
1984	160	6825	6983
1985	228	7134	7362

Source: Health and Safety Commission Report 1985–6, p. 27

1980, those under NADOR – arguably the most comprehensive – covering only 1981–82, and the series on fatal and major accidents, which is in effect consistent from 1981 to 1985. It is thus difficult to discern any impact of the legislation on accident rates over the whole period.

However, the period since 1974 does appear broadly to divide into two different phases. In the first, running from the passage of the Act to 1980 or 1981, the picture is one of continuing improvement in the overall accident rate; both fatal and non-fatal incidence rates fall. Since 1981, there is an upward trend in the combined rates for fatal and major industries overall, which is particularly severe in several manufacturing SICs and in construction.

Explaining accident rates

Despite the question marks which hang over the data, analysis of statistics on accidents raises questions concerning the factors underpinning the deterioration. Since the turning point roughly coincides with the onset of recession, one hypothesis might be that the costs of safety provision can no longer adequately be met by some employers; hence the concentration of poor accident performance in manufacturing, worst hit by recession at the time. The HSE analysis points towards consideration of other factors. The self-employed fatality rate increase in the early 1980s was 'slightly more than could be accounted for by the known increases in the number of self employed' (HSE/9, 1986: 32). It may be that the growth in self-employment makes 'self regulation' more difficult. The early 1980s was also a period of declining union membership. Since the powers of safety representatives and committees were linked to union membership by the SRSCR in 1978, this may have affected safety provision, although low levels of unionisation and safety improvement are both characteristics of the private services.

We shall return to these questions in subsequent chapters. The object of this chapter has been to attempt an assessment of the legislative impact on the basis of statistics and one must conclude that, whatever has caused the deterioration in the fatal and major accident rate since 1980, it is difficult to isolate the effects of legislation on the movement of accident figures since 1974. The six year period immediately following the Act was associated with a marked decline in the accident rate, but there appears to have been a secular trend towards decline in the early 1970s anyway. If the rise in accident rates since 1981 is associated with the operation of the Act, then it relates to that operation only within specific sectors; the rise has been uneven.

Separate from the question of the impact of legislation, there is the broader question concerning the explanation of changes in reported rates. While it might not be possible to isolate the impact of the Act, it may be possible to explain some of the variance in reported rates in terms of changes to industrial structure or processes.

There is some precedent for this. Grunberg (1983), for example, argues that there is a positive relationship, at plant level, between labour productivity and the accident rate; he does not, however, use HSE statistics. A more systematic approach is that of Nichols (1986). On the basis of HSE statistics he suggests, first, the existence of a business cycle effect, but one of some complexity. During a recession, workers may work harder as management takes advantage of slack labour markets to increase individual effort input, but may be less exposed to risk, since there is less work available. Secondly, he suggests the existence of 'structures of vulnerability', i.e. that workers in sectors characterised by low pay, weak trade union organisation and the presence of many small firms are most likely to suffer increased risk of accident during a recession. His analysis is discursive rather than rigorous, and in no sense does he test for these effects, but, measured against the relative changes in industrial accident rates since 1981, his argument is plausible.

In fact, it is extremely difficult to test for the effects Nichols suggests on an industry basis with the data available. There is a range of data problems, not only to do with the inherent problems of accident statistics, but also to do with the change in SIC classification which affects the HSE, Department of Employment and Business Statistics Office at different times. Moreover, his recession effects are quite complex, and one would need plant- rather than industry-based data to test for them. Nevertheless, one can test for a simple recession effect, and for the effect of firm size and low pay, at industry level.

We have attempted such an analysis on the data in Table 2.5, reclassified by the HSE in terms of the 1980 SIC. The data, the problems and details of the regression analysis are given in the appendix. Briefly, our findings are that increases in the fatal and major accident rate between 1981–84 are higher in industries in which there have been greater than average increases in productivity and in industries where low pay is prevalent. There is some tendency for industries where employment in small firms is high to have higher incidence increases, but the relationship is much weaker. There is no sign of a simple recession effect; output and employment changes do not appear to affect the incidence rate at industry level.

One could no doubt pursue this much further, but for many of the necessary independent variables, no measures are available. For example, changes to industrial processes, to the management of safety, and in trade union density may all affect the reported accident rate. The level of reporting itself may vary, even where legal requirements are stable. Most importantly, the fatal and major rates used here are an unknown, but probably tiny, proportion of the total number of industrial accidents in the period. Nevertheless, the results do confirm what several commentators have suggested; where firm size is small, unionisation weak, wages low and productivity increases high, there may be more risk. We shall consider these issues, and their relation to the prospects for successful self regulation, in succeeding chapters.

Conclusion

Notwithstanding considerable difficulties with the data, one can be fairly safe in asserting that the encouraging trend showing a decline in fatal and serious accidents up until 1980 or 1981 has not continued into the 1980s. There is no doubt that proportionately more people are being seriously injured in the manufacturing and construction industries at the end of the period 1981–85 than at the beginning. It is difficult to move from a description of trends to an understanding of causation.

Official statistics on accidents at work are not a wholly reliable data base from which to draw conclusions about accident causation generally. *A fortiori* they are of limited use in an assessment of the effectiveness of legislation: even were the statistics a wholly accurate record of the underlying industrial accident distribution, there would still be the problem of controlling for other independent variables. Several independent variables can be identified which do appear to affect the rate of change of incidence rates, if not the rates themselves, but the data problems facing rigorous quantitative analysis are immense. A more rigorous analysis than that attempted here would need to construct some revised measures of incidence based on estimates of under-reporting by industry. It seemed to us that, at present, no reliable estimates of this sort could be made.

One reason for this is, in fact, the development of safety institutions: there may be a relationship between institutional development and the accident rate. For example, Beaumont (1983: 132) discovered that, prior to the 1974 Act, industries with relatively high accident rates had relatively good coverage by safety committees: for a later period he notes that high accident rates and invocation of the SRSCR are also correlated. A focus on the institutions of safety regulation leads to a view that the observed level of accidents is, in part, a function of monitoring intensity. From this perspective, one would expect an initial *rise* in recorded accidents *ceteris paribus* in an industry where coverage of safety arrangements is being extended, because of the monitoring effect. One might expect this to be followed by a fall if the representative and committee structure begins to have an effect.

The prospect that it might be possible to assess the SRSC Regulations in terms of the extent to which they are associated with a *rise* in the official accident rate is rather disconcerting, particularly since there is no yardstick to judge the timescale over which one might reasonably expect reduction subsequently to commence if the institutions are to be judged a success. However, one premise upon which a system of self regulation was recommended in 1974 was that insufficient attention was focused upon the problem of industrial accidents, and one consequence of an increased focus could be an improvement in reporting rates. In the next chapter we turn to a consideration of the institutions which were fostered by the Act and Regulations.

3
Assessing the impact: safety institutions

The general duties imposed on employers by the 1974 Act were, in some cases, intended to lead to specific actions. Thus the general duty of care led to the specific requirement to prepare and disseminate a safety policy. Similarly, the rights given to employees and trade unions were to be supported by the establishment of safety representatives. There are thus identifiable actions and developments in the workplace which may attest to the impact of safety legislation.

Once more, these are imperfect measures. The formation, for example, of a safety committee in response to the Act does not in itself indicate an improvement in safety at work, nor does failure to establish one indicate a failure of the employer to fulfill the general duties of section 2 of the Act. Failure of employees to request such a committee similarly does not indicate avoidance of the duties to fellow employees under section 7. The same considerations relate to the writing of policy statements and to the employment of safety specialists, as recommended by Robens. The institutions themselves not only do not guarantee improvements, but their impact and effectiveness is very difficult to measure due to likely reporting effects.

Nevertheless, they are the best general measures of organisational response that we have, and herein lies a further problem. Beyond the requirement for a policy statement, the legislation does not specify precisely what organisational response is required from the employer to ensure that the management structure is appropriate to secure improved safety standards. On the other hand, it does require a response from the institutions for workforce involvement and indeed specifies the form such institutions will take. It is thus much easier to document the growth of workforce involvement than to identify and assess the 'organisation and arrangements' made by management. With these provisos in mind, this chapter will look at the development of safety institutions in response to the Act and Regulations. We shall look in turn at safety policy statements, management organisation, the employment of specialists and safety representatives and safety committees.

Safety policy statements

Under section 2(3) of the 1974 Act, every employer with five or more employees was required 'to prepare and, as often as may be appropriate, revise a written statement of his general policy with respect to the health and safety at work of his employees and the organization and arrangements for the time being in force for carrying out that policy, and to bring the statement and any revision of it to the notice of all his employees'.[1]

Both the Robens Committee and subsequently the HSC had seen the production of policy statements as a vehicle to effect the shift of emphasis from external to self regulation since it required management to think carefully about their own specific safety policies and practice. In this, they were to be disappointed. Two years after the passage of the Act, the Commission noted that policies were often inadequate because of insufficient information on hazards or on procedures for hazard control, inadequate specifications of managerial responsibility, a corresponding over-emphasis on the responsibility of employees and a lack of safety training at all levels. They also noted that some companies merely obtained a policy from another company either through friendly association or by payment. The 'borrowed' policy was then duplicated with the names and other specific details amended to suit its new home: more recent research has confirmed this tendency (HSE/12, 1976: 19; Dawson, Poynter and Stevens 1983a). Virtually any survey of policies, such as that undertaken by the local authority reported in Chapter 6, shows a high level of non-compliance with this section of the Act.

It is often suggested by those eager to improve standards of health and safety at work that whilst the existence of a policy does not ensure safety, its absence implies poor standards. For example the Accident Prevention Advisory Unit has emphasised the importance of policy statements as part of 'the practical expression of self regulation within an undertaking' which distinguished good and bad safety performance. A size effect appears to operate here, small organisations, particularly those in which there is little union activity, standing out as slow in fulfilling these obligations. This is complicated by sectoral differences; for example, in establishments covered by Environmental Health Officers, 'standards of compliance with obligations to produce safety policies varied considerably and some difficulties are still being experienced in convincing employers of their obligations. This applied particularly to smaller establishments where the owner was working on the premises or was self-employed' (HSE/14, 1980).

Other literature stresses the differential effectiveness of policy statements, and in particular the variation in the extent to which policies are actually implemented (HSE/14, 1980; PPITB 1983). Effectiveness is shown to be associated with careful specification of responsibility and accountability for health and safety matters, although 'effectiveness' in these terms does not – as we shall see below – relate solely to accident statistics. Leopold and Beaumont suggest that 'companies in high accident risk industries would appear to put more effort into achieving a unique and detailed policy statement than those where the inherent risk is less obvious' (1982: 26). This of course implies that 'good' policies and a high accident rate might go together in some industries, nicely demonstrating both the methodological difficulties surrounding research on effectiveness and the need to explore the internal dynamics of individual workplaces in order to understand the issues involved in attempts to improve and maintain standards of health and safety at work.

The difference between the sort of rhetoric which puts health and safety at the top of everyone's list of priorities and the practical reality of protagonists fighting to maintain its place – albeit low down – in a list of competing priorities is discussed further in Chapters 4 to 7. In fact, where serious consideration is being given to how to improve standards of health and safety at work, managers frequently turn their attention to how they can alter their actual organisation and arrangements rather than their policy.

Management organisation and safety specialists

General duties were placed upon the employer 'to ensure, so far as is reasonably practicable, the health, safety and welfare at work of all his employees' (HASAWA s2). In contrast to previous legislation on health and safety, the Act stated that the employers' duties extended beyond a responsibility for physical conditions of work to include responsibility to do all that was 'reasonably practicable' in such things as instruction, training, systems of work and supervision. The interpretation of these general duties was to emphasise the important responsibilities of senior executives, line management and supervision. 'The primary operational responsibility for ensuring safe working must rest with line management' (Robens 1972a: para. 53). In discharging this responsibility, great importance was also attached to specialist advice and expertise in diagnosing problems and deciding upon appropriate solutions. Thus the principle of efficient management was seen by Robens to depend on the development of line responsibility for health and safety supplemented by health and safety specialist activities. There is, however, nothing specific about line management accountability in the Act.

The Robens idea of line management responsibility does raise several difficulties and a number of writers have argued that there is a contradiction between the concern of line managers for production and the need to ensure the safety of employees. Nichols and Armstrong (1973), for example, argued strongly that management's overriding concern for production leads to pressure on workers to take risks. They discussed five accidents in a firm which appeared formally to be highly safety conscious and argued that pressure to take risks and court danger was a prime cause in each case. They argued that such pressures are inevitable given an overriding concern for profit, or even, as Haraszti (1977) argued in the different context of Hungary, productivity. On the basis of a comparison of two plants within Peugeot/Talbot, Grunberg (1983) similarly argued that there is conflict between the objectives of improved safety and improved labour productivity. He suggested that independent workforce organisation is the best protection of employees' safety but that, as within capitalist society the ultimate constraint is competitive success, its pursuit will eventually undermine all attempts to provide a secure workplace. Dawson, Poynter and Stevens (1984a: 34) generally found higher standards of line safety management than those implied by Grunberg, but they too found that conflicts often arose in the chemical industry, for example about whether additional expenditure or loss of production continuity were justified in the cause of improved standards of health and safety.

A key element affecting the awareness of safety issues fostered by line management involvement in health and safety is performance measurement and assessment. Representatives of the HSE itself have emphasised that

> In the move to self regulation, H.M. Inspectors of Factories
> are increasingly requiring to know that undertakings have the
> capacity to measure their own performance and to act on the
> results of the measurement. Increasingly they will concentrate
> on this aspect of inspection rather than the nuts and bolts of
> safety, although of course they will still wish to assure
> themselves that, whatever measuring system is adopted, it
> accurately reflects the reality of the situation at one workplace
> (Wade and Lindsay 1980).

However, despite such exhortation, and the existence of a number of prescriptive approaches to good practice in the area (HSE/14, 1980; Barrell and Thomas 1982), there is little evidence that such monitoring systems

47

have been adopted, still less that the adoption follows from legislation. Dawson, Poynter and Stevens (1982a, 1983a) show examples of large firms in the chemical industries which have instituted effective control systems, but such arrangements are not common.

Overall, then, there is only sparse evidence on a key area of safety provision. Line management responsibility for safety was a crucial element in safety provision for Robens, but there are some measurement difficulties and little information about the extent to which safety performance appraisal has, like output or budgetary targets, been built in to line managers' jobs. We shall return to this problem in Chapter 7.

Slightly 'harder' evidence is available on the growth of health and safety as a specialist function. The Robens Report and the 1974 Act almost certainly had a major effect in accelerating the hitherto somewhat uncertain development of a distinctive occupational group of safety specialists. Although their appointment was not required by the Act, the Robens Report (1972a: 17) had stressed the need for specialist advice 'within the management team' and many employers and managers, particularly of larger establishments, quickly began to look for more specialist advice when they were forced to think both about the implications of their general duties and their fears of criminal prosecution for dereliction of these duties. Furthermore, the Act brought in an additional 7–8 million employees not previously covered by health and safety legislation.

In 1972, the Institution of Industrial Safety Officers, formed in 1953, had approximately 2000 members. In 1981 the renamed Institution of Occupational Safety and Health, which had practically doubled its membership since Robens, estimated that 10 000 people now had the word 'safety' in their job title. But a common nomenclature disguised the large variety of qualifications, experience and activities which characterised both full-time specialists and their part-time associates who combined health and safety functions with other jobs. The Robens Report commented on the wide range of specialists from 'highly qualified professionals in very senior posts responsible for the development of safety policy and coordination at high levels' to those 'who do little more than maintain basic records, issue protective clothing and conduct routine investigations into accidents' (Robens 1972a: 17). More recent commentaries on safety specialists (Graham 1982; Beaumont, Leopold and Coyle 1982; Dawson *et al.* 1984c; Booth 1987) have all endorsed this view of an extremely diverse occupational group.

Given the current state of the occupation, comparatively few safety specialists have a strong technical background, many have been recruited from the security services or have moved into safety as a pre-retirement position from operations, production or maintenance functions within their firms (Dawson *et al.* 1984b; Graham 1982). This need not mean that they are ineffective, since their impact on other aspects of safety organisation may be considerable. Leopold and Coyle (1981), for example, note the catalytic role safety specialists can play in developing and sustaining an effective safety committee. They also note that many safety officers do receive substantial technical training; particularly concerning health matters associated with noise, dust, chemicals and ventilation.

An HSE report on the activities of safety officers in 23 companies in 1975 found that the officers who were most able to develop strong advisory roles were those in establishments where management and trade unions (if present) were very committed to health and safety. Safety officers who were effectively left to 'do' safety for their company were in very weak positions and, by implication, in establishments with relatively poor safety performance. Even advisers who were in fairly strong positions were found to be largely concerned with reacting to problems as they arose in operational areas and to have little involvement at the design stage of new machines and processes. A few, however, were invited to examine and advise on working procedures before machinery became fully operational (HSE/11, 1975).

McKinnon (1979) suggested a rosy future for the profession, considerably helped by developments in legislation, strengthening public opinion (particularly in the light of such notable disasters as Flixborough and Seveso), technological change and, he hoped, changes in managerial attitudes. However, even in 1979, the 'heyday' of concern for health and safety, he had to acknowledge that the development of the profession to a higher plane of 'advisory post(s) with direct access to the boardroom' (one of a 'number of central management services'), would only be achieved 'when it really gets through to top management that they are responsible both morally and in law for health and safety'.

It may well be that safety officers, appointed in the aftermath of the Act, have less influence now than hitherto. Beaumont, Leopold and Coyle looked at safety officers roles and responsibilities in 33 plants in 1982. They found that 'many of the safety officers interviewed suggested that, as a result of the recession, production considerations tended consistently to outweigh health and safety matters as a priority in management calculations' (1982: 38). Dawson has also dealt with the effects of recession on the role of safety specialists and discussed the implications of changes in industrial and economic structure both for the training and accreditation of specialists (Dawson 1986: 17) and for issues of professional development (Dawson 1987: 6–8). She concludes that safety practitioners are a service profession which has skills and knowledge which it must sell to its clients, who may be in-house managers in larger firms or senior executives of

49

smaller firms considering using external specialist consultants. Few of these potential clients it seems are going to come looking for the services of safety specialists since issues of health and safety are rarely 'naturally' high on the list of immediate priorities for people at work in a highly competitive environment.

Safety representatives and safety committees

As Chapter 1 showed, workforce involvement was central to the Robens analysis, even though the role of trade unions and collective bargaining caused difficulty. The form this involvement was to take was the establishment of safety representatives and safety committees. This was not an entirely new development, but it did generalise what had previously been a more local phenomenon. Apart from the coal mining industry where an Act of 1872 had given miners the right to appoint workers' inspectors, union involvement in health and safety in the workplace was, until 1977, only possible on a voluntary basis, despite a history of encouragement by the Factory Inspectorate.

The Inspectorate had urged as early as 1913 that 'the reduction of accidents can be best secured by obtaining the interest and cooperation of operatives and officials through safety committees', a sentiment voiced much later by the TUC and CBI. But despite such exhortations, the development of joint committees was patchy (Williams 1960: 188; Beaumont 1979: 56). The Inspectorate later undertook two surveys of safety committees in 1967 and 1969. In the latter year, only 27% of establishments investigated had a joint health and safety committee, although a further 20% did have a general consultative committee that discussed health and safety matters. These results formed part of the Department of Employment's evidence to Robens. The Warwick survey, though conducted in 1977–78, asked about the existence of safety committees before the Act: 44.4% of the 970 manufacturing organisations sampled reported the establishment of such committees. There were fairly large variations between industrial sectors, and committees tended to be found in larger establishments and those which had other systems for joint consultation. Such establishments were also slightly more likely to have higher accident rates, to have multi-unionism and proportionately more shop stewards (Beaumont and Deaton 1981; Brown 1981).

Surveys of developments in the immediate period after 1974 show substantially increased coverage. The Warwick survey also found that the proportion of workplaces with safety committees rose to 70% in 1977–78. A survey one year later – around the time of implementation of the SRSCR – by Industrial Relations Services found that 76% of respondent companies had safety committees; 23% of the total being a response to a trade union request. Of 68 non-union firms covered by the survey, 48 had established some joint machinery for health and safety and over half reported some arrangements for workplace inspections. The self-selection of respondents means that the results of this survey must be treated with caution and in particular one would suggest that the extent of consultation in non-unionised firms is probably over-estimated (HSIB, 34, 1978: 1–6).

In October 1979 the HSE conducted a survey on the early impact of the Regulations (Department of Employment 1981). This showed that safety representatives had been appointed in a total of 17.2% of the 5000 workplaces sampled; 81% of workplaces with safety representatives also had joint safety committees. The survey again showed variation by industrial sector and by size. Only 3.9% of the 1912 construction sites had safety representatives compared with 66.7% of the 54 workplaces in the gas, electicity and water industries. Only 5.2% of the sampled workplaces with fewer than 25 employees had safety representatives appointed under the Regulations. Although 17% of workplaces had representatives, 80% of all employees in the sampled establishments were so represented.

The effects of industrial sector and firm size are particularly interesting since the Regulations were designed to be flexible. The guidance notes illustrate solutions to the problems of dealing with very different types of workplaces (HSC/6: 11) and emphasise the need for 'flexible and voluntary' solutions. However, many small establishments clearly could not or would not make appropriate 'flexible' arrangements.

Despite the clear patterns of size and industrial variation identified overall, an analysis of the results distinguishing between committees which had been established as a result of the Regulations and those which had existed before the Regulations suggested that the new committees tended to be established in smaller plants and in industries with lower accident rates. In other words many of the new committees were in those sorts of establishments where there had been least voluntary development before the Act and Regulations. Nonetheless there were still large numbers of employees not covered and these were largely in smaller establishments.

Further analysis of these data by Beaumont (1983: 87) shows that safety representatives were still more likely to be found, one year after the introduction of the SRSCR, in industries with high accident rates, high collective agreement coverage, single employer bargaining, large establishments, in the public sector and in establishments where a member of senior management was specifically responsible for industrial relations and personnel matters. These findings and those of Beaumont and Deaton (1981) suggest that the institutional development of consultation for health and safety is associated with the development of other industrial relations

Table 3.1 *Methods of consultation on health and safety matters, (a) 1980 and (b) 1984*

(a) 1980

	All establishments (%)
A. Joint committee specifically for health and safety	37
B. Joint committee for health and safety and other matters	12
C. Workforce representatives, but not committee	21
D. No consultation or representation	27
E. Other answer	3

(b) 1984

	Public sector (%)	Private sector (%)
Within establishments		
A. Joint health and safety committee	23	21
B. Joint committee for health and safety and other matters	9	10
C. Workforce representatives, but no committee	52	34
D. No representation	10	30
E. Other answer	7	5
Joint health and safety committee at establishment or higher level	80	41

Source: (a) Daniel and Millward 1983: 145; (b) Millward and Stevens 1986: 150.

institutions. If this is any guide to what is happening now, we might hypothesise that smaller establishments and those where there are no recognised trade unions are unlikely to have formally established committees unless they are formed as a way of 'pre-empting' embryonic trade union organisations from gathering support for such structures.

More recent data on the coverage of safety committees and safety representation is given in Table 3.1 based on the two DE/PSI/ESRC workplace surveys in 1980 and 1984 (Daniel and Millward 1983; Millward and Stevens 1986). The 1980 survey indicated the widespread coverage of safety committees at establishment level, most of which had been established after the passage of the Act. Less than a third of the total had been established before 1975, and almost half of the remainder had been established after 1977 when the SRSCR had been laid before parliament. It thus appears that the legislation had some effect on the coverage of institutions for workforce involvement.

However, it remained the case in 1980 that establishments with high trade union membership and with recognised trade unions were more likely to have safety committees of some sort. Size was also important, but the trade union effect was marked even where establishment size was controlled: 30% of establishments without union recognition had some form of safety committee. There were also differences between industries. Overall, 15% of establishments having trade union recognition had no provision for health and safety consultation or representation. In construction, the comparable figure was 24%, in distribution, 29% and in financial services, 49%. Daniel and Millward concluded at the time: 'there has indeed been a growth in the provision for dealing with health and safety matters at the workplace, although a saturation point has by no means been reached' (1983: 144).

Although there was a further increase in safety provision by the time of the second survey in 1984, 'saturation' remained out of reach. The 1980 and 1984 data are not strictly comparable, but overall there was an increase in the percentage of establishments with some form of worker representation on safety matters from 70% to 80%. The increase was more pronounced in sectors where representation had been patchy in 1980 – small firms, those without recognised trade unions, and those in private services. Overall, there was a lessening of the disparities between types of workplace in terms of safety representation (Millward and Stevens 1986: 149). The differences between 1980 and 1984 on items A and C probably follow from a change in coding procedure. However, one interesting feature of the responses is the number of organisations which had representatives at establishment level but a safety committee at a higher level in the organisation.

Overall, the data imply an extension of the coverage of institutions of workforce involvement over the period, particularly in the non-union sector. Disparities between sectors have declined, but by no means disappeared. Coverage is far from universal. Indeed the GMBATU estimated in 1987 that there were about 150000 safety representatives covering approximately 40% of employees, mainly in the larger workplaces, who actually used some or all of their rights (GMBATU 1987: 28).

In summary, then, the Act and Regulations have been associated with the extension of formal mechanisms for employee involvement in that the proportion both of establishments and employees covered has been extended. However, there are still variations associated with establishment size, level of unionisation and sector of operation. Just as we looked beyond

53

formal provision in management areas, it is necessary to look at the effectiveness of operation of institutions for workforce involvement.

Still greater ambiguity surrounds the effectiveness of safety representatives and committees than surrounds the effectiveness of management. Some of the reasons for this have been touched upon in Chapter 1. The Robens approach, based on the idea of consensus, would suggest that workforce involvement would assist a committed management to improve safety through facilitating free flow of information about hazard control and by acting as a source of inspiration and commitment to maintain safety effort. However, for those who doubt managerial willingness to promote safety, institutions of workforce involvement must act not as an arm of managerial policy but as a countervailing force. Whereas the integration of self regulatory institutions is important for the former view, the safety representatives' independence of management assumes greater importance for the latter.

This distinction emerges in discussions of trade union health and safety policy. Glendon and Booth (1982) report that a number of unions in Britain which have been particularly active at both policy and grass roots level in occupational health and safety, for example ASTMS and GMBATU, have at the same time been fairly damning about the beneficial effects of safety committee operation – not least because it invites representatives to compromise. Such a view tends to stress the importance of safety representatives rather than safety committees and to emphasize the importance of procedural agreements. Rather than applauding those firms who rushed to set up safety committees, those who hold this view have seen such employers as attempting to undermine the potential power of safety representatives. Cunningham, for example, remarked that 'Management's lately-discovered enthusiasm to set up safety committees suggests that they should be carefully examined by trade unionists. It should be remembered that they have only a *consultative* role, not a negotiating one' (1978: 25). This approach sets safety squarely in the bargaining arena, although it does not conform to the Robens view of the effects of bargaining, in which safety issues are 'traded off'. Certainly, ineffective safety committees appear to exist, if not obviously for the reasons trade unions fear.

An emphasis on the need for independent workforce organisation for health and safety, and scepticism both about managerial motives and the value of safety committees is consistent with attempts which were made to encourage informal groupings of safety representatives, both within and between establishments, in order to establish a strong and independent trade union base in health and safety. The first of such groups, the Coventry Health and Safety Movement, was set up in 1977, and at one time there were as many as 40 similar groups. However, changes in political and economic life in the 1980s have seen a decline in their scope and number.

For those who stress independence, one of the more important features is the relationship between shop stewards and safety representatives. Several unions seek to amalgamate the two roles to avoid organisational divisions: however, they do not always manage to implement such a policy. For example, in 1980 the (then) AUEW surveyed their estimated 12 000 safety representatives and found that, in spite of their policy to nominate existing shop stewards, 24% of safety representatives had not received trade union training. There were also reports of representatives not receiving paid time off either for training or to carry out their duties. 17% of workplaces had no safety representatives. Small companies, as always, featured strongly in the group of workplaces which were marked by poor or non-existent provisions (Glendon and Booth 1982).

One of the most detailed studies of safety representatives – of 225 GMBATU representatives from the Glasgow region in 1979 – is reported in several publications by Beaumont (1980, 1981a, 1983). He asked his respondents about their views on their most important functions. Considerable importance was attached by most safety representatives to the function of communicating workers' complaints to management. Most representatives felt that the workforce was an important source of information on hazards. Only a third of those sampled said they thought routine inspections were their most important single function; 52% felt that pursuit of individual complaints was the more important factor.

The study also explored the safety representatives' views on negotiation, consultation and problem solving and found that these activities were seen more as alternatives than as complementary. Negotiation was more likely to be adopted as the representative's approach in response to situations

(a) where safety representatives saw management as strong defenders of management prerogatives, keen to limit union influences in decision making;
(b) where safety representatives believed that there was a basic dissimilarity between the aims of management and trade unions on health and safety;
(c) where representatives believed that management were relatively unconcerned with health and safety;
(d) where there had been little union involvement prior to the 1974 Act;
(e) where representatives were also shop stewards (54% of the sample were also shop stewards).

Workforce support obviously mattered more to this sample where they felt that negotiations were involved: just over 20% of Beaumont's respondents reported some form of industrial action over health and safety in the previous year. Two-thirds of the sample – disproportionately from smaller firms and ones where labour relations were viewed as harmonious – considered that unions and management were seeking to accomplish similar things in health and safety. The remainder saw an essential difference in objectives. Again we see a strong relationship between approaches to workplace industrial relations and to health and safety.

Whereas the union fear was that management would disregard safety issues, employers' fears about safety representatives concerned their power and the extent to which they would seek to trade off safety issues against others in bargaining. Castle (1978), for example, criticised the Regulations for giving safety representatives and safety committees 'power without responsibility'. He foresaw a time when safety representatives would rarely acquiesce in accepting risks but would always demand action, and furthermore that in their powers of inspection 'parliament has invested the more dictatorial amongst them with greater power than any plans afoot for industrial democracy'. For good or bad there is no evidence that any of these fears have been realised.

Moreover, despite anxiety amongst some employers and managers about the burdens which the HASAWA would impose, there is no evidence that the legislation is in fact particularly burdensome. Daniel and Stilgoe (1978) reported generally favourable reactions to the health and safety legislation even from small firms which are more prone to such complaints. In a DE survey of 300 firms focusing on companies with fewer than 50 employees only 2% mentioned health and safety legislation as one of their 'main difficulties' in the running of a business. Moreover while 28% of the sample had experienced the enforcement of standards of health and safety, only 4% had found this troublesome (Clifton and Tatton-Brown 1979).

The effectiveness of institutions for workforce involvement is thus, as with those of management, indeterminate in the absence of reliable data on accident statistics. A well developed safety representative network may be seen as the first line of defence of workers' safety or as a costly attempt to gain bargaining leverage by manipulation of safety issues. A smoothly functioning committee may be seen as evidence of effective practice or as an illustration of a workforce being 'conned'.

However, whatever the balance of consensus or conflict over safety, one could argue that evidence of training is important to considerations of effectiveness, even if the issue re-emerges in discussions about the source and nature of the training provided. In fact, following the emphasis given to safety representative training in the Robens Report, the SRSCR reinforced the legal right for trade union appointed safety representatives to be permitted time off without loss of pay to undergo TUC approved training

Table 3.2 *Attendance at TUC courses for union safety representatives: 1975–86*[a]

1975–76	5370
1976–77	7803
1977–78	10 398
1978–79	27 361
1979–80	18 738
1980–81	12 067
1981–82	8934
1982–83	6737
1983–84	7824
1984–85	7870
1985–86	7307

[a] Includes stages 1 and 2 but excludes follow-on courses.
Source: TUC general council report, 1986.

courses. This was associated with a rapid increase in the numbers trained in safety matters by the TUC in 1978–79; as Table 3.2 shows.

However, as Table 3.2 also indicates, the increase was not sustained and numbers fall away substantially after 1979. Such a trend could simply indicate the satisfaction of a single peak in training demand, but other factors appear to be at work.[2] Glendon and Booth (1982) cite two cases in which tribunals have decided that safety representatives, having been on a company course, are not entitled to paid time off to attend courses approved by the unions. They suggest that the problems of getting time off, particularly for training, have increased during the recession.

Moreover, the idea that safety training demand has a single peak may be mistaken given available evidence on turnover of safety representatives. Leopold and Beaumont (1984) conducted a pilot study of representatives from GMBATU. They suggested that between 12% and 26% of known safety representententatives were in the process of being replaced. Only 20% of the sample had served for more than five years in office and they tended to be older, employed with the company for a relatively long period, to have held another union post previously, to be in a relatively large establishment, with a relatively large number of other safety representatives and to receive considerable full time union officer support. Over two-thirds were willing recruits to the role but, for many, initial expectations had been disappointed. The majority of those who remained in office reported unsatisfactory relations with either management, or rank and file, or both.

The reduction in safety training since 1979 is thus likely to mean that the number of safety representatives with adequate training has declined. It may also mean that those who remain in office for some period of time lose enthusiasm and effectiveness.

The general link between the institutions of self regulation and those of workplace industrial relations – both in terms of extent and performance – raises questions about the ability of the institutions to survive and prosper while workplace trade unionism is weakened by recession. There is, of course, some debate about the precise extent to which workplace organisation has been undermined by recession since 1979 (Batstone *et al*. 1986; Terry 1986), but it seems clear that such organisation has had to accommodate substantial changes in working practices and technology in the last few years (Edwards 1984). Questions thus arise both about the effects of such changes and about the ability of safety representatives to influence them.

Some of the best evidence comes from Batstone *et al*.'s questionnaire study of over 1000 shop stewards in manufacturing, telecommunications and the civil service. They find substantial evidence of negotiation over the health and safety effects of technical change; in all of their industries, over 50% of respondents claimed to have done so. In a minority of cases, there had been disagreements over it. Particularly in white collar areas, health and safety figured strongly in union proposals regarding new technology. Overall, 'the data suggest that technical change is associated with improved health and safety among manual groups, and the reverse for non-manual' (1986: 196, 205, 233). Evidence is available that some workplace institutions for self regulation are still operational, though the impact on overall safety standards remains in doubt.

Conclusions

The growth of the institutions of workforce involvement is thus reasonably well documented. The Act and Regulations substantially encouraged their development away from those areas where previous voluntary mechanisms had existed, but many firms and sectors remain relatively untouched. In addition, there is some indication that the period since 1979 has seen less growth than in the five previous years. By contrast, it is difficult to document any parallel impact on management organisation. Such changes are not easily surveyed, since the Act merely specified the duty to illustrate organisation and arrangements for safety in the policy statement; it did not specify what those arrangements might be. In both cases, the assessment of effectiveness is difficult. The survey data cannot give such an assessment, and in any event the criteria both for assessment and the measurement of effectiveness are difficult.

These lacunae mean that we know more about institutional form than about safety awareness and effectiveness. We also know more about events in large, unionised organisations than those in small and non-unionised firms. Finally, we know more about the period of institutional proliferation immediately after the Act and subsequent Regulations than about more recent events.

Three issues emerge as worthy of more detailed discussion. The first is that of 'effective self regulation'. Robens specified no particular organisational form for improvements in safety in particular workplaces beyond suggestions about the form of workforce involvement through representatives and committees. A number of interesting questions surround the issue of appropriateness of safety policy and safety organisation within the scope of self regulation and in the face of different sorts of hazards. Where interests differ between employers and trade unions, it is not easy to decide on how to discuss effectiveness. Nevertheless the relationship between forms of management organisation and of workforce involvement are central to safety improvement.

A second important issue concerns the associated differences in size and unionisation. The available evidence raises questions about the response to safety legislation in small companies, while the legislation itself promotes a distinction between unionised and non-unionised workplaces. On the assumption that small establishments may, for a number of reasons, experience problems in legislative compliance, that they may frequently be non-unionised and that unionisation makes a difference to safety provision, then industries characterised by large numbers of small firms present particular difficulties for self regulation.

A third issue concerns developments since 1979, both in legislative and economic terms. From both points of view, a climate broadly supportive of institutional proliferation and resource provision has been replaced by one in which safety issues receive a lower priority. The auxiliary legislation upon which certain aspects of safety legislation were premised has disappeared or fallen into disuse: fewer safety representatives are trained, and it may be that union support services are less readily available. Moreover, if there is a cost associated with the provision of a safe and healthy workplace, then it may be the case that recession-hit firms are less able to support it, and recession-hit unions less able to insist: the result may be a deterioration in safety standards.

The legislation: background and impact

There is some evidence, both from the statistical analysis of the previous chapter and from the institutional analysis of this, that aspects of economic and industrial structure have a profound effect on safety which requires closer attention. We shall discuss these issues in subsequent chapters. Chapters 4–6 will look in detail at events in three sectors, chemicals, construction and retailing. Chapter 7 will develop a model of local self regulation and indicate the areas where it is least likely to flourish.

PART 2

Developments at local level

Assessment of the extent to which a self regulatory system has developed at the level of the firm must look at the three areas in which action was promoted by legislation. These are

(a) safety policy documents;
(b) management organisation, including the role of specialists;
(c) employee organisation and involvement through safety representatives and safety committees.

Studies of these developments in the three contrasting industrial sectors of chemicals, construction and retail follow in this part of the book. Its objective is to present the findings of these studies and to use them as a basis for Chapter 7 which provides a prescriptive model of effective health and safety management and indicates at local level where the limits of self regulation are likely to be encountered.

4

Safety in chemicals

The chemical industry was the setting for the first Imperial College research project into safety at work.[1] The fieldwork was conducted between 1980 and 1981 before official statistics revealed the levelling off in safety standards and performance noted in Chapter 2, although our case studies suggested that things were changing. This chapter is included for two reasons. First, it formed the basis for the derivation of a model of effective self regulation at the level of the enterprise which was subsequently revised in the light of the second study and which is the subject of Chapter 7. Secondly, the chemical industry provides significant points of contrast with construction and retail. In this and the following two data chapters, we follow broadly the same format. Initially, the industrial context and the background to the cases, including the safety performance of the industry, is outlined. Subsequently we deal with managerial policies and organisation, and then with the institutions and quality of workforce involvement. The chapter closes with an assessment of the impact of recession.

The chemical industry

Industrial structure

In contrast to construction and retail, the chemical industry is characterised by oligopoly and employment concentration. In 1979, 59% of the workforce were employed in establishments with 2000 or more employees whereas 98% of construction employees were found in establishments employing fewer than 100 people (Table 4.1). Nonetheless there are also a significant number of small establishments in the specialist chemical areas with 75% of all establishments employing fewer than 100 (Table 4.2). In addition, there is a substantial element of subcontracting for maintenance and construction and reconstruction of plant. In the ten years from 1970 the UK chemical industrial production rate grew by 3.4% as compared

Table 4.1 *Industrial concentration, establishment size and employment in the chemical and construction industries.*

Size group	Establishments (number)	Total employment (thousands)	Employment of operatives (thousands)	Gross output (£ million)
Chemicals and allied industry (order V)				
1–99	2434 (75%)	34.6 (8%)	19.4	1 423.2 (8%)
100–999	429 (13%)	81.4 (20%)	47.5	3 833.7 (22%)
1000–1999	128 (4%)	51.6 (13%)	29.7	1 753.3 (10%)
2000–9999	195 (6%)	134.5 (33%)	77.8	5 398.2 (31%)
10 000 and over	54 (2%)	99.5 (26%)	62.8	5 099.0 (30%)
Totals	3220 (100%)	402.6 (100%)	237.1	17 231.9 (101%)
Construction (order XX)				
1–99	100 942 (98.3%)	626.6 (47%)	446.6	4 239.8 (42%)
100–999	860 (0.84%)	129.3 (10%)	98.0	1 029.2 (10%)
1000–1999	713 (0.69%)	296.6 (22%)	222.7	2 418.7 (24%)
2000–2499	98 (0.14%)	145.3 (11%)	108.9	1 232.0 (12%)
2500 and over	25 (0.03%)	139.0 (10%)	102.7	1 137.4 (11%)
Totals	102 638 (100%)	1336.7 (100%)	979.0	10 057.1 (99%)

The ratio of operatives to total employed in chemicals is 59%; and in construction is 73%.

Source: Business Statistics Office: Business Monitor: Report on Census of Production, Summary Tables 1979, Tables 6 and 14; HMSO.

with an overall industrial production growth rate of 1.1%. However, by 1981 recession had hit the industry.

In 1979 the chemical industry employed 402 600 people in the UK. The industry is capital intensive and much of its activity is dependent on research and development. Consequently the industry as a whole employs comparatively fewer unskilled and semiskilled manual workers and comparatively larger numbers of skilled and professionally trained workers, a strong point of contrast with both construction and retail. Another difference is that trade union density is greater in chemicals than in construction. Union membership is more concentrated in the larger chemical establishments.[2] The discussion in Chapter 3 has already suggested that a combination of an above average level of unionisation, together with an above average accident rate, could be correlated with a relatively high level of voluntarily established joint health and safety

Table 4.2 *Fatal accidents reported to HM Factory Inspectorate under the Factories Act: incidence rates[a] by industry: 1971–80*

	Incidence rates per 100000 at risk				
SIC order	1971	1974	1977	1978	1980
III Food, drink & tobacco	4.5	4.2	4.0	3.1	2.8
IV Coal & petroleum products	7.4[b]	12.2[b]	19.8	8.2[b]	21.9
V Chemicals & allied industries	8.4	17.2[c]	5.0	4.9	2.4
VI Metal manufacture	13.7	13.8	12.3	10.4	7.2
VII Mechanical engineering	3.5	3.1	3.4	3.0	3.5
VIII Instrument engineering	0.9[b]	1.0[b]	1.1[b]	—	1.2[b]
IX Electrical engineering	1.4	0.5[b]	0.8[b]	—	0.5[b]
X Shipbuilding & marine engineering	12.4	11.8	10.3	3.8	7.3
XI Vehicles	2.3	1.8	0.9	1.7	2.2
XII Metal goods not elsewhere specified	3.6	3.6	2.9	2.7	3.3
XIII Textiles	4.1	4.2	2.3	1.9	0.6[b]
XIV Leather, leather goods and fur	5.2[b]	2.8[b]	3.0[b]	6.3[b]	—
XV Clothing and footwear	—	0.6[b]	0.3[b]	—	—
XVI Bricks, pottery, glass, cement etc.	7.6	6.8	3.4	7.5	3.3
XVII Timber, furniture, etc.	4.3	6.7	3.5	4.1	2.2[b]
XVIII Paper, printing and publishing	2.4	2.0	2.2	3.9	2.0
XIX Other manufacturing industries	2.4	1.1[b]	2.4	0.4[b]	1.9[b]
All manufacturing industries	4.3	4.5	3.4	3.1	2.7
XX Construction	19.6	16.0	13.1	12.2	13.0

[a] Incidence rates based on fewer than five fatal accidents can be misleading and should be treated with caution.
[b] Incidence rates based on fewer than five fatal accidents.
[c] Includes 28 fatalities in the Flixborough Explosion.
Source: Health and Safety Executive, Health and Safety Statistics, 1980, HMSO (Table 3.2).

committees prior to the 1974 Act and 1977 Regulations. The Warwick survey of workplace industrial relations found that 50.7% of the 69 chemical establishments sampled had voluntarily established safety committees before 1974, and 37.7% had established committees between 1974 and the survey in 1977/78. Only 11.6% were found to have no committees in 1977/78. This compares with 44% of 970 manufacturing establishments with voluntary established committees, 36.7% with committees established in the 1974–78 period, and 17.9% of sampled establishments with no committees at all (Beaumont and Deaton 1981).

Table 4.3 *Incidence rates for 100 000 at risk for accidents to operatives reported to HM Factory Inspectorate under Factories Act: 1972–80*

All reported accidents: incidence rates[a]			
	1971–75	1976–78[b]	1979	1980
Chemicals	3678	4020	3960	3420
All manufacturing	3556	3570	3340	2860

[a] Incidence rates based on number of operatives.
[b] Average.
Source: Health and Safety Executive Manufacturing and Services 1978 (Table 3.2, 3.3). Health and Safety Executive Statistics 1981–2 (Table 1.1B).

Hazards

The extensive use of toxic and flammable substances and the development of complex transformation processes dependent on finely controlled, but extreme, levels of temperature and pressure might suggest that the potential for damage to the safety and health of employees is high. However, as Table 4.2 suggests, the fatality rates for the period 1971–80 are significantly less than for construction and by the end of this period, having experienced a generally steady decline, only a little above the average rates for all manufacturing industry. A notable discontinuity in the chemicals series for this period is caused by the inclusion of 28 deaths from the Flixborough disaster in 1974.[3] Occurring as it did in the same year as the Health and Safety at Work Act, the Flixborough disaster adds further complications to those already discussed in Chapter 2 to attempts to establish the effect of health and safety legislation on behaviour and outcomes in this industry. There is general agreement that, at least in the short term, its occurrence made most people in the industry more 'safety conscious', and more concerned about the safety of their plant and working practices. One effect of these developments could well be an increase in the willingness to report accidents. This could be one explanation for the trend of a greater increase in the incidence rates of all reported accidents in the chemical industry 1976–78 compared to all manufacturing industry (Table 4.3).

Another factor in this disproportionate increase in chemical lost time accident (LTA) rates could be higher rates of economic activity in the chemical industry than elsewhere. This may also be a factor in the drop in

Table 4.4 *Fatal and major injuries to employees reported to enforcement authorities by industry: 1981–84 (incidence rates for 100 000 employees)*[a]

	1981	1982	1983	1984 p[a]
Chemicals	331	351	383	375
	(82.0)	(91.4)	(105.7)	(104.2)
Construction	1796	2050	2294	2369
	(164.0)	(204.0)	(220.7)	(232.6)
Distributive trades	252	229	207	224
	(9.3)	(8.6)	(7.5)	(7.8)
All manufacturing	4218	4193	4349	4729
	(70.8)	(74.6)	(79.3)	(87.4)
All industries	12764	12743	12 890	12678
	(60.3)	(62.1)	(62.4)	(60.9)

[a] Incidence rates based on number of employees and thus not directly comparable with previous incidence rates based on number of operatives.
Source: Table 2.1A HSE Statistics 1983.

accident rates in 1980, as economic activity began to decline and the effects of the recession were felt more strongly and widely. Although the LTA rates showed an increase in 1974–78, the rates for group 1 (serious) and fatal accidents showed a greater decline in the chemical industry (13% and 40% respectively) than for all manufacturing industry (6% and 22% respectively).

The period 1981–84, although occurring after our case studies of chemical establishments were conducted, is nonetheless of interest in terms of general trends. Table 4.4, which provides selective information from Table 2.5, shows that the incidence rate for fatal and major accidents in chemicals 1981–84 has increased by 27% from 82.0 to 104.2, compared to an increase of 23% for all manufacturing industry.

Many of the accidents which occur in chemical works are not related to the effects of chemical processes, but are attributable as in other factories to falls, materials handling, over-exertion and trapping. However, the 1985 Report of the Chief Inspectors of Factories comments that whereas it

has traditionally been thought that only 20% (of all reported accidents) are truly processes related ... special analysis of the more serious accidents, fatalities and dangerous occurrences in the industry during 1983 showed that 65% were process related (HSE/6, 1986: 47).

Estimates of the magnitude and scope of the problems of occupational health in the chemical and related industry are difficult to make. The effects of exposure are frequently delayed, and often vary with the timing and nature of exposure as well as with the personal characteristics of the health of the individuals at risk. The operation of the RIDDO Regulations should offer a source of more information on health, whilst it is hoped that the proposed COSHH Regulations will help to secure improvements to occupational health in this industry where it is clear that many workers come into contact with dangerous substances. Monitoring the use and effects of dangerous substances and maintaining high standards of protection are thus important activities for people in this industry.

Another significant concern for both the HSE and those directly employed in the chemical industry is with major hazards and major incidents and their impact on the public as well as employees. Events in Bhopal in 1984 once again focused international attention on the extensive dangers associated with chemical plants.[4] Work in this area in the UK is reflected in the preparation and promulgation of the CIMAH Regulations 1984. The limits of this book and its focus on accident experience and more limited concepts of the safety of employees mean however that these important subjects of occupational health and major hazards can only be given passing reference.

The case studies

The emphasis in these studies was on achieving an understanding of the processes involved in establishing health and safety programmes in selected workplaces, rather than on a broad and representative picture of developments across the industry. After initial visits to some ten establishments, detailed case studies in eight different establishments were completed during 1980 and 1981. Special attention was paid to the roles of line managers, safety specialists and safety committees. The intention was to identify the various pressures on these groups in different contexts and the factors which were likely to lead to improving or declining standards of health and safety at work. Table 4.5 provides background details of each establishment and shows that the study included large and small establishments, involved in the manufacture of a wide range of chemical and related products. It also covered different processes and technologists, from the relatively labour intensive batch production of chemicals to the highly automated process control of oil refining. A similar degree of variety was found in the organisation and arrangements associated with safety. Each site had a safety policy but there were considerable differences in their content and implications. The involvement of specialists varied with

Table 4.5 *The case studies: details of chemical establishments*

Establishment	Size (approx. no. of employees)	Main activity	Safety specialists employed
A	1100	General batch chemicals	1 safety adviser with staff of 1 safety officer and 1 environmental health officer
B	1000	Man-made fibres	1 safety officer
C	2000	Detergents	1 safety manager with staff of 1 safety adviser, 1 safety engineer
D	1100	Plastics	1 safety adviser
E	930	Oil refining	1 safety officer, 1 safety supervisor
F	1800	Oil refining	1 safety and environment manager with staff of 1 safety officer and 3 inspectors
G	150	Industrial gases	1 operations manager who is part-time safety adviser
H	307	Cosmetics	1 safety officer, 1 welfare/ occupational nurse

establishment size, history and the complexity of technology and materials. All but one site had recognised trade unions, but within the unionised firms, safety representatives, shop stewards and managers played different roles in respect of safety. All sites had some form of safety committee structure but again there were variations in role and structure.

Data were collected as shown in Table 4.6 through personal interviews with a total of 126 managers, supervisors, safety representatives and safety specialists and from the responses to a total of 618 self-completion questionnaires which were distributed to a wider sample of these groups within each establishment. Interviews were also conducted with specialists and managers in the headquarters of parent companies where appropiate. Observations were made of work in production areas and meetings of safety committees. The study was confined to health and safety issues as they affected direct production workers and those employed on maintenance in production areas. Issues relating to employees in other work places such as offices, laboratories or distribution depots were not considered.

The discussion of the case study material is divided into five main sections. The first deals with the views of employees about the hazards and

Table 4.6 *The case studies: interviews and questionnaires*

| | | Respondents to questionnaire | | | |
| | | | | | |
Establishment	No. of people interviewed	Managers, incl. safety specialists	Supervisors, technicians	Shopfloor (safety reps. and committee members)	Total
A	20	44	35	18	97
B	16	24	31	11	65
C	16	53	60	33	146
D	16	36	31	23	80
E	15	34	41	10	85
F	11	45	29	22	96
G	8	3	10	2	15
H	24	14	15	5	34
Total: *N*	126	243	251	124	618
%		39%	41%	20%	100%

safety problems they faced at work. The subsequent sections focus on aspects of self regulation, beginning with the development of health and safety policy and practice. This is followed by a discussion of the roles of line management, safety specialists and workforce representatives and the chapter concludes with some general comments on the organisational context of health and safety and the impact of the recession in the chemical industry.

Hazards

Questionnaire respondents who were engaged directly in production and engineering maintenance were asked to identify 'the most important health and safety problem or hazard' faced by 'the people for whom they (managers/supervisors) were responsible or whom (safety representatives) they represented'.[5] A total of 348 respondents replied in the pattern shown in Table 4.7. The largest category of respondents (37%) identified aspects of the chemicals used on site, particularly their toxicity, fumes, gases and the dangers of fire and explosion. The second largest (29%) group of respondents focused on the attitudes and behaviour of people, for example, as one supervisor commented, 'familiarity breeds contempt and this causes the worst accidents'. Specific reference was also made to a reluctance to

Table 4.7 *Health and safety hazards or problems identified by questionnaire respondents*

The nature of the hazard of problem identified by questionnaire respondents	All respondents (%, N = 348)
A Chemicals (toxicity, corrosivity, fire, explosion)	37
B People (attitude, careless behaviour, ignorance)	29
C Plant, machinery and systems of work (mechanical, electrical, transport, materials handling)	17
D Place of work (housekeeping, noise, ventilation, access, building fabric)	12
Other	4
Total	100

wear protective clothing or to follow prescribed procedures as well as to a lack of information and poor or non-existent training. The third group concerned hazards or problems associated with plant, machinery and systems of work, for example being crushed by machinery or encountering 'live' electrics. The final category focused on the problems of securing and maintaining reasonable housekeeping standards. Some respondents thus focused attention on the 'people' component of hazards, using words such as 'apathy', 'complacency', 'awareness' and 'training', but a larger group focused on material aspects of the working environment. Consideration of the interview data and written comments on the questionnaires showed that the majority view was that accidents and ill health largely arose through the interaction of these two aspects of the working environment.

There was variation between the cases with more respondents from less technologically complex plants paying more attention to chemical hazards. Of more interest than this difference between the establishments, however, was a clear relationship between positions in the hierarchy and perceptions of hazards across establishments. Substantially larger proportions of senior and middle managers than of first line supervisors and safety representatives saw hazards in terms of attitudes, knowledge and behaviour. In contrast, larger proportions of safety representatives and first line supervisors focused on the chemicals produced or the mechanical material environmental as major health and safety problems.

The focus on chemicals as a source of hazards is interesting since although it contrasts with the picture revealed by overall statistics for all accidents in the industry, where process related incidents are relatively infrequent, it accords with the findings of the HSE special analysis of serious accidents and fatalities which showed 65% to be process related (HSE/6, 1986:47). Only one fatal accident had occurred in any of our eight plants in the five year period immediately preceding field work; it had been the result of electrocution. Information collected about fatalities which had occurred at other worksites supported the view of other studies of accidents in the chemical industry, that accidents relate as often to problems of securing and maintaining a safe place of work, as to the specific properties of chemicals (HSE/1, 1980: 51).

Information was sought from respondents both about what had been done in the last five years to improve health and safety and about actions they would like to see taken in the future. Responses indicated that people at all levels thought in terms of 'hardware' measures, directed at characteristics of plant, equipment, materials, substances and 'people' measures concerned with training, instruction and motivation. It is a theme of this book that the latter are an essential adjunct to any policy if the hardware measures, which limit hazards in a more direct and obvious way, are not only to be provided, but actually utilised, maintained and, where necessary, adopted. In the chemical case studies we noted some declining interest in efforts to maintain motivation and positive commitment. This was particularly marked in those sites which were most hit by economic recession where safety appeared to be given a diminishing priority. But it was also a trend in other plants. The nervous days of adjusting to the 1974 Act and considering the horrors of the Flixborough disaster had receded into history. Subsequently managers and workers' representatives became concerned with other problems and different sets of priorities.

The development of safety policies

It will be recalled that the study of chemical establishments was not specifically concerned to monitor the effects of legislation, though there was broad interest in identifying the factors which lay behind recent developments in policy and practice. Questions on this issue met with contradictory responses. A typical opinion was expressed by one manager: 'we didn't need the law to interfere in health and safety, our company has always taken it seriously, we've had safety committees for 20 years and always done what was needed'. Nonetheless, the majority of respondents to the questionnaire, including managers, identified HASAWA and the SRSCR as the most important influences on health and safety policy and practice in the recent past (Table 4.8).

One interesting conclusion emerges. Before the chemicals study was undertaken it was assumed that differences or changes in technology and materials, and hence the nature and extent of hazards, would be associated

Table 4.8 *Respondents' view on most important influences on health and safety policy and practice in the last year and in the last five years*

	Last year ($\%; N = 560$)	Last 5 years ($\%; N = 560$)
Legislative framework, Act and Regulations	15.2	50
Changes in internal organisation and administration	31	21.1
Accident/actual incident (mostly on site)	8.2	6.6
Change of technology/plant	11.2	5.1
Change in attitudes	12.2	5.2
Safety specialist activity	1.5	4.3
Company financial position	2.0	0.8
External enforcement	2.0	1.0
Others	3.1	2.3
None – can't think of any	13.4	3.6
Total	100	100

with significant developments in safety policy and practice. This was only borne out insofar as more health and safety specialists were employed in plants with what could be called more serious hazards. Other significant influences on health and safety policy – apart from legislation – included developments in internal administrative practice, for example the effects of 'permit to work' systems[6] and the generation and communication of information about hazards, working practices and safety performance. In Chapter 7 it will be suggested that such administrative developments, which no doubt were related to the legislation of the mid 1970s, are extremely important because of their impact on strengthening the motivation of managers and workers to place a higher priority on safety and health.

Policies, organisation and arrangements

All the eight establishments studied in 1980 and 1981 had safety policies which had originated in their present form from the time of the Act, although two of the establishments had prepared some sort of policy document a decade earlier. However, in retrospect several of the managers interviewed commented that the policy was a missed opportunity for change (Dawson, Poynter and Stevens 1984a). They now regretted that policy statements had been over-general in their requirements and conservative in their impact. The caution of their predecessors or even of these same people ten years previously can be explained by four different factors. First, in responding to the legal requirements of a policy document they had not wished to imply criticism of what they had done in the past; the preservation of corporate image encouraged policies to be framed in terms of continuity with the past rather than change. Secondly, in the early 1970s managers had been fearful about the likely costs of implementing the HASAWA. Thirdly, they had been concerned about the effects of policy statements on the liability of individuals and companies to criminal prosecution and hence shied away from including anything too specific. Finally, they were apprehensive about the impact of statutory rights for workforce involvement and hence kept their policies as general as possible so that workforce representatives did not have too detailed an agenda for criticism and change.

Fears that to be explicit or adventurous in policy statements would open the door to criminal prosecutions, great financial costs or ready-made sources of grievances for trade unionists had in fact proved largely unfounded. Certainly neither the external enforcement agencies nor trade union appointed safety representatives had become the scourge of management, as many had feared. The fact that such expectations were not realised is evidence that the hopes of those drafting the Act had also been, to an extent, unfulfilled. It was in this context that some of the managers and specialists interviewed in 1980 expressed concern about the impact of recession and tighter financial controls on any 'unnecessary' expenditure at the local level, and wished that they or their predecessors had been more explicit and adventurous in writing their policies a decade earlier.

Although there was full observance of the legal requirement to produce a safety policy, this was not usually seen to be very significant. The scope of formal commitments bore little relationship either to the level of awareness about safety practices and procedures or to the extent to which safety policies were used as a point of practical reference. It was not uncommon for policies to be given out to new recruits only to be filed or thrown away. Even in the more safety conscious firms it was common for those who did not have any special health and safety interest or responsibility to be completely unaware that a policy existed. Most of those who knew of its existence were ignorant of its details or purpose.

Beyond the formal policy, it is important to consider the organisation and arrangements for carrying it out. Responses to a list of 14 aspects of their plant's organisation and arrangements for health and safety showed most respondents to be largely satisfied with the provisions in their workplace. Only two features attracted significant negative comment. These concerned 'education and training in health and safety' and 'the consideration given to health and safety at the design stage'. Both of these issues reflect a view that people on the shopfloor felt neglected, though in different ways. There was considerable feeling that not enough was done on the shopfloor to train and refresh workers and supervisors about how to secure good standards of health and safety, particularly following the introduction of new materials or processes. Similar feelings of neglect were expressed in relation to changes in plant or equipment. 'There's no consultation with shopfloor representatives when new machinery is designed, faults only show when it's installed' (interview with safety representative).

There was similar criticism of access for maintenance to lines and vessels, the positioning of valves and other aspects of basic engineering design. There was also some dissatisfaction about the poor attention given to occupational health. One would expect this to become a matter of increasing anxiety as concern and knowledge grows about occupational diseases, which may become evident only in the longer term.

In interviews the researchers formed the view that expressions of satisfaction with the organisation and arrangements for safety and health reflected low or vaguely conceived expectations and a dearth of standards against which present performance could be evaluated. Many people seemed to be commenting on whether the arrangements had actually been formally established 'on paper' rather than how effective they found them. Furthermore as most of the arrangements were relatively new they were seen as 'better than nothing'.

Some interesting differences between levels in the hierarchy and age of respondents were revealed. Management respondents or those who were older, were systematically more satisfied with all arrangements, than were respondents who were lower in the hierarchy and/or younger. When respondents were grouped according to company, differences also emerged, even though the effects of position and age were clear in every case. Companies F and D stood out as having comparatively higher levels of satisfaction overall, whereas companies C and E appeared at the other extreme with greater levels of dissatisfaction. These differences are not explained by technology, since there was an oil refinery at both extremes. Insofar as there was a common feature of C and E, it was a general feeling, revealed particularly in the open ended interviews, that no-one of any importance really seemed to care about health and safety and that little was done to commit resources to secure improved standards. It was not that what was done was inappropriate but that more action and communication were desired. In particular many of the interviewees felt that they were not given enough information. Someone complained that the policy failed to give a 'clear account of the company's attitude on the relative importance of safety compared with production pressures'. Another observed that he could not be satisfied (with resources put to health or safety) 'if I don't know how resources are allocated'. Furthermore, there was a view that information about new products or materials was always late, 'never seems to arrive until the material is in use'.

These comments direct attention once more to the parts played by the key actors – senior and line management, safety specialists and representative institutions for workforce involvement. These were, in the Robens philosophy, to be the principal elements of self regulation. How far was this concept working in chemical industry in the early 1980s?

Management organisation

The policy in all eight establishments was that line managers were formally responsible for ensuring the health and safety of their employees. Beyond the policy document however, none of the sites explicitly included safety considerations in managerial job descriptions. Furthermore there was enormous variation in the extent to which the practice of line responsibility for health and safety was practised and supported. The differences were not easily explained by size of workforce, type of technology or hazards, or level and type of workforce involvement. The main point of difference seemed to be whether line responsibility was supported and encouraged, and where necessary enforced, by significant senior managers in the factory and headquarters. If it was clear that the 'performance' of a manager in health and safety mattered to superiors, and particularly if this showed itself in something more than a tirade of recriminations if an accident occurred, then the principle of line responsibility took on some meaning. Where this happened, managers took the trouble to find out whether inspections had been conducted in their areas and what they showed. They certainly appeared to listen more to specialists and sometimes gave more time and weight to the views of safety representatives or safety committees although, as will be seen, their attitudes to workforce involvement were not simply influenced by their view of the importance and nature of their own role in health and safety.

The researchers observed that the importance of active encouragement and enforcement from senior managers was not seen to have been of particular significance at the time of the passage of the Health and Safety at Work Act. In that period, managerial fears had been largely concentrated on two subjects; first the possibilities of individual and corporate prosecution and secondly the consequences of statutory workforce involvement. However, by 1980 it was clear that managers had little to fear from either development. Indeed, having recovered from their fears about the legislation and the Flixborough disaster, some senior managers were now wondering what, if any, real improvements in health and safety had been achieved in their establishments.

Three examples may be given of establishments where there was concern that significant improvements in health and safety should be made, and the spotlight was being turned on senior executives and line managers. Managers in establishment G were acting on the recommendations of a company-wide report that good safety performance would only come from commitment from all levels, particularly from line management. It was noted that poor safety performance was actually the signal for recrimination from senior executives whereas good performance was rarely acknowledged. Accordingly, monthly reporting procedures were introduced which covered positive as well as negative indications and safety became an item for discussion and comment in annual appraisals.

Establishment C provided a similar example. It was part of a UK company which had recently become a subsidiary of a large US multinational concern. One of the new American directors had spearheaded a safety campaign for change with the target of reducing the accident frequency rate by 40% within five years. A programme of departmental and site safety objectives were agreed and performance monitored through accident statistics and inspection reports. During the first year of the programme lost time accidents were reduced within the company by 12% and minor injuries by 22%.

A newly appointed senior executive was also a significant factor in a third establishment (A), where greater emphasis had recently come to be placed on the role of line managers in every aspect of work. A new manufacturing director had instituted a system of more integrated and cohesive shift teams with line managers having clear responsibility for meeting targets both for production and for safety. A 24 hour incident and accident reporting scheme was introduced and used on a departmental and shift basis to identify safety problems and establish responsibility and accountability.

These three examples illustrate the general findings of the chemicals study that significant developments in workplace health and safety depend crucially on the part played by members at all levels of the management team and require action in respect of motivation, just as much as, if not more than, action at the technical level. In establishments which had not received a sustained management initiative, procedures instituted in the flurry of activity associated with the passing of the 1974 Act were becoming less significant. For example, in one establishment inspections which had been set up as the responsibility of line managers and supervisors had been passed on to a safety officer who had little power or influence even to get people to pay attention to his findings, let alone to plan remedial action.

The line managers said they were too busy to undertake or even to oversee inspections and they often gave similarly low priority to acting on their recommendations. In this same establishment the safety committee was supposed to conduct inspections of selected areas before each of its monthly meetings. But by 1980 these inspections were often cancelled when members just simply did not turn up. When inspection reports were made, they were no longer necessarily followed through by a series of recommendations. If they were, recommended action was not always carried out.

Safety specialists

Specialist positions in health and safety have a much longer tradition in the chemical industry than in many other sectors. As the industry expanded during the post-war period, so the likely occurrence of fires, explosions and toxic releases encouraged the appointment of specialists in safety, environmental pollution, toxicology and occupational health. Seven of the eight plants studied had at least one full-time specialist position. The sole exception was establishment G, with a payroll of 150 engaged on the preparation of industrial gases, which had a part-time safety adviser who was also an operations manager (Table 4.5).

All the safety specialists encountered in the research were placed formally in advisory roles, and direct responsibility for safety was always vested in line management. When the specialists wanted to secure changes, none of them took executive action alone. The more effective specialists tried to work through an appropriate line manager to get support for their recommendations. Specialists with less training and fewer qualifications tended to confine themselves to processing information and reacting to requests. The better qualififed specialists, on the other hand, were more active in making suggestions and in monitoring activities independently.

Questionnaire respondents were more or less equally divided over whether they were satisfied with an advisory role for specialists. There were two typical complaints. Managers argued that they should be more concerned with the practical difficulties of implementing their suggestions and advice. The safety representatives and blue collar safety committee members, particularly if they felt they were dealing with line managers who were unenthusiastic about health and safety issues, argued that the specialists should take a stronger role in the implementation and enforcement of improved standards. An 'enforcement' approach was also given more general support in two case studies (B and C) where respondents thought there were serious health hazards. On the other hand, respondents at all levels in D, H and F, where the hazards were thought to be more 'straightforward', were more likely to be content with an advisory role.

The degree of specialist involvement in deciding upon appropriate technical ways to control hazards varied between the eight sites studied. However, it was quite exceptional to find a specialist who was actively involved in giving advice on general management practices, such as monitoring, measuring and maintaining managerial performance in safety, even though these activities are crucial in securing improved safety standards.

The chemical case studies showed that the role of the specialist in giving advice is often beset by difficulties. Specialists are pushed by conflicting forces to adopt various strategies, which they are then handicapped from pursuing because they usually lack effective power and influence. Specialists who were working in larger establishments, or those which were part of larger companies where senior executives clearly attached importance to health and safety, were more qualified and experienced and had more influence. Furthermore, senior management commitment to safety was more likely to be found where the hazards were manifestly due to the characteristics of substances and processes as well as to human factors.

Safety committees and safety representatives

Table 4.9 shows that all eight sites had safety committees although in establishment H there were no recognised trade unions. In this case safety representatives and committee members were appointed by management. Managers also had a hand in appointing some representatives and committee members, particularly amongst supervisors and senior managements, in establishments A, C, D and F. In the other three sites all safety representatives were appointed in some way through the trade unions. Table 4.9 shows that the percentage of safety representatives to total workforce ranged from 1.6% in B with approximately 59 employees per representative to 4.6% in A with approximately 27 employees per representative. Certainly site B was beset with health and safety problems, but these were felt to be less to do with few safety representatives and more to do with low commitment at all levels, and to a poor economic climate. Nonetheless these factors are clearly related to one another.

Several of the establishments in the study had had joint committees to deal, at least partly, with safety matters long before 1974. However, they were given a new look and brighter image in the flurry of activity which surrounded the 1974 Act and the 1977 SRSCR. One new aspect of the committee structure which appears to be directly associated with legislation was the proliferation of several 'local' committees to serve

Table 4.9 *Chemical case studies: workforce involvement in health and safety*

Establishment	A	B	C	D	E	F	G	H
Recognised unions in relation to:	—shopfloor —supervisors —craft —management	—shopfloor —supervisors —craft	—shopfloor —supervisors —craft —management	—shopfloor —supervisors —craft —management	—shopfloor —supervisors —craft	—shopfloor —supervisors —craft —management	—shopfloor —supervisors —craft	—No recognised union
Safety committees	1 site 8 locals	1 site	1 site 14 locals	1 site 4 locals	1 site 3 locals	1 site 10 locals	1 site	1 site
Trade unions appointed reps.	31	17	49	34	28	17	4	—
Management appointed safety reps.	20	—	17	7	—	50	—	9
Total safety reps.	51	17	58	41	28	67	4	9
Safety reps. as % of total workforce	4.6%	1.6%	2.8%	3.7%	3.0%	3.7%	2.6%	2.9%

particular geographical or departmental areas. Area committees had long been a feature of the two oil refineries but were specifically established in sites A, C and D in response to the legislation. All the committees met formally at regular intervals of between six weeks and three months.

Respondents to the questionnaire were asked about their views on a range of items related to the structure, activities and consequences of committee operation. Overall there was more satisfaction with such structural elements of the operation of the committees as their composition and the frequency of the meetings, rather than with the activities undertaken by the committees. In particular there was dissatisfaction about decisions not being put into practice and about communications between site committees, local committees and the workforce. Younger respondents, and those who were not committee members themselves, were less dissatisfied with all aspects of the operation of safety committees.

Complaints about communication and the way decisions were put into practice focused attention on a common problem. This was the lack of integration of the committees' activities with other aspects of structure and process in the plant. There were many complaints that committees had no way of getting their recommendations implemented. One respondent linked the two problems together: 'decisions are made, then the carrying out of the decision is lost due to poor communications on how and who is actually to carry out the decision as well as lack of back up, especially if the decision is unpopular' (interview with supervisor).

The interview and questionnaire data together with observations led to the conclusion that although safety committees served important functions in bringing representatives of different interests together and raising important issues, they were less successful in ensuring that standards of health and safety were improved. This was largely because they usually had no executive responsibility, no budget and no ability to ensure that their recommendations were carried out. As a consequence members often became disaffected and resigned their position. A high turnover of safety representatives and committee members was evident in several of the larger sites even in 1980 when the newly (or re-) constituted committees were comparatively young.

Respondents were asked specifically about the tasks which they felt safety committees both should and did perform; 601 responded. In all cases there were more people who felt committees should undertake some specified action than there were people who actually felt they did so. In contrast we did not encounter many people who felt that committees did more than they should. The problems identified were thus disappointed expectations, rather than complaints that committees were 'overstepping the mark'. Whereas 87% of all respondents felt that safety committees should provide a channel for communication on health and safety matters, only 57% felt that the committees did serve this function. 62% felt the committees should advise management on health and safety matters, and only 43% considered they did so. 55% of all respondents and nearly all workforce representatives felt that committees should provide a place for management and unions to negotiate on health and safety issues with 47% considering this was done already. Again with disproportionate representation from union representatives, 40% of the total supported the view that committees should be able to direct management to take action to improve health and safety; 24% of respondents thought this sort of direct action was being accomplished.

Analysis of the data to investigate different patterns of response found that the single factor which best differentiated between people who felt that safety committees should not perform (certain) functions was respondents' position.[7] Overall proportionately fewer managers compared to workforce representatives or non-managerial committee members favoured an active role for safety committees. The difference was strongest on whether safety committees should negotiate and weakest on whether they should communicate, a function on which everyone was more or less agreed. People who were not members of safety committees generally favoured a more active role than those who were members. Committee members had their expectations tempered by a realisation of what was feasible (Dawson, Poynter and Stevens 1983a).

Respondents who strongly favoured line responsibility were least in favour of an active role for safety committees. It was as if they saw these two developments as being contradictory. This could be either because of a fear that line managers would seize the opportunity to 'pass the buck' to committees, or else because of a wish to preserve managerial prerogative. Observation in committees and interviews bore out the view that managers generally had a more restrictive view of safety committees. Managers often made a distinction between what they thought were 'genuine' safety matters, and those which they called 'political' or 'pseudo' safety matters, which in their view were raised simply by safety representatives in order to try to 'make a fuss'. For the former 'genuine cases' there were, they implied, absolute standards whereas relative and politically determined standards prevailed for the latter. In discussions the researchers suggested that all issues were essentially subject to some negotiation or differences of view if only between members of the management team. However, this view was generally not accepted by managers. Many managers, even those strongly committed to safety, nonetheless said that safety became devalued if it became 'political', by which they seemed to mean the subject of collective bargaining. This opinion, which was fairly widespread, has resonance with the Robens philosopy that there is a 'greater natural identity of interest' in safety matters with 'no legitimate scope for bargaining' (Robens 1972a: para. 66).

In some companies the split between 'political' and 'real' safety was institutionalised. For example a 'technical safety committee' was established in site B with a membership drawn exclusively from management. This committee was established in the mid 1970s when the company safety committee had been expanded to include an overwhelming majority of workforce representatives. In these changed circumstances it was felt that the committee was not a suitable place to establish safety standards. Thus the additional management committee was founded to ensure that essential technical and managerial consideration could be given to 'real hazards'. Workforce representatives would, it was argued, be out of place on this committee, since they lacked the necessary skills and knowledge.

The fact that the pursuit of safety makes demands on scarce resources means inevitably that judgement and compromise are important. It is important to decide who is a legitimate participant in exercising judgement and deciding on compromise. Safety is thus inextricably linked to general views on, and experience of, industrial relations and management prerogative. Material relevant to this issue was collected during the study of the chemical establishments. All questionnaire respondents were asked whether they agreed or disagreed with two statements. The first concerned the ends or objectives of safety policies: 'Management and workforce have a common interest in matters of health and safety'. The second concerned the means for achieving objectives: 'Management and workers will always be in conflict over what measures are necessary to ensure health and safety at work'.

A commonality of interest between management and workforce was identified by 36% of respondents; furthermore they did not believe that conflict over the measures to be taken was inevitable. For example, a supervisor commented: 'No one party can make the Health and Safety at Work Act become an everyday part of industrial life. It has got to be approached with team work and team spirit. Consequently to make it successful the differing views to a problem have to be fused together to make safety "common sense" which 99% of the time it is.' Approximately one-third of the respondents identified a commonality of interest in objectives, but felt that there was inevitably conflict over measures necessary to secure health and safety. Only a small group (4%) saw conflict as likely over both ends and means.

The group who believed in common interest and consensus on means were disproportionately drawn from management whilst representatives of the general workforce were disportionately represented amongst those who saw a degree of conflict at least in achieving objectives. The two most frequently mentioned subjects of conflict on health and safety objectives were: whether additional expense for safety provisions was justified, and whether production continuity should be lost. For example, in one plant there was considerable conflict between departmental managers and safety representatives over whether sufficient money could be found in the short term to rectify a problem of airborne contamination in a man-made fibre plant. In other cases conflict arose over whether work should be interrupted in order to rectify fully a mechanical or electrical problem which, when it was noticed, looked fairly minor.

The conflicts which respondents observed were sometimes attributed to uncooperative attitudes. For example, one safety representative put it as follows:

> Although top management seems to put an effort into health and safety this effort seems to fail when it comes to middle management carrying its policy through. I tend to feel that to some members of management health and safety is a waste of time and something to be taken now and again. This view is supported by looking at the area safety books which have some items dating back two or more years and we have to resort to threats to get items fixed.

Another safety representative spoke of his frustration at the lack of response from managers if he pointed out significant problems:

> When I bring a glaring example of where we should have an improvement to the attention of the manager, he stares at me as if I've descended from another planet. On the only occasion so far when I've served him with a report form [of a near miss] he seemed to take it as a personal affront ...
> management seem to consider that they and they alone decide what is defective and what steps should be taken. They resent interference in their considered function (interview with safety representative).

On the other hand managers laid the blame for an uncooperative atmosphere on safety representatives, particularly those whom they considered 'used' health and safety issues for what they see as ulterior motives:

> Safety representatives and safety committees can be a route for individual dissatisfaction or grievance ... A few [reps] use their

position to enhance their power and this leads to conflict (interview with manager).

Another manager commented:

> safety is and always will be used by unions and union negotiators to promote conflict. Until attitudes change, real progress made jointly between management and employee will be rare.

The following statement of a safety representative is typical of those who believe in common objectives which are then subject to conflict over how they should be achieved:

> although management are striving towards a better policy and improved relationships with safety representatives on this site, I do not personally think this will ever be achieved.
> Management always look at the costs of changing a practice whereas safety representatives will always look at what danger there is to an individual or group and the precautions that may be taken.

In many ways safety representatives and safety committees were not found to be the dominant force for change which many people had either hoped or feared. Interviewees felt that their institution had possibly raised the general level of awareness about safety matters within the workplace and had led to some issues being discussed, but that generally they had not had a profound effect on standards of health and safety. The views of managers already discussed have considerable bearing on this situation, as indeed do the views of the safety representatives themselves.

In all but one of the seven sites with recognised trade unions, most of the safety representatives were also shop stewards, and they saw themselves as shop stewards first and safety representatives second. As shop stewards they were faced with a range of difficult problems. The economic climate made them acutely aware of the problems associated with both recession and changes in technology. Their concerns were to preserve jobs, to secure retraining, to establish greater degrees of participation and consultation in changes and to achieve improved terms through bargaining over employment conditions. Not only were they trying to pursue divergent interests, but sometimes the interests of safety actually conflicted with their other interests. In one establishment which was suffering from the general recession as well as particular problems of loss of markets, there was general concern about the use of methylene chloride and associated toxic gas emissions. The prescribed threshold limit value[8] was rarely achieved and yet no affordable way of modifying the plant could be found. An informal arrangement was established whereby people knew that they should not spend 'too long' in this part of the factory at any one time; paper work was done in another part of the factory and maintenance activities were kept to a minimum while the largely mechanised plant was in production. The safety representatives involved in these discussions did not stand out against this decision but accepted the need for an essentially unsatisfactory 'solution' because of a scarcity of funds and a feeling that nothing must be done to threaten the survival of any part of the establishment.

This *ad hoc* arrangement was a typical manifestation of the effects of economic recession. As a result, health and safety problems were more likely to be tackled by administrative or personnel arrangements than by incurring direct expenditure and changing some part of the hardware of the process or materials. It was reported that hardware measures had been common in the mid 1970s, but were now only seriously considered if they related to very dangerous hazards, or were required by the enforcing authority. Where the hazards were associated with health problems, which often take a long time to become apparent, neither the criteria of 'great danger' or external requirements were particularly helpful.

Where safety representatives were not shop stewards, in establishment E, there was no sign that they were any stronger in representing a more independent force in safety matters than their counterparts who were. Economic and industrial relations considerations were still very important to them but, lacking experience and status as shop stewards, they were sometimes ill equipped to take a very active part in discussions.

A different situation was found in establishment H, where there were no recognised trade unions. The safety committee had developed out of a working party set up in 1978 to consider the implications of the health and safety legislation. The committee at the time of the fieldwork was chaired by the welfare officer, a qualified nurse who provided first aid as well as welfare facilities. Its members, drawn from all levels of the company, were appointed by management. Most of the workforce lacked any experience of participation in consultation or bargaining and they were generally extremely quiet and tentative in meetings. The committee was not seen by many of the general workforce as an opportunity to discuss safety matters but rather as an ordeal which they had to endure if they were forced to take office. Management largely regarded the committee with indulgence or indifference and felt it was good to give members of the workforce the opportunity to discuss health and safety matters, particularly as experience had showed them it did not foster antagonism. Furthermore, having survived an unsuccessful attempt by a trade union to secure recognition and bargaining rights, many managers felt that the committee, like the new 'all status' canteen, was a fairly harmless way to resolve grievances and remove possible sources of confrontation and union strength.

Committees which were chaired by senior managers and which had representation from managerial as well as shopfloor grades were more stable, and more likely to withstand the apathy which characterised most plants from time to time. A strong managerial presence signalled a degree of commitment and provided channels for processing information and occasionally for ensuring action. The committee least able to suggest and secure improvements in health and safety conditions was found in establishment B. Here the chairman was a departmental manager, and the safety and welfare specialists were *ex officio* members. Otherwise the committee was made up solely of safety representatives. Given this constitution the representatives were arrayed as suppliants, requesting improvements to the manager who invariably explained why little action could be taken. This committee was the furthest from being a problem solving collective. Ironically their numerical majority helped to diminish the influence of the safety representatives and appeared to contribute to their reticence in pressing for necessary improvements, in the face of fears of redundancies and commercial liquidation.

The overall picture and the impact of recession

All the chemical plants in the study had responded at a formal level to the health and safety at work legislation, and to the Regulations for workforce involvement. There were safety policies in every establishment, specialists had been appointed at local, and even at regional and national levels. Mechanisms for workforce involvement had been established. Yet to an extent in all the plants, but most noticeably in B and C, there were grounds for doubting the extent to which these formalities indicated a serious and established concern to improve standards of health and safety at work.

There was evidence in the early 1980s that people were once again showing the same apathy which the Robens Committee had been so eager to try to eradicate. The mood in many workplaces was one of weary familiarity with the standards and procedures which had been established in a period of heightened activity, prompted by legislation and the Flixborough disaster in the mid 1970s. None of the plants studied had recently suffered a significant increase in accidents although they were not achieving the dramatic decline they would have welcomed. Relations with the Inspectorate had shown that whatever the provisions of the HASAWA, there were important reasons why violations of the law would only occasionally lead to prosecutions. First, violations had to come to the attention of the Inspectorate and Inspectors' visits were infrequent. Secondly, even if a visit revealed a problem, it was known that Inspectors rarely started enforcement or criminal proceedings, unless a case of clear negligence was combined with serious injury. Several of our interviewees commented that Inspectors clearly preferred cooperative compromise to punitive enforcement.[9]

At the establishments in the study, safety representatives and managers were both often concerned with other matters, and specialists lacked strength and support. Without a central and continuous force to maintain standards of health and safety, they were slipping further down the list of priorities for the expenditure of scarce resources of time and money. Internal inspections were less frequent, committee attendance declined, and reports were left without action being taken.

A major contributory factor to this decline was the impact of recession. Several of the establishments studied had already had experience of recent redundancies reflecting contracting markets and poor prospects. All levels of the workforce expressed some concerns about their future employment prospects. Their fears were justified: several of our main informants have in fact been made redundant in the years since the fieldwork was undertaken. Given these fears, few were prepared to push the company to additional 'non-productive' expenditure. And the Inspectorate was reported to be sympathetic to companies who felt they simply could not pay to make some advised changes in machinery, layout, or ventilation.

An interesting observation is the relationship between the impact of the recession on expenditure and gradual changes of attitude. If money cannot be spent on improved equipment one might argue that this is all the more reason why people should be 'more careful', and 'more safety conscious', in order to compensate, through behaviour, for physical or technical shortcomings. In fact, the opposite seems to occur. When suggested actions are not taken to make plants physically more safe, people too appear to become less concerned with observing safety procedures. If less is being spent on safety it appears to become a less important issue in the minds of all concerned.[10]

Recession may mean a reduced workforce but it often also signals a search for new products or materials, or the development of new processes. Thus a reduced cash flow does not mean that the hazards will stay the same. Yet a focus on 'cost cutting' often means that the health and safety implications of proposed change are neglected. It was precisely at such a time that one of the companies introduced a substitute material which had two considerable advantages. It was cheaper and technically superior to its predecessor. There were fears that it had carcinogenic properties, but no-one spoke out strongly against its introduction and no-one pushed to establish precisely what knowledge was available. Even with acknowledged hazards, people were less vociferous about the need to reduce associated risks.

Conclusion

Our conclusion, and that of some of the more concerned senior managers in the establishments we studied, was that the push to maintain a strong emphasis on health and safety at both the procedural and substantive levels has to come from within the management hierarchy. This may then create an atmosphere conducive to the development of a strong specialist function and provide a setting in which workforce representatives can act in a positive way. Without this essential bond of senior management and line responsibility and accountability however, it is very difficult to maintain commitment to safety, particularly in times of economic recession. We shall return to the problems involved in achieving effective self regulation in Chapter 7 after considering the results of our studies in two more sectors: construction and retail.

5

Safety in construction

In the construction industry, 1983 was the year of Site Safe, a national safety campaign initiated by the HSE and the industry advisory committee, CONIAC. By drawing attention to the risks inherent in construction work and demonstrating the methods and procedures available to reduce them, it was hoped that the campaign would help to improve the industry's safety record.[1] As Chapter 2 has shown, in 1980 the incidence of fatal accidents in construction was almost six times that of manufacturing. Unfortunately, the hoped-for improvements in safety did not occur. The incidence of the combined category of fatal and major accidents in construction rose in Site Safe year itself and again in 1984. In 1984, construction was the highest risk industry in the UK and the combined incidence rate for fatal and major accidents had increased by 42 % in the period 1981–84 (see Tables 2.4 and 2.5).

Some have suggested that the failure of the campaign followed from its organisation and operation (Glendon and Hale 1984). However, an explanation of the high and rising rate of accidents in the industry must look beyond the campaign itself, and focus on the structure and organisation of construction. Unlike manufacturing, site work seldom involves a stable set of activities, materials and personnel. The continuous and cumulative nature of the work leads to dramatic changes in activities undertaken and in the working environment. In addition, the majority of operatives on many sites are not in the direct employ of the managing contractor; they may work for subcontractors or be self-employed. Union membership in the industry is relatively low and falling. Finally, the prospect of inspection is, in some cases, low. On small sites lasting six weeks or less, contractors are not even obliged to register the fact that work is in progress, and the probability of routine inspection is thus remote.[2]

In this chapter, we shall look at the provisions for health and safety within the industry, using official data and results of case studies conducted in a number of organisations in 1983–84. The first section describes the structure of the industry, its industrial relations and the nature of accidents in construction. The second section of the chapter analyses the development of the institutions of self regulation within the case study companies.

The construction industry

Industrial structure

The construction industry comprises a number of different and to some extent quite separate product markets. Whilst some of the major contractors straddle these sectors, medium and small firms generally operate within fairly narrow boundaries. The major sectoral division is between civil engineering and building work, with the latter being further divided into public, private, commercial, industrial and domestic work.

The industry thus includes a wide range of industrial activities undertaken by firms of vastly different sizes. Multi-million pound civil engineering projects like the Thames Barrier and small, domestic refurbishments are all included.[3] It experiences cycles of demand but, as Table 5.1 shows, output (in real terms) and employment have fallen during the period since the HASAW Act. The recession of 1980–82 was particularly sharp, and both employment and output have risen since then.

There is little doubt that these published figures underestimate both activity and employment at any one time. The casual and intermittent nature of the work has always been associated with an unknown amount of 'moonlighting' and recent estimates suggest that the recession may have encouraged this practice. The figures of Table 5.1 also conceal considerable sectoral variations. As Figure 5.1 shows, the decade from 1974 experienced marked differences between the market for private and public housing, while particular sectors, such as the vast 'repairs and maintenance' sector, have virtually escaped the effects of recession.

The industry has always contained a large number of small firms, but their share of employment and of output has increased in recent years. Firms of fewer than 60 employees accounted for 34% of work done in 1975: by 1985, this had risen to 53.2%. Over the same period, the share of work accounted for by firms of over 600 employees fell from 33.4% to 20%.[4] This shift is reflected in the employment shares of large and small firms. Table 5.2 presents figures from *Business Monitor* over a similar period. Again, the very small firms have increased their share at the expense of the very large ones. The size distribution of firms in the industry in 1982 and 1984 is given in Table 5.3. It is evident that the absolute number of very small firms (i.e. fewer than 20 employees) is rapidly increasing despite the failure of the industry to grow in real terms.

Table 5.1 *Output and employment in construction: 1974–84*

	Gross output (£million)	Output index (at 1974 prices)	Employment[a]
1974	12 932.1	100.0	1 508 466
1975	14 899.3	93.7	1 464 817
1976	15 778.9	84.2	1 396 921
1977	16 783.6	77.4	1 334 394
1978	19 658.3	83.7	1 336 825
1979	23 402.8	87.9	1 336.748
1980	26 963.1	85.8	1 306.422
1981	25 966.1	73.8	1 196 411
1982	29 263.5	76.6	1 158 247
1983	32 831.4	82.2	1 190 763
1984	36 005.0	85.9	1 181 122

[a] Average employed during the year including worker proprietors.
Source: Business Monitor, PA 500, 1984, Table 1.

Part of this change may be due to the differential sector performance shown in Figure 5.1; there are more small firms involved in repair and maintenance, for example, than in civil engineering. However, the greatest part has to do with the growth of subcontracting and self-employment across the industry as a whole. In his 1982 Report the Chief Inspector of Factories noted a trend for large companies to let 'substantial parts of their work to subcontractors – often their own employees in a different guise' (HSC/3, 1983: v–vi). A more recent HSE study shows that over 87% of sites with more than 60 employees use subcontractors (see Table 5.9). Many of these subcontractors are self-employed tradesmen, or labourers.[5] In 1975, 32% of 'firms' in the industry had one employee; by 1985 this had risen to 43.5%, with the absolute number tripling across this period. Even these figures may underestimate the real growth. One estimate, from Inland Revenue returns, suggests a vastly greater figure of 600 000 self-employed in 1982, approximately equivalent to the total of directly employed private sector operatives.[6]

This change in the nature of construction employment may in part be due to the recession of 1980–82, with large contractors unwilling to become involved in maintaining high levels of permanent employment. However, it also relates to substantial changes in the nature of contracting in the industry, particularly by large firms.

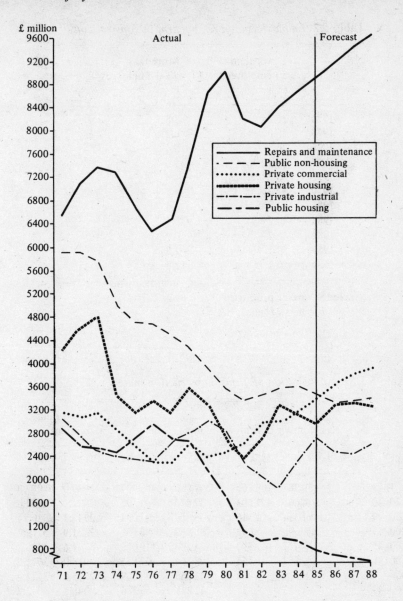

Figure 5.1 Value of output by contractors and direct labour on construction work at 1980 prices.

(Sources: Building and Civil Engineering EDC, Construction Forecasts, 1986–88, NEDO/HMSO 1986)

Table 5.2 *Employment shares by firm in construction*

	Fewer than 50 employees[a] (%)	More than 5000 employees (%)
1974	36.7	8.8
1975	36.0	6.2
1976	36.3	5.6
1977	36.2	5.6
1978	38.3	4.4
1979	37.3	4.6
1980	41.7	6.6
1981	44.2	5.1
1982	46.2	4.9
1983	50.1	2.8
1984	50.1	2.8

[a] Includes worker proprietors.
Source: Business Monitor, PA 500.

Table 5.3 *Size distribution of firms, construction industry, 1982 and 1984*

Size group (employees)	Number of firms		Employment[a]		Gross output (£ million)	
	1982	1984	1982	1984	1982	1984
1–19	139 988	168 155	397 986	466 237	7930.0	10 977.9
20–49	4 601	4 302	137 473	131 595	3322.3	3944.0
50–99	1 384	1 316	93 969	91 081	2746.1	3 165.4
100–199	698	642	95 959	88 951	2671.9	3 179.2
200–499	411	390	124 277	119 073	3741.6	4333.2
500–999	157	154	108 544	107 855	3018.0	3671.5
1000–2499	71	64	101 366	90 069	2735.2	3172.9
2500–4999	13	17	42 218	53 336	1048.7	2042.7
> 5000	7	5	56 455	32 925	2029.6	1518.2
Total	147 330	175 044	1 158 247	1 181 122	29 263.5	36 005.0

[a] Includes self-employed.
Source: Business Monitor, PA 500, 1982, p. 8; 1984, p. 14.

Contractual relations

The 'traditional' contracting process on major projects begins with the client commissioning a design from an architect. On reaching agreement a quantity surveyor will then prepare a bill of quantities outlining the relevant materials and specifications, and a selected number of major contractors are asked to submit tenders giving a price for the complete structure. When the contract has been awarded (usually to the contractor offering the lowest price) a number of nominated and specialist sub-contracts are then let. The former are packages of work given to subcontractors nominated by the architect irrespective of the main contractor's wishes. The latter are decided by competitive tender to the main contractor.

Under the 'traditional' system of contracting, main contractors have tended to supply their own labour and operatives in the general trades (e.g. bricklayers, carpenters, etc.) with subcontracting confined to specialist trades (e.g. electrics, plumbing, etc.). However, there is much evidence to suggest that this is no longer common practice and on many large sites main contractors now supply only the management personnel, contracting out all of the construction operations to a variety of subcontracting firms. This process is further complicated by the practices of subsubcontracting and of labour only subcontracting, where self-employed labourers are hired daily for a lump sum payment, often by 'firms' having dubious financial or legal standing.[7]

Thus the decline in directly employed private sector operatives is linked to these changes in forms of contracting. Most larger contractors, and an increasing number of medium-sized contractors, now offer their services as managing contractors on what are variously termed management fee, design and build, construction or project management work.[8] Under these contractual conditions, the management contractor provides the technical and managerial expertise, whilst other firms are contracted to undertake the actual construction work under their overall supervision. Even where firms do not advertise themselves as managing contractors, they frequently assume this role in practice, and seldom directly employ many of their own operatives. Proponents of this contractual form argue that the absence of direct employment responsibilities and the release of inevitable tension between the management contractor's interests as both subcontractor and guardian of clients' interest frees the managing contractor to concentrate entirely on the management of the project.

Although this system of contracting is widespread, particularly for major projects, other organisational forms are also found. Small or medium-sized general building firms may decide to pursue their own small contracts in the domestic, local authority or industrial sector, using their own labour where possible. However, one effect of the recession is the increasing penetration of this sector by major construction companies and a consequent squeeze of the tender prices within it.[9]

All sectors of the industry are subject to the pressures accompanying competitive tendering. In major project work it is often the source of numerous contractual disputes. Since profit margins are cut to a minimum in order to win contracts, delays to work due to inclement weather, poorly detailed design, the supply of materials or simply poor workmanship lead to a plethora of penalties and compensation claims, putting severe pressure on poorly capitalised and under financed companies. Whilst local council direct labour organisations (DLOs) stand somewhat apart from these general considerations, recent legislation and the growth of privatisation has undoubtedly increased the competitive pressure on them.[10]

There can be little doubt that the recession has also encouraged the trend for increasing the proportion of self-employed operatives in the industry since it has increased unemployment amongst building workers whilst simultaneously reducing their chance of finding employment in other sectors.

These recent changes in the organisation of construction work bring a further degree of fragmentation to an industry well known for its fluctuating levels of activity and disparate structure. Construction has always had relatively high labour turnover and low levels of training. The ease of capitalising a building firm has ensured that a high number of small firms constantly leave and enter the industry. Such employment conditions naturally affect those institutions and procedures developed to allow effective collective bargaining to take place.

Industrial relations

Collective bargaining for manual workers is well developed in the construction industry, with nationally agreed terms in both building and civil engineering. Such terms are applicable at site level, and there is only a limited amount of supplementary or local bargaining. There are three employers' associations in building; the Building Employers Federation (formerly the National Federation of Building Trades Employers), the Scottish Building Employers' Confederation, and the Federation of Master Builders. The main employers' association in civil engineering is the Federation of Civil Engineering Contractors, which covers most of the large- and medium-sized firms. In addition, there is a plethora of joint machinery covering the range of specialist trades, each of which have their own employers' associations. The principal unions in the industry are the

TGWU, GMBATU, UCATT, FTAT and the EETPU, who constitute the employees' side of the various national joint boards.

Whilst the institutions of collective bargaining have remained unchanged, the bedrock of union representation – never completely solid – has been eroded in recent years. Price and Bain calculate that union density in construction increased from 30.1% to 36.7% between 1968 and 1979 (1983: 54). More recent statistics compiled on a similar basis are unavailable, but figures published by the Department of Employment imply a considerable fall in the membership of unions organising the industry between 1979 and 1982 of approximately 25%. The 1983–84 figures show a continued, slower decline.[11]

The loss of construction employment is only part of the reason for this fall. The growth in subcontracting and self-employment also helps to explain declining union membership. As a result, although most of the major firms engage in collective bargaining, and although industry-wide terms are set, there must be some doubt about the influence of national industrial relations institutions at site level. If safety institutions depend on such influence, then the climate for self regulation at site level is not propitious. In fact, when one looks at the type and severity of accidents in construction in the 1980s, there is some suggestion that a failure of self regulation, rather than a set of intrinsically unmanageable hazards, lie behind them.

Accidents in construction

Deficiencies of accident statistics have already been discussed in Chapter 2. Whilst these make it impossible to isolate a legislative effect and extremely difficult to isolate trends in the accident rate itself, some preliminary conclusions can be drawn from a study of them. The first is that as Chapter 2 has indicated, the construction industry fatal accident incident rate, though falling during the 1970s, was approximately five times that of manufacturing industry. By contrast, the non-fatal accident incidence rates were similar. Between 1981 and 1985 the combined fatal and major incidence rate in construction has risen markedly. While the manufacturing rate rose by 31% and that for all industries was broadly static, incidence rates rose in construction by 45% in the period 1981–85 (see Tables 2.4, 2.5).[12] This trend has been of such great concern to the Factory Inspectorate that in his Annual Report, 1986–87, the Chief Inspector of Factories identified construction safety as one of the three major priorities for his Inspectorate.

A second, very obvious and profoundly depressing observation about the recurring pattern of accidents has been made time and time again; it is

Table 5.4 *Type of accidents in construction, 1981–84*

Type of accident	All reported injuries (%)[a]		Major injuries (%)[b]		Fatal injuries to employees (actual no.)	
	1981 (N = 45 599)	1982 (N = 40 810)	1983 (N = 2176)	1984 (N = 2286)	1981 (N = 106)	1982 (N = 100)
Asphyxiation	0.01	0.02	0.14	0.22	3	4
Over-exertion etc.	24.61	25.68	2.90	2.23	—	—
Caught/trapped by collapse	0.31	0.37	1.33	2.28	12	12
Caught/trapped in between objects	6.13	5.81	6.76	8.27	5	4
Electric current	0.30	0.45	2.34	2.89	5	3
Fall or slip to same/higher level	14.77	13.09	9.83	8.53	1	—
Fall or slip to lower level	15.09	15.97	42.83	42.83	52	53
Harmful substances	0.30	0.37	1.24	1.27	—	—
Other	4.32	4.48	2.98	2.75	2	—
Powered vehicle	0.24	0.29	0.74	0.74	20	14
Struck by object/material	23.46	23.14	23.21	22.00	6	8
Striking an object	9.23	9.00	3.49	3.37	—	—
Extreme temperature	1.23	1.33	2.21	2.67	—	2
Total	100.00	100.00	100.00	100.00	106	100

[a] All injuries to employees as reported to H.M. Factory Inspectorate. These are not available for 1983 and 1984 owing to changes in reporting regulations.
[b] Major injuries to employees as reported to H.M. Factory Inspectorate.
Source: Communication from Health and Safety Executive, November 1986.

Table 5.5 *Accident rates per 1000 workers at risk, certain construction occupations, 1979[a]*

Occupation	Accident rate per 1000 at risk
Electrician	26.03
Bricklayer	53.88
Plasterer	44.62
Steel erector	151.28
Carpenter	42.19
Plumbing and heating	54.32
Slater/tiler	117.34
Painter/decorator	32.34
Glazier	108.00

[a] Calculated from Construction Industry Training Board figures for operations by craft. These differ from the SIC classification.

illustrated in Table 5.4 and was a central point in the Site Safe package:

> The general pattern of accidents remains very little different from earlier years ... it is possible to write in advance the epitaphs of the men who will be killed each year, in falls through roofs, when painting under roofs, by contact with overhead lines and in trenches. Declining accident figures so often only reflect declining construction activity.[13]

From Table 5.4, it is clear that the most common causes of construction accidents are over-exertion and falls of persons or objects. Fatalities tend to be caused either by falls or by accidents with powered vehicles. These are areas where working rules and standards exist, and in many cases accidents were associated with non-observance. Because of the importance of falls of persons or materials in accident causation, some construction operations are more hazardous than others. Table 5.5 shows accident rates for 1979 for certain construction operations. It would appear that people who work at heights or with fragile substances are most at risk.

A third important point concerns the fear expressed by the proponents of Site Safe, that increased levels of activity would be associated with a rise in the number of accidents:

> unless strenuous efforts are made to maintain the resources committed to safety and to improve safety performance a

Table 5.6 *Fatal and major injuries to the self-employed and non-employed in construction, 1981–84*

	1981		1982		1983		1984P	
	Self-employed	Non-employed	Self-employed	Non-employed	Self-employed	Non-employed	Self-employed	Non-employed
Fatal injuries								
Construction	11	12	18	13	20	11	17	7
All manufacturing industry	6	4	2	4	10	8	5	2
Major (non-fatal) injuries								
Construction	40	36	51	33	56	66	70	71
All manufacturing industry	8	22	21	40	18	60	30	59

P = Provisional
Source: Health and Safety Statistics 1983, Table 2.1B.

storm of accidents will be unleashed when the industry as a whole begins to expand again.[14]

This fear is justified by the data already presented (Tables 2.4, 2.5; Chapter 2). Table 2.4 also shows that the falling incidence rates of the 1970s are no longer in evidence; the combined fatal and major incidence rate in construction has arisen markedly since 1981. Under NADOR, the fatal and major injury rate rose from 164 per 100 000 at risk in 1981 to 204 in 1982, when it was three times the manufacturing average. Subsequently, it rose to 220.7 in 1983, 232.5 in 1984 and 238.4 in 1985. It seems therefore that the rise in the accident rate goes beyond what might have been expected due simply to a rise in the level of activity and employment after 1982. Safety performance has deteriorated.

A fourth point is that available evidence suggests that the size of the firm, the size of the site and the size of the workgroup are major factors in determining the distribution of accidents within any type of employment activity or the industry as a whole. Whilst the confusion of employment relationships at any one building site make it difficult to isolate the effect of size alone, the vulnerability of the small firm has been a constant theme in official reports on safety in the construction industry. In 1956 for example, the Factories Report observed that

> the small contractor seems to think that safety organisation is a thing right outside his orbit, if he is aware of its existence (quoted in Williams, 1960: 170).

Whilst the 1977–78 HSE Construction Health and Safety Report commented that

> in general the problem no longer lies with the major firms; they have the motivation and the resources. The problem now is getting the message across to a multitude of small firms (para. 7, page 7, HSE, 1979).

The HSE calculated that almost 80% of all fatal accidents in construction in 1977 occurred in small and medium-sized firms and in 1981 the Chief Inspector of Factories cited evidence to indicate that operatives working in 'small workgroups' were most at risk.[15] Thus, while a lack of detailed analysis prevents a more definite interpretation of patterns of accident trends and distribution in construction itself, the rise in numbers of small firms may be related to the rise in accident rates.

The increase in self-employment is also likely to be an important factor, but not one which is reflected in the statistics shown in Tables 2.4 and 2.5, since these relate to accidents to employees. Table 5.6 shows that the figures for fatal and major injuries to the self-employed in construction for the period 1981–84 are consistently higher than those for all manufacturing industry. The same can be said of the category of 'non-employed'. This can mean the unlucky 'passer-by', visitor or trespasser but – equally likely in construction – may mean someone who, when dead, is found not to have been 'employed' by anyone on the site. Their status is thus unclear but there may be some evidence to suggest that they were in fact engaged by 'someone' on a casual 'cash – no questions' basis. The Birmingham Coroner's Court, for example, dealt with two cases of death on construction sites in just one month (September 1985) where there was uncertainty about the employed status of the deceased. In one case a painter who had clearly been engaged to work on the site, fell to death, but his exact employment status was difficult to determine (Birmingham City Coroner's files 1 368/85). In the other case a demolition worker was found dead after a fall in a demolition site. The director of the firm responsible for the demolition claimed that the deceased was not engaged to work on the site at that time although he had been previously so employed. He further claimed that the deceased must have been trespassing when he fell to his death (Birmingham City Coroner's files 1 356/85). The trend for the combined fatal and major category for the self-employed and non-employed in construction is just as alarmingly upward for the period 1981–84 as is the trend for the same category of accidents for direct employees in the industry.

In summary, then, the construction industry is characterised by a growth in small firms and in subcontracting, a fall in union membership and a rise in the combined rate of fatal and major accidents since 1981. It might be expected, then, that the institutions of self regulation – in particular those of workforce involvement in health and safety – might be poorly developed, and that safe systems of work would come increasingly to rely on management responsibility and external enforcement. In fact, as our cases will show, the structure of activity in the industry often makes it difficult for managers and inspectors to afford the necessary attention to safety matters.

The case studies

Case studies were undertaken in 13 companies which ranged in size from publicly quoted large contractors with well known names to small private companies with direct workforces of fewer than 50. One direct labour organisation of a London local authority was also visited. Headquarters visits involved discussion with owners, directors or managers and, where possible, safety specialists. Interviews were also conducted with managers, specialists and, where possible, workforce representatives on at least one site from each of the same 13 companies. The researchers also had the opportunity to observe work in progress on these sites. Unlike the studies of chemical companies, the studies of construction and retail establishments did not include the administration of self-completion questionnaires.

The sites were chosen in an attempt to cover a wide spectrum of activity. They included one large civil engineering contract, three large building contracts in excess of £8 million in the London area, and a variety of medium and smaller contracts for both new building and refurbished work. All sites except for the civil engineering contract were in the London area or south-east England. The main features of the case study companies are summarised in Table 5.7.

It can be seen from this table that our case studies are unrepresentative of the industry as a whole. Most obviously, small firms are under-represented. However, on many of the larger sites, as the proportion of total workforce to direct employment shows, many subcontractors (themselves small firms) were employed. All of our sites had been visited by an Inspector at some time. This too is likely to make our sample untypical and suggests that our access was gained among a set of firms who felt that their safety organisation stood up to external inspection. We did not visit un-notified sites. It may well be then that our data overestimate the level of safety provision in the industry. We shall return to this point later.

The organisation of the data follows that of the previous chapter. We look in turn at safety policies, management organisation, specialist provision and workforce involvement.

Safety policies

It may be recalled that the requirement to produce a formal policy statement on health and safety is contained in section 2(3) of the HASAWA. All the firms we studied had discharged their statutory duty by providing and issuing their employees with a company safety policy. Whilst many of the larger firms' policies predated the Act, it was freely acknowledged that the statutory duty had encouraged revisions which had considerably improved their scope and content. Safety policies of the smaller firms were, however, usually specifically compiled to meet the legal duty.

Our case studies are in this respect also unrepresentative of construction industry practice as a whole; a significant proportion of the industry's population is exempt from the requirements of section 2(3) by virtue of size alone, since firms with fewer than five employees are not required to provide a safety policy.[16] This particular exemption probably affects a

Table 5.7 The case studies: details of contractors
(a) Information by firm and by site

Case	Description of main contractor, annual turnover (1982–83)	Contract value (£ million) nature of site	Workforce (operatives)		Union rep. on site	Safety rep. on site	Safety committee on site	Safety specialists		
			Total no. on site (including subcontractors)	Total no. directly employed				in head office	in area office	on site
1	Large contractor £169M	£35M Large office site, London	149	42	No	No	No	Yes	No	1PT[a]
2	Large contractor £169M	£6.2M Refurbishment London	90	9	No	No	No	Yes	No	No
3	Large contractor £616M	£8M Office and resid. development, London	52	14	No	No	No	Yes	Yes	No
4	Joint venture: 2 Large contractors £N/A	£35M road Wales	600	220	Yes	No	Yes	Yes	Yes	1FT[a]
5	Large contractor £N/A	£18M Office/shop/hostel development, London	150	N/A[a]	No	No	No	Yes	Yes	1FT[a]
6	Large contractor £177M	£34M Conference Centre, London	300	N/A[a]	Yes	Yes	Yes	Yes	Yes	1FT[a]

	Description of firm		Project			Union reps	Safety reps	Safety committees	in head office	in area office	on site
	contractor £44M		Hostel, London			No	No	No		No	No
8	Medium sized contractor £44M	£3M	Office building, London	60	12	No	No	No	Yes	No	No
9	Medium sized contractor £22M	£1.25M	Arts centre, Berkshire	40	12	No	No	No	No[b]	No	No

(b) Information by firm (detailed site information not available)

Case	Description of firm	Annual turnover (£ million)	Workforce directly employed	Union reps.	Safety reps.	Safety committees	Safety specialist		
							in head office	in area office	on site
10	Small firm, Essex	0.5–1	12	No	No	No	No	No	No
11	Small firm, outer London	0.75	20	No	No	No	No[b]	No	No
12	Small firm, London	2	90	No	No	No	Yes	No	No
13	Large firm, London	245	N/A	No	No	No	Yes	Yes	Yes
14	Local authority DLO, London	37	1250	Yes	Yes	Yes	Yes	Yes	No

[a] PT = part time; FT = full time; N/A = not available.
[b] Regular use made of external firm of safety consultants.

large number of employees, since smaller firms tend to attract self-employed labour which effectively reduces their employment size. A firm with an actual labour force of ten people might have only four 'legally defined' employees because the other six remained self-employed. All those we spoke to, whether directors of smaller firms, representatives of trade unions or employers' associations or those from the HSE, were all convinced that the response to the safety policy requirement amongst small firms was very low.[17]

A second major point of importance when considering safety policies concerns the origin of the policy itself. Both the HASAW Act and the Robens Report were of the opinion that safety policies should reflect more than a formal response and should demonstrate serious consideration of the individual firms' peculiarities. As the APAU Report puts it:

> It is important that the policy reflects the uniqueness and the special needs of the company for whom it is written. The document cannot be bought or borrowed nor can it be written by outside consultants or inspectors ... only they [the firm] have this deep and continuous insight into the complete relationship between the job being done and the men who do it which will enable them to write the policy with the conviction which is needed (HSE/14, 1980: 5).

The role of both specialist safety firms and employers' associations is relevant here. Some construction employers' associations have actually prepared a 'model' safety policy and made it available to their members. The safety specialists we interviewed generally felt that the danger of member firms merely adopting the policy without the necessary depth of organisation to implement its contents, outweighed the benefits of legal compliance. In their opinion, such documents were of no value if they merely represented 'paper organisation' without any real commitment to health and safety. Though none of our firms admitted to obtaining their own policy this way, several had commissioned a safety policy from specialist safety firms, and tended to regard it as a 'paper commitment', the main purpose of which was to meet the conditions of contract imposed by larger firms or local authorities to whom they subcontracted. In general then although our case study firms had complied, it was felt that the effective response to section 2(s) of HASAWA had been patchy, especially in smaller firms.

All the safety policies we studied were signed by a company director carrying ultimate responsibility for health and safety matters. Scope and content varied according to company size. Larger companies with a separate safety department usually produced an annual safety report with a sophisticated analysis of accident frequencies and types of risk, which often included accidents to their subcontractors amongst the returns. These annual safety reports provided the most tangible evidence of a form of safety policy review, though the bulk of the work contained within them concentrated on accident figures and types of causation rather than the effectiveness of the safety organisation itself. Figure 5.2 shows an extract from the 1982 safety report of one of the large contractors in our study. The report focuses on accidents by cause, timing and location, gives estimates of incidence rates, lists hazards and specific dangerous occurrences and gives publicity to Inspectorate action such as prosecutions and prohibition

Analysis of 16 accidents (over 3 days off work) (22 in 1981)

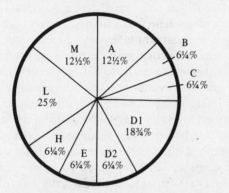
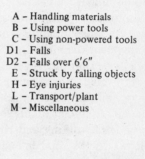

A – Handling materials
B – Using power tools
C – Using non-powered tools
D1 – Falls
D2 – Falls over 6′6″
E – Struck by falling objects
H – Eye injuries
L – Transport/plant
M – Miscellaneous

Falls on the ground continued to figure prominently in the statistics and there was an increase from nil to 25% (4 accidents) in transport/plant accidents. Three of these were due to operator error and one to unforeseeable failure of equipment.

Incidence rates of over 3 day accidents per 1000 employees for the period 1979–82 are shown below:

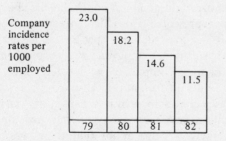

Figure 5.2 Analysis of accidents in 1982 by a construction company.

(Source: one of the construction companies studied)

107

notices. It also spells out the requirements on subcontractors to produce safety policies, attend safety meetings and participate in company training. The figure shows a breakdown of accidents by cause and a substantial reduction in 'lost time' accidents from 1978 to 1982.

Monitoring of the safety policy in smaller firms was usually undertaken in an informal or casual manner if at all, save in those cases where pressure for improvement came from outside bodies. In our experience, such pressure came primarily from clients, mostly in the public sector, or from some of the larger contractors in the private sector. It was generally held, by those we spoke to on sites, that the Health and Safety Executive Inspectors rarely concerned themselves with written safety policies.

The safety policies of the larger firms were usually compiled in two volumes. A separate short statement of objectives, organisation and responsibilities was usually available to give to employees or subcontractors when necessary. Since these large companies were often part of a larger holding group, the document often covered a variety of employment activities and groups including manufacturing and office work as well as primarily construction-based activities. The responsibilities of the safety department and the various levels of managerial responsibilities, together with safety procedures and organisation, were generally contained in this volume. Directions for job-specific training, safe methods of working and particular hazards were compiled in a second volume. In the smaller and medium-sized firms there was usually one document which was much slimmer, confining itself to a company statement, safety organisation and the various spheres of responsibility. In all documents, employees were reminded of their responsibilities under sections 7 and 8 of the HASAWA.

Management organisation

The two major variables affecting site management organisation were the size of the site itself and the size of the company controlling it. The number of contractual relationships represented is also highly significant and is the most obvious reason to consider construction a 'special case' for health and safety. As we show later, large firms may employ a variety of mechanisms in order to ensure subcontractors' compliance with safety policies, but subsubcontracting is more difficult to control. Moreover, the statutory responsibility of the managing contractor is by no means clear even where a formal contractual condition involving safety is imposed on other contractors. Nonetheless there was no doubt that there was general agreement on all sides that the senior line manager on site (whether called site agent, contracts manager or site manager) was *de facto* ultimately responsible for all aspects of the work on site, including health and safety.

Construction activities do not lend themselves to close supervision. Unlike typical factory work with a stable labour force, finite tasks and a fixed physical environment, in construction even apparently repetitive work like bricklaying or joinery can be undertaken in a wide variety of different contexts. The control of the first line supervisor, typically a ganger, is thus potentially much weaker than the factory-based equivalent; increases in subcontracting and the consequent attenuation of clear lines of responsibility have exacerbated the problem. On the large sites studied in this research managerial staff in the direct employ of the managing contractor were often working with self-employed or subcontracted craftspeople and labourers. The small firms, several of whom had a number of non-notifiable sites in operation at any one time, could only offer broad estimates of the total workforce on them at the time of the interview.

There are thus severe problems of coordination and control. The process of line management in construction has come to consist less of direct supervision of activity and more of attempts to impose pressure on subcontractors through financial penalties for inadequate performance. There is thus a tendency for reactive rather than preventative management. In safety terms, this implies blacklisting unsafe contractors or penalties for unsafe practices rather than the direct control of particular activities.

Construction work is cumulative; each stage of the work is organically linked to the next and the sequence of operations and the simultaneous occurrence of several operations create hazards. A delay or mistake at an early stage in the work may create a hazard for later operations; people working at higher levels on one particular task may be unaware of those working below. Time constraints create problems of scheduling and put pressure on operatives doing 'bottleneck' work. These problems are exacerbated by the presence of numerous different firms with their own methods of work and peculiar financial pressures. Managers are primarily concerned with cost and with the progress of the contract. On large sites, it is extremely difficult directly to observe the whole range of activities; managers thus tend to try to control outputs rather than methods of work. The techniques for such control are primarily contractual; however, in practice much depends on the attitudes of line managers to safety issues. On small sites, there may be less contractual complexity, but there may also be scarcity of resources and expertise. We shall analyse the two size categories separately.

Developments at local level

(a) Large firms and subcontractors

There has been an increasing recognition of the importance of health and safety considerations amongst construction management in the larger companies. At the highest levels, this commitment has been expressed most obviously in the support shown for the Industry Advisory Committee, CONIAC. Given this commitment and its expression in the expansion of training programmes and safety departments, it is not surprising that many of the managers interviewed in our large firms claimed to pay a great deal of attention to health and safety. Although there are some grounds for qualifying their rhetoric there is no doubt that the younger breed of site managers are 'converts' to the health and safety cause, at least to the extent that they agree that health and safety should be considered along with other managerial objectives. There was a general recognition, for example, that deliberate flouting of the various statutes was a criminal (rather than civil) matter and that they, as controllers of the site, could be held responsible for these transgressions.

It was also recognised that enforcement action or accidents themselves could bring the site to a long and potentially costly halt. In some cases, individual site managers felt that a poor accident record would reflect on their ability as managers and possibly count against their promotion prospects, though only one of the firms we studied explicitly included consideration of a manager's safety record in its appraisal system.

'Conversion' to the cause of health and safety can of course mean several different things. Site managers contravening specific statutory standards, for whatever reason, are not condoned or defended by their companies. Equally, line managers who encourage or ignore unsafe behaviour and hazardous work were likely to be reprimanded by their superiors. In one of our case studies, for example, a foreman was severely reprimanded for encouraging operatives to ride in the shovel of an earth-moving machine. There is, however, a form of sliding calculus which site management seem to use in which they balance an assessment of the risks involved in a particular contravention against the benefits to be gained from it. For example, if an urgent task needed to be completed, it was generally admitted that there would not be a very profound enquiry into the manner of its completion.

Site management operate in an extremely competitive and highly pressured environment, their reputations and futures depending on successful completion within the time limits set by the contract. Given these types of pressures and the enormous variety of tasks they are expected to undertake, it is not unexpected that considerations of health and safety are quite often of marginal significance, except when they directly affect, or are likely to affect, the progress of the work. This does not mean that site managers are indifferent to the health or safety of the operatives. At least one of our interviewees took an active interest in such questions and all, to differing degrees, were willing to use their authority to rectify breaches of the various regulations or to deal with potentially hazardous behaviour if they were brought to their attention. However, unless such work involved, or was likely to involve, serious danger, such considerations remained peripheral.

The position of foremen or supervisors and lower levels of line management generally were slightly different, since they were often more aware of and involved in the working practices of the operatives themselves. In many cases though, the benefits of this intimate knowledge were lost through lack of commitment, ignorance, lack of direct authority, pressures for completion, or simply the sheer variety of work in progress. It is an unfortunate fact that safety training appears to be poorest for operatives and for first line supervisors who experience or supervise the riskiest activities.

One of the key issues for larger companies is the extension of control to subcontractors. The attempts of larger companies to improve the health and safety performance of their subcontractors included both direct and indirect forms of control. The former centred around a pre-contractual examination of the subcontractor's safety organisation and systems of work; the latter involved the extension of the main contractor's lines of responsibility and the identification of a subcontractor's own line management.

The most tangible evidence of some form of health and safety monitoring in subcontracting could be seen from the increasing use of safety clauses in contracts. By making possession of a safety policy a necessary condition of tender, main contractors attempt to ensure that their subcontractors have some tangible commitment to health and safety. For example, the large contractor involved in case 6 required all subcontractors explicitly to include costings of 15 safety items in their contract tenders, as well as to conform with a number of accident reporting requirements. The 'general conditions' outlined were as follows:

> Subcontractors must furnish [company 6] with a copy of their safety policy.

> Subcontractors will be required to provide the name of the person responsible for safety on each site.

> The subcontractor is advised that it is the duty of [company 6] management/supervision/safety officer to stop their works if there is any actual or likely contravention of the requirements of current health and safety legislation.

> Subcontractors will be required to discuss and agree safe systems of work with [company 6] management and safety department prior to commencement on site.

In cases involving dangerous or unusual types of work, some large firms demanded an outline of the system of work to be adopted (a so-called 'method statement') prior to operation, thus attempting to ensure that the subcontractor is both technically competent and safety conscious. Other types of contractual obligation developed to ensure some degree of control over subcontractors limit the further sub-letting of tenders awarded to specific firms.

Systematic sub-letting of contracts is a common practice in construction and whilst its main effects are commercial and financial, the practice inevitably affects health and safety organisation. There is little point in main contractors imposing health and safety controls on their subcontractors if these same subcontractors sub-let part of the work to firms not sanctioned by the main contractor. There are some indications that main contractors are developing a blacklist of subcontractors with poor safety records, a practice which seems confined to large firms with strong safety departments.

As regards indirect forms of control over subcontractors, all of the large companies we studied attempted to ensure that their subcontractors maintained a minimum level of health and safety performance. It was a general requirement that all subcontractors' personnel adhere to the main contractor's safety procedures and adopt any suggestions and improvements made by site management or the company's safety officers. Most of the larger companies insisted that subcontractors working on their sites nominate a supervisor or competent person to act as a link between the site management and the subcontractor. In theory this practice extends the influence of line management and identifies the particular responsibilities of the subcontractor itself. The potential benefits of this are not, of course, confined to, or even informed by, purely health and safety considerations; they simply open a channel for communication which can be used to discuss any aspect of the subcontractor's behaviour. Our evidence suggested that most of the information flowing through this channel related predominantly to commercial preoccupations and only marginally touched on health and safety.

In our cases, there were no attempts to ensure that the supervisors or gangers appointed by subcontractors had any knowlege or expertise in health and safety or that they were necessarily competent supervisors. In many cases site managers did not know the identity of individuals on their site or even in some cases the identity of particular subcontract companies.

We learned of several cases where subcontractors' supervisors had been found flouting safety procedures, and yet no action had been taken by either the managing contractor or the person's own higher management. There appeared to be considerable differences between policy statements, some of which specified dismissal or contract termination as the result of failure to comply, and the actual behaviour of managers and employees on sites with such policies 'in place'.

(b) Smaller companies

Management in the smaller companies in the study operated in a different fashion, since the lines of communication were much shorter, the structure much simpler and often the commercial pressures were felt more clearly and immediately at site level. A distinction can be drawn between those firms for whom subcontracting to major companies' sites comprised the majority of work and those who concentrated on the domestic or small contract work. Several of the smaller firms we studied had a particular antipathy for the majors and the whole practice of subcontracting, preferring to tender for local council, domestic or light industrial work. With one particular exception, the safety organisation of these firms had not been bolstered or affected by contact with outside bodies. The exception was company 11, which had employed a safety consultant in an attempt to improve its safety procedures and records, so that it complied with standards expected by certain major contractors and public sector clients.

In general, we found that management in smaller firms was both informal and unstructured; where health and safety was concerned it was primitive or non-existent. None of our small firms had separate safety departments with specially trained personnel; any managerial control of health and safety was exercised through normal line management. In all such cases there was no intermediate link between the directors and supervisory management at site level; effectively this meant that health and safety was left in the hands of the foreman or ganger, reinforced only by the casual visits of the director or owner of the firm or the factory inspector. Quite often the director, or person identified in the policy as having final responsibility for health and safety, had no special knowledge or training in the subject. Their commitment to health and safety was often confined to vague warnings about 'looking after yourself' or 'working as safely as possible'. There were no formal assessments of safe working methods or operative behaviour.

There were some indications that the interest shown in safety varied with the type of work undertaken. Several of the larger firms claimed that smaller firms subcontracting to their sites were more careful in their working methods and ostentatious in demonstrating their awareness of safety when working for them than when working on their own small sites. Not surprisingly smaller firms rebutted this accusation, maintaining that they always took all the necessary precautions to safeguard their employees' safety.

The specialists: safety departments, advisers and consultants

Whilst there are no general statutory provisions governing the appointment of safety advisers or safety departments, certain industries including construction have been governed by particular legislation explicitly designed to foster forms of safety organisation. The Building (Safety, Health and Welfare) Regulations 1948 provided for the appointment in writing, by an employer of more than 50 persons (subsequently lowered to 20 in 1961), of an experienced person to advise on statutory standards and supervise safety arrangements generally. According to the wording of the Regulations, the general duties of the person chosen must not be such as to interfere with the efficient discharging of these safety duties. The immediate response to this statute was an explosion in the numbers of 'safety supervisors', as they came to be known, despite the fact that the legislation did not cover works of engineering construction. Unfortunately, there is considerable evidence to suggest that the growth of safety supervisors was not commensurate with a *real* growth in safety organisation or commitment, as the 1955 HMFI Report observed:

> In too many cases, and even among the larger firms, the appointment of a responsible person under Regulation 98 appeared to be purely nominal. It was not uncommon to be told that every foreman had been appointed. This does not constitute compliance with either the spirit or the letter of the Regulation. For directors, agents, managers or site foremen, such an appointment means additional work which usually they cannot find time to do (HMFI Report 1955: 62).

The Inspectorate felt that the Regulations laid the basis for effective safety organisation. In the same Report they said that

> where a suitable person has been appointed as a full time safety officer the results in accident prevention have been satisfactory.

In their 1966 Report, 'Accidents in the construction industry', the Factory Inspectorate commented:

> The effectiveness of safety organisations varied considerably ...

the key to the situation is undoubtedly a positive safety policy, the appointment of an effective safety supervisor and the backing he receives from management followed by adequate training at site level ... (1966: Conclusion 6).

Following the Robens Report and the HASAW Act, numbers of safety advisers and specialist safety officers in the industry rose quite considerably. There is little doubt that both their training and their general competence are now at a higher standard than they were in the period prior to the Act, but still much of the industry is not directly covered by specialist appointments. Their incidence and effectiveness is generally confined to the larger companies, who have their own safety departments, or exercised through specialist safety firms or safety groups.

Our case studies suggest that the incidence of strong specialist safety departments is confined to some of the very large companies. Companies in this size band each had a central safety department with regionalised safety officers and a separate departmental budget. Medium-sized, but still quite considerable, companies like cases 7, 8 and 12 had very small safety departments, usually combined with other service functions, employing perhaps one or two safety officers based in head office. Company 11 employed an outside specialist safety company to perform the tasks of safety monitoring and advice. The smaller firms we studied had no safety specialists or safety departments and relied totally on managements' ability to ensure that legal standards were met. There is little doubt that company size is the major variable affecting the incidence and depth of specialist safety departments/advisers. For this reason it seems logical once more to examine the evidence of our case studies in their respective size categories.

(a) Large companies

Whilst the powers and duties of the safety officers employed by the companies we studied varied considerably, the organisation and procedures adopted followed a basic model common to them all. Typically, the department was headed by a senior manager operating at one or two levels below the board of directors, with lines of communication upwards to a named director, his immediate superior and horizontally to other service managers (for an example, see Figure 5.3). The safety department had its own budget with secretarial support and a number of regionalised departments, each employing safety officers responsible for the company's activities in that region. The regional safety officers visited or inspected the company's sites on a regular/specified rota varying between a fortnight and a month and sent their reports both to the site managers and to the manager of the safety department. The reports would give an overall assessment of the site's safety provisions, together with a number of specific

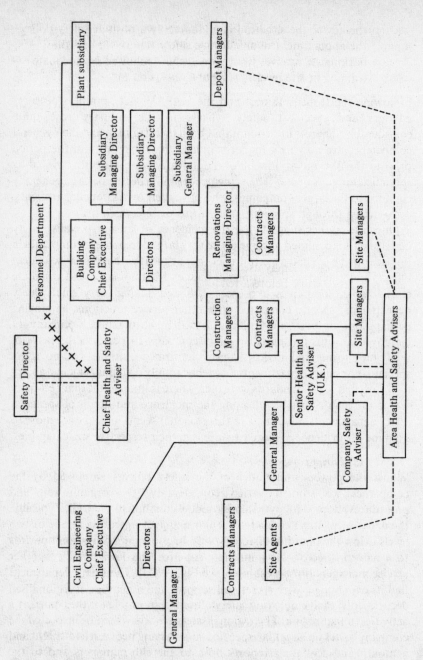

Figure 5.3 Safety organisation and line management in construction company 3.
(Notes to Figure 5.3 are on p. 117.)

recommendations or identified faults needing rectification. These would be monitored on the next visit and further reports sent to indicate compliance or non-compliance. In addition to this monitoring function, safety officers were expected to advise site management on their legal duties and suggest alternative systems of work where necessary.

Most of the safety departments were also responsible for overseeing company safety training. Much of the managerial safety training was supplied by outside specialists, usually in the form of block release. Courses for lower levels of line management and operatives, were undertaken by the company itself and usually lasted for half a day. It was common to find that the safety department prepared an annual review of safety performance and for this to be the only tangible example of monitoring. A breakdown of accident statistics, Inspectorate action or new regulations were also sometimes included. One fairly recent development relates to the use of contractual safety requirements as mentioned earlier; safety department personnel are increasingly used to examine subcontractor's safety policies and systems of work before a tender is granted.

There were considerable variations in the attitudes and expectations of the safety departments we studied, especially in relationships between safety officers and site management concerning their respective powers and responsibilities. Though these formal differences were less marked in the practices and daily experiences of safety officers, they were nonetheless indicative of some divergence in the perceptions of a safety officer's role and the importance of safety considerations in general.

The two major preoccupations of the safety officers we interviewed were those of monitoring and advice, though far more examples were given of the former than the latter. Monitoring involved a number of specific and separate tasks. First, it involved ensuring that all activities were undertaken in a safe manner and that statutory standards were observed, e.g. setting of abrasive wheels, scaffolding, tower cranes and statutory records. Secondly, it meant checking that the company's safety procedures were actually observed, that accidents were reported, that subcontractors were observing conditions specified in their contract, etc. Thirdly, monitoring involved checking that defects identified in previous reports had been rectified and attended to. The advisory function covered much the

Notes to Figure 5.3
Dashed lines (−−−−−) indicate advisory links; lines of crosses (× × × × ×) indicate liaison links. Workplace Safety Supervisors are functionally responsible to the Safety Department. Senior Health and Safety Adviser (UK), in the absence of Chief Health and Safety Adviser, is directly responsible to the Safety Director.
(Source: construction company, case 3)

same areas, either devising systems of work to alter present practice or, less commonly, planning systems of work for hazardous and difficult activities to be undertaken in the future.

Within these general activities, however, there were wide variations in the formal powers of safety officers. At one end of the spectrum was the company which firmly limited the role of the safety officer to that of *adviser* to site management. Consequently the adviser had no independent power to prohibit activities or stop the work in progress, to demand that certain modifications be made or that work be done in a particular way. At the opposite end of the spectrum was the company who gave their safety officers a *watchdog* role; formal power to suspend any activity they thought unsafe or hazardous, to demand any improvements they thought necessary or insist on certain conditions being observed if they thought it appropriate. In the latter company, a safety officer had recently been dismissed because the safety director was not satisfied with his competence and 'toughness'. In practice, we found that formal differences in role and power were of less significance than might be supposed, since the influence of the safety officer and safety department as a whole was always tempered by commercial considerations.

In practice these commercial pressures could be seen in a number of ways. On the one hand, the formal power of the 'watchdog'safety officer was constrained by the commercial logic of site economics and the need to maintain an effective relationship with site management. Both safety officers and site management realised that completion dates and financial penalties placed severe limits on 'pure' health and safety matters. Naturally the harder the safety officer pushed 'pure' safety, the more the site management resisted; for them safety was a cost to be endured, once the serious dangers had been eliminated. A form of balance was attained, where the safety officer practised a form of self censorship, and the site management responded to the 'sensible' suggestions he made. Similar considerations also affected the way safety officers dealt with subcontractors. Generally site management were very reluctant to discipline efficient subcontractors purely for safety reasons, unless of course their activity threatened the progress of the site as a whole. In one case, a site manager had physically ejected the safety officer from the site, the culmination of a particularly bad relationship where a balance had not been attained. Interestingly, the site manager was not penalised and the safety officer was not supported by his superior who, knowing the rules of the game, considered that the safety officer himself was to blame for the breakdown.

In the same way the 'adviser' type of safety officer had more power than the formal role would suggest. *In extremis*, a safety officer could invoke the aid of the safety manager to bring pressure to bear on the site management knowing that blatant disregard of statutory provisions endangering the workforce would not be condoned by higher management. Similarly, persistent failure of site management to rectify faults identified in regular inspections could be drawn to the attention both of the safety director and of the commercial line management.

Similar considerations were important in the relationships between the safety manager and those in higher management. The departmental budget and the status of the safety department were reliant on a 'sensible' and 'helpful' attitude. It was common practice for safety managers to make a case for one or two items of extraordinary expenditure each year and, since these could not often be justified purely in terms of compliance with minimum standards, the safety department chose this ground carefully and relied heavily on its reputation for 'reasonableness' cultivated throughout the year.

(b) Medium-sized companies

Safety departments in the medium-sized companies were much smaller, usually combining the safety function with other types of service. Typically it was headed by a manager, qualified in a technical building skill such as surveying, and staffed by one or two safety inspectors. Unlike the major construction firms, the medium-sized firms we studied confined their operations to a particular region, so that there was no need for a decentralised safety function. The safety department was not funded by a separate departmental budget, being treated as a service function to be funded when necessary. Whilst the job descriptions and responsibilities of the safety officers we interviewed included such items as supervising training, collecting information and giving instruction, it was evident that the majority of their time was taken up with making site inspections and preparing reports. This followed the normal procedure outlined above: one copy of the report was left with the site manager and another sent to the safety department; the defects and weaknesses outlined would then be checked on the next visit. The frequency of these visits varied between a fortnight and a month, though particularly dangerous sites or activities might be subject to closer scrutiny. We found little evidence to suggest that safety officers in medium-sized companies conducted training courses or disseminated information to management or employees. Although safety officers in medium-sized firms, as in the large companies, collected accident statistics and investigated serious accidents, we found no collation and examination of accident trends or rates. Since this type of operation was the only indication of a form of safety policy review, we can only conclude that such reviews are limited in scope and confined to the larger firms.

All the safety officers we studied in this size category had the formal power to 'stop the job' if they felt it necessary, although none of our companies could furnish us with a single example of the use of this executive power on the basis of direct experience. Not surprisingly then, safety officers in medium-sized firms were subject to the same constraints as those in larger firms. One of our medium-sized firms (9) did not have its own safety specialists, but relied instead on external consultants.

(c) Small companies

None of the smaller companies we studied had specialised safety departments or safety inspectors, though each had – as already indicated – a safety policy outlining the duties of line management. The general view in these smaller companies was that the scope of their operation did not justify the expense of a separate safety specialist. The companies here were certainly not ignorant of their statutory duties or apathetic to health and safety considerations in general. There is some evidence that commitment to safety varies considerably in this size band. For example an unpublished APAU study of safety groups in the construction industry found that some companies which employed fewer than 20 people and therefore under present Regulations had no statutory duty to appoint safety supervisors, nonetheless did so. Others – even though above the limit of 20 employees – disregarded their statutory duty. There can be little doubt that our case studies were among the better small firms as far as safety provision is concerned.

Employee/workforce involvement

An initial assessment of the SRSCR's impact on safety organisation was gained from a survey undertaken by the HSE.[18] The comparatively poor response in the construction industry was partially attributed to the preponderance of small workplaces in the sample and was not interpreted as an indication of ignorance of or antipathy towards the Regulations themselves. Evidence collected from our case studies, some four years later, suggests that these inferences were optimistic then and are certainly less relevant in the late 1980s. We found little evidence of workforce involvement in either statutorily based or voluntarily developed health and safety machinery, even where trade unions were recognised. Participation in voluntarily developed safety machinery, either at site or company level, was usually confined to management personnel. Only three of the sites we visited had any form of union organisation or representation although several of the main contractors 'recognised' unions at national level. Of these three, two were strongly organised, one being case 14, the direct labour department of a local council, and the other, case 6, a management-fee contract where trade union organisation was encouraged and supported by site management. These two sites had both safety representatives and safety committees: the other site, case 4, had a union representative and a safety committee, but no safety representative on site.

By far the most common form of workforce involvement took the form of casual, informal consultation with line management. 'Employees know that they can approach me any time and point out danger spots', was the sort of common statement by managers in our case studies. Given that such casual encounters were genuinely believed to constitute 'workforce involvement', it is perhaps not difficult to explain the sporadic incidence of voluntary joint safety procedures and formal provisions for employee involvement. With one exception, site-safety meetings were composed entirely of management representatives. The lack of statutory safety representatives even in those cases with a sizeable number of union members, is more difficult to account for. Unlike voluntary procedures, their establishment does not depend on employer initative but on union recognition. We did, however, find a certain amount of evidence to suggest that the attitude of the employer exercises a certain influence, even in the latter case.

Most of the discussions concerning statutory safety representatives were retrospective, conducted in the past tense simply because the present was inappropriate. All of our large companies had managed sites where statutory safety representatives had been appointed, but even here such sites tended to be semi-permanent, large, complicated, prestigious and usually in progress for several years. This size effect partly explains the comparatively few safety representatives encountered in our medium-sized firms.

The influence of size was illustrated by reference to the Thames Barrier Project, where it was said that statutory safety representatives were firmly established and well organised. The three separate worksites had been represented by a safety representative on each shift, with a total of nine statutory representatives conducting inspections and setting up safety committees. By comparison, all but one of the representatives we interviewed, were unaware of their statutory rights and untrained. Despite the various difficulties of organising a sprawling and fragmented industry, the adequate levels of trade union membership, well established collective bargaining machinery and obvious hazards of the work itself led us to expect a much higher response. We were not alone in these expectations, since construction managers themselves told us that in the past they had viewed the possible effects of safety representatives with some concern.

There is of course a long history of both casual labour and hostility to trade unionism in building, at times combining to reinforce each other and defeat the objectives of those seeking to organise the industry. In recent times, relations between the employers and the unions reached a low in the 1972 strike partly because of the growth of 'lump' labour and the unions' attempts to stamp it out. At issue in this particular dispute was the increasing irrelevance of substantive joint agreements and the corresponding deterioration in the standing of the national bargaining machinery.

Since the 1972 strike there has been a certain rapprochement between the two sides at national level and joint agreements, national negotiating machinery and other subsidiary joint committees have retained some relevance. The activities of the joint health and safety advisory committee (CONIAC) for example have been praised by both employers and trade unionists. But despite this cooperation at national level, company management, especially at site level, seems relieved to find workforce involvement through safety representatives so underdeveloped in the industry.[19]

Construction managers we interviewed put forward a number of reasons for the lack of voluntary safety procedures. They argued that though legislation had made provisions for workforce involvement there was a lack of interest or demand from the employees. Workers, they said, did not want responsibility for safety and they thought that in any case a lack of workforce involvement made no difference since safety was adequately controlled by management.

In seeking to explain the lack of statutory safety representatives, union officials point to the pressures of being a trade union activist in a recession. Several trade unionists we interviewed alleged that blacklists circulated to warn future employers of union activists. The most effective safety representative we interviewed suggested that his lengthy spell of unemployment was partly explained by his record of active trade unionism. On another site, the trade union safety representative admitted that the fear of antagonising site management severely restricted the scope of his activities.

The weakness of trade unions at site level and their consequent failure to take advantage of the provisions available in the SRSC Regulations is mirrored by the general lack of consultative procedures common in other industrial sectors. This lack of concern with industrial relations matters at site level makes voluntary consultation on health and safety matters even less likely. Management skills in the construction industry emphasise technical and commercial excellence and the effective coordination of those tasks necessary to complete the job. Personnel skills and the encouragement of forms of workforce involvement are often ignored.

The activities of those safety representatives we did find varied considerably. On one large site, the safety representative was ignorant of the legislation, had not attended any training courses, did not conduct any inspections and was not invited to the monthly site safety meeting which consequently consisted entirely of managerial personnel. At the other extreme on a large management-fee contract, we interviewed an experienced safety representative who had attended numerous safety courses, was fully conversant with his rights under the legislation and active in the monthly safety committee. This particular committee included representatives of the major subcontractors working on the site and dealt with basic safety problems such as the scaffolding structure, problems caused by the stacking of materials and the inevitable difficulties of coordinating the working practices of many different firms and activities. Though the activities of both the safety representative and the safety specialist ensured that this particular site had one of the most effective safety organisations of those sites we studied, this standard of organisation would appear to be the very minimum necessary for establishing a safe place of work. That most do not reach these standards is a cause for great concern, and must be a factor in explaining the industry's safety record, indicating a limited basis for self regulation.

Inspection and enforcement

In circumstances where some of the institutions of self regulation are poorly developed, one might expect to see a great deal of enforcement activity by those Factory Inspectors who specialise in construction work. It is true that all of the case study sites had been visited by an Inspector, in some cases more than once. Several of the companies involved in the study had been issued with improvement or prohibition notices at some time, though this was by no means regarded as common practice and only in a minority of cases did these notices relate to work on the sites we visited. In one case, inspection occurred in response to a notified accident. Nonetheless the hand of the Inspectorate lay rather lightly on the case study sites. There may be several reasons for this. The most obvious is that the cases are self-selected for reasonable safety standards and that Inspectors were directing their attention elsewhere. However, it was a consistent complaint of managers on our sites that smaller 'cowboy' operations escaped inspection altogether, despite their reputation in the industry for poor standards.

A second reason lies in the resourcing of the Inspectorate. In 1984, there were only 88 Inspectors nationally available to monitor over 100 000 firms in the construction industry, and several of these Inspectors had additional responsibilities for other industries. Although the number of sites is likely

123

Table 5.8 *Enforcement and prosecution activities, construction industry, 1981–85*

	1981	1982	1983	1984	1985p
Notices					
Improvement	124	96	130	133	99
Deferred prohibition	13	29	27	45	38
Prohibition	458	709	819	890	886
Informations					
Laid	585	823	721	657	684
Convictions	531	734	651	590	567

Source: private, HSE Communication, November 1986.
Note: p = provisional.

to be much lower than the number of firms, the smaller sites come only casually to the attention of Inspectors who have a substantial workload in any event. It seems likely that some sites are never visited, and some only rarely, because the Inspectorate is overstretched.

Table 5.8 shows the enforcement and prosecution activity of the Inspectorate in the construction industry from 1981 to 1985. Despite falling resources, there has been a rise in several types of enforcement activity, notably the use of prohibition notices. Informations laid and convictions have also risen, although in both cases there has been a decline since 1982 after a sharp rise from 1981 to 1982. Mounting concern about poor standards of health and safety, particularly on small construction sites, led to the Chief Inspector of Factories announcing in 1987 that the Construction Inspectorate were planning a big inspection initiative. They were intending to target certain locations in which they would seek to visit all construction sites, however small.[20] In identifying construction safety as a particular problem for the Factory Inspectorate, the Chief Inspector of Factories in his Annual Report 1986–87 announced an intention to increase the number of Factory Inspectors engaged on construction work from the present 85 to 100.

In planning the division of their time for 1987–88 HSE Construction Inspectors announced they aimed to spend 40% on routine investigation, 47% on reactive work, including the investigation of accidents and complaints and work associated with follow-up visits and legal proceedings, 9% on special projects and 4% on new plant and substances.[21]

None of the people interviewed in our case studies commented at the time on any changes in the pattern of inspection or enforcement activity.

Some line managers presented stereotyped views of Inspectors. Some were seen as 'legalistic', 'bookish' and 'out of touch' with the realities of construction; others were criticised for not dealing strictly enough either with 'careless' employees or with the 'cowboys' who got the industry a bad name. Safety specialists in the larger companies appeared in general to be on good terms with local Inspectors and their senior area directors. Those interviewed made several references to the help, advice and cooperation they had received from members of the Construction Inspectorate on particular safety problems and issues. One group safety report, for example, noted that the HSE were a 'helpful and cooperative body as long as they can see that companies are complying with the legislation and aware of potential hazards'. These sorts of close links are further illustrated by an experiment in 1984 and 1985 when the HSE agreed that one major contractor should arrange 'self policing' for health and safety.[22]

In general, site managers in our case studies complied with suggestions or instructions from the Inspectorate, at least in the short term. However, in one easily observable way, the wearing of hard hats, there was often open disregard for the working rule agreement[23] and indeed for one of the most obvious safety precautions it is possible to take.

Conclusion

The question arises of the extent to which the experience of our cases can be seen to be typical of the sector as a whole. In terms of the size distribution (30–1250 employees), we have clearly undersampled very small firms, but we made contact with some of these as subcontractors to our main contractors. In terms of unionisation and the development of workforce involvement, our sample is probably broadly typical. However, in other respects it is not. Our large contractors generally had falling accident rates up to 1983. The small sites had often not been in operation for a lengthy period but it appeared from the accident books we inspected and from the opinions of the managers we interviewed that accident rates were not rising sharply, whereas they were at this period in the industry as a whole.

In addition, all of our sites had been inspected. This is almost certainly untypical given the limited resources of the Inspectorate. Taken together with voluntary offers of access, and the willingness of line managers to give up time to discuss safety, it seems reasonable to conclude that, within each size category, we have cases in which concern with, and provision for, safety was higher than average.

One of our strongest findings from the cases was the pronounced size effect on safety provision, subcontracting, and union membership. As Table 5.9 illustrates, this does appear to be the case more generally. The

Table 5.9 *Effectiveness of a working rule agreement on wearing safety helmets on construction sites*

Size of site (no. of employees)	No. and (%) of sites in each size range	No. and (%) of employees	% sites in each size range with subcontractors	% sites in each size range with unions	% sites in each size range where increased use noted	% unionised sites where increased use noted	% sites with subcontractors where increased use noted	% sites where encouragement occurred	% sites where enforcement occurred
1–7	175 (22)	613 (2)	8	7	6	30	60	52	10
8–13	184 (23)	1932 (7)	59	15	22	45	68	35	24
14–24	203 (26)	5409 (19)	69	3	38	25	61	55	24
25–34	88 (11)	2596 (9)	84	41	63	43	85	57	20
35–59	76 (10)	3572 (13)	67	54	52	43	100	63	30
60–79	20 (2.5)	1390 (5)	90	30	65	38	85	65	25
80–114	16 (2)	1552 (5)	87	87	87	93	93	75	25
115–1000	16 (2)	3093 (11)	94	81	63	50	100	75	50
1000+	4 (0.5)	7900 (28)	100	100	100	100	100	100	100
Totals	782 (100)	28 057 (100)	mean 56	mean 21	mean 33	mean 45	mean 84	mean 52	mean 18.5

Source: HSE 18, 1985.

table also illustrates a positive relationship between site size and observance of the safety helmet rule – perhaps the most easily monitored working rule in the industry. Although we have no data, it does seem reasonable to conclude that the relatively high safety standards on our case study sites relate partly to the fact that we did not sample the first three size categories listed in that table.

The pillars of local self regulation laid down by the Robens Committee were management responsibility, specialist advice and workforce involvement. Looking at the construction industry in 1983, we found some management responsibility at top level, particularly in the large companies, but only limited amounts at middle and line management level. We found an unrealistic reliance on safety specialists since it was not always backed up by senior line management commitment and little or no real development of workforce involvement. The types of self regulation envisaged in the Report have not been embraced by the construction industry. The weaknesses of trade union organisation at site level and the antipathy of construction management to organised workforce involvement have severely hampered the development of effective safety representatives and safety committees in larger companies and on larger sites and virtually precluded it altogether in smaller firms.

In attempting to construct an explanation both of the industry's appalling safety record and of its poor response to self regulation, a number of separate factors immediately present themselves. Apart from the confusion of employment relationships, the sprawling spectrum of activity and the inherent danger of the work itself, there is little doubt that the industry covets and promotes an image of toughness, individuality and independence. Bravado and the running of risks, by ignoring or deliberately flouting safety procedures, are seen as natural expressions of this culture. As an explanation for individual accidents and the industry's safety record as a whole, this holds an easy, obvious and popular appeal. But whilst it is possible to observe people who work as if their safety, or more especially the safety of others, is of little consequence, this attitude is itself the product of a number of complex factors. As previous writers on construction safety have observed:

> Encouraging workers to obey safety rules and to be cautious in hazardous situations seems unlikely to alter construction workers' priorities since it leaves unchallenged the methods of working which give rise to and encourage unsafe work practices ... widespread use of incentive bonus schemes – often calculated on an individual basis – and the practice of lump working undoubtedly contribute to risk-taking and unsafe

127

behaviour ... Given the interests of contractors in reducing completion time and workers in making as much money as possible out of the available job, 'cooperation' between the 'two-sides' seems likely to encourage unsafe systems of work as much as heightened safety unconsciousness' (Codrington and Henley 1981: 303).

The issue of safety helmets is a perfect illustration of the problems faced by those seeking to improve safety provisions in the industry. Despite an agreement between construction trade unions and employers at national level and its incorporation into the working rules which govern industry wide conditions of service, available evidence clearly demonstrates a widespread flouting of the rule. The refusal of operatives to wear safety helmets and the failure of site management to enforce their wearing are the source of much frustration to those officials who sit on the industry wide committees. But it is clear that without legal enforcement of the ruling, commercial pressures, the pattern of extensive subcontracting, weak trade union organisation and the 'culture' of the industry will combine to defeat the good intentions of such officials. Implicit in this illustration is the tension between self regulation and outside enforcement and the role of the Inspectorate in both. We shall examine these issues in Chapter 9.

6

Safety in retailing

Retail stores were chosen as the third area for case studies because they both represent a low risk industry and provide large numbers of smaller workplaces with low levels of trade union membership. Looking at retailing made it possible to consider an industrial structure quite different from construction and chemicals with a distinctive workforce and a different machinery for the enforcement of health and safety standards through Environmental Health Officers (EHOs) employed by local authorities.

The retail sector employs around 2.3 million people in a wide variety of manual, service and administrative occupations. Workers in retail are to be found in firms and enterprises from the largest to the smallest in the land. The development of this sector and its current structure need to be considered before discussing its safety.

The retail industry

Development and structure

Small retail stores had little significance for the British economy as a whole before the great urban growth of the nineteenth century. It was only then that fixed shops and groups of stores took over retailing from fairs and travelling hawkers (Davis 1966; Alexander 1970; Winstanley 1983). Early in the twentieth century, the economic historian Thorold Rogers recalled the breakdown of direct dealing between producer and consumer as occurring within the memory of a generation. By that time there already existed the familiar myth that there was once a golden age when the retail trade was made up of 'family-run neighbourhood shops, possibly handed down through successive generations' and for some reason so located as to be described as 'corner shops' (Jefferys 1954). Each generation since the mid nineteenth century has regretted the decline of the smaller retailer, ever

129

Table 6.1 *Percentage of retail trade by type of organisation*

	1957	1975	1981
Department stores	5	5	5
Multiples	24	40	45
Independents	57	41.5	38
Cooperatives	12	7.5	6
Mail order	2	6	6
Total	100	100	100

Source: Keynote, *Multiple Stores*, Survey (1982).

since a concentrated mass market has allowed the development of forms of bulk supply.

The first alternative to the small retailer came through cooperative societies who were able to organise bulk purchase to undercut competition and share profits with customers. Private multiple retailers were also able to make economies from bulk supply methods and firms such as Liptons and Maypoles emerged in the 1870s. By 1880 there were around 1500 branches of such chains; in 1920, 25 000; in 1950, 45 000; in 1980, 150 000. Taking advantage of economies of supply, the share of the retail market of these multiple shop retailers rose from around 4 % at the turn of the century to 8 % in 1920, 19 % in 1950, 30 % in the early 1960s, 40 % by the late 1970s, and is over 45 % in the 1980s. A small but nonetheless significant section of the market has been held by department stores whose origins go back to the mid nineteenth century. At the turn of the century they accounted for around 1.5 % of retail sales, in 1920 they reached 3.5 % and since 1950, between 5 and 6 % (Livesey 1979: 103).

Another form of multiple retailing to emerge in the 1920s were variety chain stores like Woolworths and Marks and Spencers who benefited not only from economies in supply but also from new sales methods, including modern advertising techniques. It was the various forms of multiple stores which benefited from the advent of the supermarket in the 1950s and 1960s, at first in food lines exclusively, but more recently in a greater diversity of products. These developments can be illustrated in Tables 6.1 and 6.2.

Whilst the number of multiple store chains has declined slightly, there has been a dramatic increase in the proportion of sales attributable to multiple stores. This growth has not been so much in the old grocery retailers of the nineteenth century, the Maypoles and the Liptons, nor yet

Table 6.2 *Changes in retailing, 1971–84*

	1971	1976	1978	1980	1982	1984
Retail businesses (thousands)	368	262	235	240	233	231
Outlets (thousands)	510	390	350	362	350	343
Turnover († hundred million)	17.0	34.0	44.6	39.4	69.8	82.3
Single outlet retailers (thousands)	n/a	231	208	198	203	202
Small (2–9) outlet multiples (thousands)	n/a	29.4	25.5	28.9	28.6	28.2
Large (10+) outlet multiples (thousands)	n/a	1.4	1.2	1.3	1.1	0.9
Persons engaged (thousands)	2845	2503	2424	2419	2264	2326
Persons engaged as % of employed population[a]	13.14	11.35	10.58	10.77	10.82	11.21

[a] Employees in employment, June each year.
Source: SPO 25 (1982): Annual Abstract of Statistics, 1987.

the variety chains of the 1920s. The growth has come by diversification of products and increase of size of a number of groups, usually with one basic starting point. Thus Marks and Spencers has gone into food, W. H. Smith's into electronics and Woolworths into accessories for do-it-yourself and gardening. This expansion in multiple stores cannot be expected to continue indefinitely. The department store seems likely to retain a stable if relatively small share of the retail market. Meanwhile, competition between the large supermarket chains seems likely to increase their overall share of the retail trade, particularly as they move into larger and more automated units, and employ new technology methods like electronic point-of-sale systems.

One recent phenomenon which can be noticed in the structure of the retailing sector is franchising, particularly in larger department stores. There are examples of larger stores that sub-let small sections to other, usually smaller firms, sometimes using them as show cases for well known brands, sometimes as risk takers to be taken over if successful. There are some parallels with the construction industry, and one or two examples are illustrated in the following case studies. However, franchising in retail is not so important as subcontracting in construction and is generally much more closely integrated into the activities of the larger enterprises.

Another clear trend is a decline in the size of the workforce, although

Table 6.3 *Retail trade by business and form of organisation, 1984*

	Businesses (thousands)	Outlets (thousands)	Persons engaged (thousands)	Total turnover (£ billion)
Total	230.8	343.1	2326	82.3
Single outlet	201.6 (87%)	201.6 (59%)	813 (35%)	24.2 (29%)
Small multiple	28.2 (12%)	73.7 (21%)	249 (15%)	10.6 (13%)
Large multiple,	0.9 (0.4%)	67.8 (20%)	1164 (50%)	47.5 (57%)
of which co-ops	0.1 (0.04%)	5.8 (1.7%)	108 (5%)	4.3 (5%)

Source: British Business, 11 July 1986.

figures in Table 6.2 and elsewhere illustrate that this has not fallen as quickly as the number of outlets (Robinson and Wallace 1976: 10, 14). Table 6.3 shows that the great majority of the workforce is in large or medium multiples which have 68% of the turnover. The small single outlet businesses, though including 87% of the individual shops, only had 36% of the workforce and an even smaller proportion of the turnover.

Within this workforce of 2 326 000 (in 1984) there is a rather low union density, which has probably tended to diminish in recent years. Taking the larger sector of distribution as a whole which includes more work units and probably more trade unionists than simple retail, Bain and Price have calculated union membership for different industries and compared it with employment as a whole. Table 6.4 shows that trade union density in distribution has always been low, and in recent years has been around half of the level in industry as a whole. The density in retail is almost certainly even lower. Robinson and Wallace quote a figure of 7% membership in large stores and multiples in the mid 1970s (1976: 58).

The main trade union in retail is the Union of Shop Distributive and Allied Workers (USDAW) whose total membership in 1980 was given as 450 287. USDAW has a white collar section called Supervisory Administrative and Technical Association (SATA), and some other white collar workers are in APEX and ASTMS. Drivers and some others are in the Transport and General Workers Union or the United Road Transport Union, and the Bakers Food and Allied Workers Union has some members. There is also a separate organisation for the employees of W. H. Smith's which claimed 8929 members in 1979.

One of the main avenues for trade unions to exercise their influence in retail is through wages councils which determine minimum wages in

Table 6.4 *Union membership and density in distribution in certain years,*
1892–1979

	Distribution			All industries
	Potential union members (thousands)	Union members (thousands)	Union density (%)	Union density (%)
1892	427.9	4.4	1.0%	10.6%
1921	1721.5	155.6	9.0%	35.8%
1948	2089.1	325.8	15.6%	42.5%
1968	2762.9	294.5	10.7%	44.0%
1974	2753.9	330.0	12.0%	51.0%
1979	2872.2	428.3	14.9%	55.4%

Source: Bain and Price 1980, Price and Bain 1983.

sectors where there is a lack of strong trade union organisation. The Food
and Allied Trade Wages Council covers over 500 000 workers in food
shops, bread shops, newsagents, tobacconists and confectioners. Seventeen
employers' associations and the main trade unions decide on minimum
wages. Similar regulations are made through a Retail Trade (non-food)
Wages Council where 26 employers' associations and the four main unions
set similar standards for about 600 000 employees. Other industrial
relations procedures in the industry include particular arrangements with
larger employers, a National Wages Board with the Cooperative Societies,
Joint Industrial Councils in the retail meat trade and in pharmacy, as well
as a Multiple Grocery and Provisions Joint Committee and an agreement
between the Shoe Retailers Association and USDAW covering about
150 000 workers.

In general, employment conditions in retail are relatively poor. Just as in
the 1970s, these relative conditions reflect

> predominance of female employment, the high proportion of
> part-time and juvenile workers, the fragmentation of
> employment units, the limited incidence of collective bargaining
> and the determination of statutory minimum remuneration by
> Wages Councils (Robinson and Wallace 1976: 3).

Since the passage of the Act, and indeed back at least to 1968, when
systematic data were first collected, earnings in retail have been low

Table 6.5 *Earnings in retailing as a percentage of national averages, 1974–84*

	Male (%)	Female (%)
1974	81.2	88.1
1976	81.0	86.8
1978	81.2	89.3
1980	81.4	90.7
1982	81.1	90.8
1984	80.1	91.8

Note: Figures are based on average weekly earnings for full-time manual males and females on adult rates whose pay for the period was unaffected by absence. Figures for all industries and services, and for retail distribution, SIC 1968 for 1974 to 1982, SIC 1980 thereafter.
Source: New Earnings Survey, Analysis by Industry, various years.

compared to relevant national averages. Table 6.5 gives New Earnings Survey data on male and female averages. Male workers in retail average approximately 80% of national average earnings across the period: female workers have improved their relative position slightly, but still fall short of the female national average. It is widely believed by those who work in the industry that the pro rata rates for part-time and temporary workers are considerably less than those for full-time workers.

Hazards

Retail shops are not considered very dangerous places and any study of reported accidents bears this out. Table 6.6 sets out the number of accidents reported to local authorities under the Offices, Shops and Railway Premises Act and gives details of those in retail including the main categories of accident. Just as with construction it is notable that annual figures are strikingly uniform and even within quite low totals, the numbers of accidents and the proportions attributable to various causes showed virtually no change in the period following the 1974 Act. There are some notable hazards concerned with the use of knives and saws particularly in butchery, moving escalators in large stores and some cleaning substances, but the vast majority of accidents in retail stores do not involve machinery or materials. One chain of department stores calculated for us that 57% of their accidents are caused by falling or tripping. This pattern was found in

Table 6.6 *Accidents reported to local authorities, 1975–80*[a]

					Causes of accidents in retail					
Year	Total under OSPRA	Of which fatal	Total in retail	Of which fatal	Handling goods	Falls of persons	Hand-tools	Falling objects	Machinery	Transport
1975	17 198	16	6076	5	1575 26%	1876 31%	664 11%	363 6%	426 7%	228 4%
1976	18 359	20	6533	3	1794 27%	1872 29%	659 10%	429 7%	412 6%	320 5%
1977	19 159	34	7066	5	2030 29%	1960 28%	728 10%	459 7%	458 7%	351 5%
1978	17 679	15	7722	3	2178 28%	2174 28%	835 11%	537 7%	512 7%	400 5%
1979	18 865	27	8245	5	2301 28%	2387 29%	870 11%	565 7%	520 6%	362 4%
1980	18 337	17	7986	5	2180 27%	2194 28%	865 11%	597 7%	544 8%	412 5%

[a] Local authorities report these to HSE on a voluntary basis (see Chapter 2).
Source: Health and Safety Statistics, 1975–81/82.

Table 6.7 *Accidents reported in a supermarket chain:*
October 1981–September 1982

Total reported accidents	2256
Total involving staff	1433 (64%)
Total involving lost staff time	596 (26%)
Location	
Sales floor	517 (30%)
Meat	398 (18%)
Outside	309 (14%)
Warehouse/unloading	284 (13%)
Causes of accidents to staff	
Knives	321 (22%)
Collision with fixed objects	193 (13%)
Falling objects	144 (10%)
Wet floor or debris	138 (10%)
Slicers/saw	118 (8%)

Source: Internal Document: *Supermarket Chain.*

other stores, where it was also clear that as a general rule, less than half of the accidents involved customers.

Another chain of about 100 supermarkets provided a detailed analysis of reported accidents in their stores between October 1981 and September 1982. Table 6.7 summarises some of the main points. Among other interesting phenomena revealed by Table 6.7 is that 36% of accidents involved customers. Other retailers gave us rather higher, but less precise, figures for this. One particular chain which gave the impression of a lower proportion of customer accidents did not, however, collect any figures centrally on the grounds that there was too much disparity between reporting methods in the different stores.

As discussed in some detail elsewhere, changes in the basis of accident statistics have made comparisons between the 1970s and 1980s quite difficult. Furthermore, the return of statistics from local authorities, who inspect retail outlets, to the HSE is voluntary, hence figures are not available for all areas. However some recent figures for the HSE, set out in Table 6.8, show, even allowing for variation in the number of authorities reporting, that the total number of major and fatal accidents to employees and the public in retail shops showed no sign of declining in 1981–84. Indeed one could argue that it had increased, with 409 local authorities reporting 586 fatal and major accidents in 1981 and 409 (not necessarily identical) authorities reporting 633 in 1984.

Table 6.8 *Major and fatal injuries reported to local authorities*
(*Annual voluntary survey by HSE*)

	1981	1982	1983	1984
Major injuries to employees	1220	1458	1160	1329
Major injuries to public	248	206	246	322
Fatal injuries to employees or public	40	32	48	42
Total major or fatal injuries to employees or public	1508	1696	1454	1693
Of which in retail shops	586	673	504	633
No. of LAs replying (out of 461)	409	414	374	409

Source: 'Health and safety in LA enforced premises 1984', HSE Statistics Unit, May 1986 (and previous issues).

The case studies

It was not possible to consider a fully representative sample of all possible variations in types of store, forms of organisation, range of merchandise and the like. Nonetheless, the research attempted to cover most aspects of the industry except for the very small businesses often run by 'families'. Twelve enterprises were covered at head office level and fifteen establishments at store level. In some cases visits were paid to two establishments within the same enterprise and in one case a visit to the head office of a chain of supermarkets was not followed by a study of one of its establishments. Outline details of the companies and stores covered in the course of the research are given in Table 6.9. This shows that visits were paid to stores in the north and east of England as well as in London and the south-east. Large, medium and small branches of chains of department stores and supermarkets were covered as were a town centre clothing store, two very small establishments specialising in the sale of motor car accessories and two stores specialising in butchery, which were also small.

The visits to the head offices consisted, where possible, of discussions with safety specialists, inspection of policies and procedures and discussion of company organisation and practice. Two of the organisations in our study (enterprises 3 and 5) did not have any safety specialists at all, so discussion was held with personnel directors and others with more general

137

Table 6.9 The case studies: details of retail enterprises and establishments

Enterprise (parent company)	1	2	3	4	5
Type of retail enterprise	Large chain of multiple stores	Chain of department stores	Part of manufacturing and distribution chain of outlets for motor car accessories	Chain of women's clothes outlets	Small chain of foodstores
National/regional safety/health/hygiene specialists	1 hygiene and safety officer	Head office and area office safety specialist	Personnel manager with specific responsibility for health and safety	1 security and health officer	Personnel officer with minor concern for health and safety

Establishment	A	B	C	D	E	F	G
Size (1983 figures) Employees: Total	70	62	559	3	5	17	20
Full time	30	25	335	1	2	12	12
Location of outlet	Central London	Central London	Large town, NW England	Small town, E. Anglia	Large town, E. Anglia	Town, Berks	Central London
In-store safety/health/hygiene specialists	First-aiders	First-aiders	Store nurse Store doctor P/T safety specialist[a]	None	None	None	None

Table 6.9 (*continued*).

	6		7	8	9	10	11	12
Enterprise (parent company)								
Type of retail enterprise	Chain of food and general supermarkets		Chain of dept. stores	Chain of multiple stores	Chain of butchers	Chain of multiple stores	Chain of multiple stores	Chain of food supermarkets
National/regional safety/ health/hygiene specialists	Head office and regional fire, safety and health officers, and environmental consultants		Head office health and safety officers and medical staff	1 head office fire and safety officer	Head office part-time safety and health specialist	Head office environmental and safety officer	Head office health and safety specialist	Head office health and safety specialist
	H	I	J	K	L	M	N	O
Establishment								
Size (1983 figures) Employees: Total	70	300	2380	400	4	14	120	280
Full time	30	210	1760	150	3	2	70	130
Location of outlet	Outer London	Small town, Herts	Central London	Central London	Outer London	Outer London	Outer London	Town, Surrey
In-store safety/health/ hygiene specialists	None	None	Store doctors Store nurses Safety officer	Store doctors Store nurses Safety officer	None	None	First-aiders	Part-time fire, safety and health adviser

a P/T = part-time

responsibilities. Some firms did not deal with safety as a separate issue, but combined responsibility with that for fire, hygiene or security.

In the stores, we usually spoke with at least one member of the store management team, with anyone who had been given any special responsibility for health and safety and with any of the few safety representatives who could be found. We also observed working practices within the stores and, where possible, looked at accident reports, safety policies and any other relevant documents. Unlike the studies of chemical companies, studies of retail and construction establishments did not include the administration of self-completion questionnaires.

Safety policies and written documents

All the firms in our study had safety policies. Some were clear and well thought out, others had been 'copied' from an available model and in one shop the manager indicated a dusty copy of the Offices, Shops and Railway Premises Act as his understanding of his shop's safety policy! Beyond general statements only a few policies provided details on specific hazards or methods of dealing with them.

The policies we saw showed considerable disparity, and the differences were not correlated in any very obvious way with firm size or ranges of activity. One policy in establishment A which went to considerable lengths to detail the duties and responsibilities of employees might have been less important than it appeared, since the safety representative we met in that firm did not recall having seen it. One impression derived from looking at the policies is that they often bore the clear imprint of the phrases and concerns of the 1974 Act. In one case we were told that 'nobody ever heard of health and safety' before this legislation. There appears to have been very limited formal activity in respect of occupational safety and health in retailing beore the Act.

A number of other features in the written policies are of interest. It was only in the smallest firm that we found that the policy itself gave instructions on the use of particular machinery, for example, for cutting or packaging, though the larger firms included such matters in accompanying manuals. 'Responsibility for implementing the health and safety policy', read the policy of one large supermarket chain, 'rests with line management at every level'. Some other policies placed particular responsibilities on store managers, though in one case the district managers and the board are the only people mentioned. One other chain of department stores gave no role to top management at all, but simply said that branch managers had to ensure 'overall implementation'. This was clearly reflected in the firm in question, we found on visiting the stores that individual managers were more aware of safety issues than most.

The larger companies were naturally in a better position to provide details, often in manuals, about specific hazards and methods of dealing with them. Two important issues, however, did not come up in any regular way. One of these was the matter of training which only came into one or two of the policies and accompanying documents. Insofar as safety was mentioned it was usually only a small and subsidiary part of more general training programmes. The greatest prominence given to training was in the written policies in the butchery outlets – where the company safety specialist was also the training manager – though it was not evident that this had a strong effect in the stores themselves. The second issue which did not figure in most of the policies was the rights as opposed to the duties of members of the workforce. Some did refer to safety committees and to safety representatives, in all cases management appointed. One policy appears to imply that representatives may be trade union appointed, but such possibilities normally appeared quite remote.

Another interesting document found in enterprises 3 and 9 related to company 'safety audits'. These consisted of lists of items to be covered by inspections carried out either by store managers, or else by management specialists or even safety representatives. It is perhaps not surprising that the best such document was provided for us by the same firm that produced the best statistics of its own performance. The 'audit' included almost everything from the contents of first aid boxes to lighting in the car park and plungers in mincing machines. A total of 420 points needed consideration in the audit of a large supermarket. A similar but less comprehensive list of 182 headings was found in the 'safety audit' of another supermarket chain. In this case there was a perfunctory reference to training, but no monitoring of the results of any enquiries. Some firms, especially the smaller ones, had general manuals covering legal and other obligations of individual stores, and including a section on health and safety. The 'audits' were by no means a guarantee of effective safety, but they did show one way of checking local conditions and monitoring and assessing them.

Company organisation, line management and safety specialists

The case study organisations varied greatly not only in their size and activity but also in their level of centralisation and their apparent adhesion to fixed rules and procedures. The level of central control and specialist activity was, as one might expect, a function of size, history and activity.

Developments at local level

As Table 6.9 shows, the large firms, often parts of conglomerates, generally had safety specialists amongst those who operated out of their head offices. However, there was no uniformity in the way such specialists fitted into their respective organisations. Typically they were recruited from a career in the fire or security services. Only one head office specialist had a recognised safety and health qualification and others in a second company had been recruited from the ranks of environmental health officers. Apart from chains 2, 7 and 8, specialist emphasis at head office tended to be on fire and security and and to a lesser extent, health, with safety being 'tacked on' to these other concerns.

The powers and influence of headquarters specialists varied a good deal according to the general level of central control, the ethos of the company and their training and experience. A few of them had subordinates who covered regions or specialist areas and undertook systematic visits to individual branches, but in most cases they worked at the head office of the organisation concerned and visited individual shops only to deal with particular problems or emergencies. Their main functions in respect of safety and health were to ensure that laws and regulations were enforced within individual firms, to investigate hazards and accidents, to sort out insurance and legal claims, and to deal with outside agencies such as the Environmental Health Officers of local authorities. Some specialists collected statistics and monitored developments within their operations and a few checked management arrangements and workforce involvement at a local level. In most cases, however, they were predominantly concerned with reacting to individual accidents, specific problems or recent changes in laws and regulations. Their varied background, training and role was reflected in a comparatively limited feeling of professionalism or shared identity amongst safety specialists. However, the safety specialists in the larger firms were beginning to work together. The British Retail Association, which represents companies with perhaps 25% of the workforce in the industry has a health and safety committee made up of the safety officers of the larger firms.

Moving from company headquarters to store level it was only in the larger stores that there was any in-house specialist advice on health and safety. Beyond trained first-aiders, this extended more to part-time medical doctors and nurses with an emphasis on health rather than safety. Part-time specialist responsibility for safety was, however, sometimes given to a member of the management team in the larger stores.

The smaller chains naturally had fewer specialist functions of any sort. These companies dealt with issues of safety as part of personnel management. They tended to have store managers who were given

142

considerable power with discretion in hiring and firing and in purchasing policy, presentation of stock and the like. Though one could not expect specialist health and safety managers in such systems one could, and did occasionally, find safety rules capable of having an impact at local level. However, safety does not loom large amongst the concerns of the managers of smaller retail outlets, except insofar as they may have to contend with local authority Environmental Health Officers. One particularly memorable response to the question concerning specialist advice came from the manager of establishment G with 20 staff: 'we don't have anyone trained in first aid but we do have a first aid box and we sell plasters'. Had our case studies included very small businesses the point about the size effect on safety provision could probably have been made even more strongly.

Some chains of department stores have a very clear corporate structure and image extending from central headquarters down to individual counters in the smallest stores in the remotest part of the country. In these cases it was obvious that, within financial and bureaucratic constraints, the suggestions of safety and health specialists from head office were likely to have some impact within individual enterprises. In one of the larger chains in our survey one could trace a clear chain of influence from the specialist at the head office down to second or third rank management in individual stores. This was in a firm generally reputed to have good health and safety provision, and certainly with comprehensive staff welfare provision.

Central influence on local policies and practices is much less clear within more decentralised operations. One large chain of department stores much affected by economic recession had decentralised some of its decision making, and at a store level it was clear that local managers left to their own devices were little concerned with staff welfare and safety. The cooperative movement has the most decentralised forms of management structure of all and the most comprehensive provision for staff welfare but even this did not appear to lead to a high level of health and safety provision in the establishment we studied.

There is in fact some indication of a move towards more centralisation within the retail trade. Modern sales methods and the computerised recording of transactions tend to reduce local discretion. It is common to find that store managers are under 30 or even under 25, and are given limited powers and a short time in which to succeed, or to fail. Much more important as line managers are those given district or area responsibilities, usually covering six to ten shops. In a number of cases these district managers were given all the responsibility for reporting accidents, dealing with inspection agencies, and generally looking after personnel and related matters.

Working practices and employment conditions

Our interviews and observations within the retail sector revealed that a high proportion of part-time and casual labour often made it difficult to develop health and safety procedures, monitoring or training. For example one supermarket in the survey had 30 full-time and 40 part-time workers requiring supervision. In another, with about 30% part-time workers, monitoring and training was difficult since long opening hours meant that large numbers of employees did not work between the 'normal' hours of 9 a.m. and 5 p.m.

There was enormous variation in the amount of general training given to shop assistants, supervisors and managers. Most but not all larger enterprises had specific plans and requirements to train all their staff and some of these included health and safety as one of the subjects in the training courses. General training for both managers and assistants was often not available in the smaller establishments and very little, if anything, was done specifically for health and safety.

Apart from being relatively untrained in their jobs, members of the retail workforce are also subject to other pressures. For example a tough 'hire and fire' policy in some companies, recession, recent changes in technology, a reducing workforce size in individual establishments, closer monitoring of individual performance and less task variety for employees were all to be found. At the same time we were told in a number of chains and individual stores that the general 'quality' of the workforce had improved, perhaps as a consequence of the recession. We also found that less pressure has tended to be placed on employees through bonus payments, which were only to be found in small franchise operations and in some city centre stores where staff turnover was in any case very rapid. In contrast to the trend away from bonus and commission payments for shop assistants, it is now more common for shop managers to be set specific financial and sales targets for their operations and for them to be rewarded or sanctioned in the light of their results. This involves both bonus payments and considerations of promotion.

Another feature of employment conditions is the development of franchising within large stores. Within stores C and F over 50% of space was 'sub-let' to franchise operations and small-scale franchising for particular operations was found in store G for delicatessen items, store J for perfumes and store O for other specialist goods. Local managers who played host to these franchise operations varied in their opinions about their safety responsibilities. To one manager subcontract labour was 'no such concern of his whatsoever', but another was actually aware of his legal obligations for the health and safety of his franchisee's employees, including his liabilities as the controller of the premises under section 4 of HASAWA.

Employee/workforce involvement

One obvious result of the employment pattern in retail has already been mentioned – the weakness of trade union activity, with a membership density roughly half of that in employment as a whole. Table 6.10 gives details of trade union activity in general and workforce involvement in health and safety in particular for the stores included in this study. As is perhaps common where trade union organisation is finding difficulty in establishing itself, we found some unexpected practices. Thus in enterprise 6 (store H) where there is national recognition and a local closed shop we found that individual store managers were not even aware that union dues were being checked off the pay of their employees. This is not to say that managers were unaware of the impact of trade union activity and that even in cases where membership was small, there was some indication of increased consultation with the workforce and adherence to minimum wages and working conditions. It does, however, provide an indication of the limited impact of organised workforce activity in individual stores.

The main trade union in retail, the Union of Shop Distributive and Allied Workers, finds it very difficult to secure and keep members in a workforce which is often transitory, temporary or part-time. The Union did not at the time of the study employ any specialists to deal with health and safety, no doubt reflecting the fact that it is not considered to operate in particularly hazardous workplaces. There were, however, people in the national office covering issues such as training and individual compensation, who were well aware of the main problems. The Union conference has also called for the employment of safety specialists in the regions but the resources have not yet been found for this. Consequently health and safety representatives at local level receive only limited support from their trade union and they rely more on their own management for information and training. In a number of the larger chains in our survey we were told that this picture was quite different in warehousing and distribution where there was a more stable workforce often more used to the ways of trade unionism, and usually members of the Transport and General Workers Union. However, we found no evidence that any unions had solved the problems of dealing more effectively with health and safety in the retail stores themselves.

The only trade union safety representative we encountered who did have a clear and independent view of his functions was in store C, a large department store. Interestingly he was hardly even aware of the limits to

Table 6.10 *Retail case studies: trade union and workforce involvement*

Enterprise (parent company)	1	2	3	4	5
National agreements with trade unions	National recognition and agreed negotiating rights	National recognition and agreed negotiating rights	Limited involvement on basis of very patchy membership	None	None

Establishment	A	B	C	D	E	F	G
Local recognition of trade unions and level of activity	Recognition but only 3% membership	Recognition approximately 80% membership	'Check off' closed shop but no meeting of union branch for 12 months	Nothing formal	Nothing formal	Nothing formal – a few members	None
Number of safety representatives	One	One	2 positions, 1 filled	None	None	None	None
Safety committees	None	None	Committee of management representatives with one safety representative included	None	None	None	None
Regular health and safety inspections	None	None	3 monthly inspections by safety representative and management	Management audit	Management audit	None	None
Other non-union forms of workforce involvement	Consultative staff affairs groups		Staff councils	None	None	Weekly half hour training/discussion sessions	None

Table 6.10 (continued)

Enterprise (parent company)	6		7	8	9		10	11	12
National agreements with trade unions	National recognition		None (although union recognition in other areas e.g. haulage)	None	National recognition		National recognition and full negotiating rights	National recognition	National recognition but little activity
Establishment	**H**	**I**	**J**	**K**	**L**	**M**	**N**	**O**	
Local recognition of trade unions and level of activity	'Check off' closed shop	Recognition but little activity	None	None	National recognition but no local activity		Recognition with closed shop	Recognition but little activity	
Number of safety representatives	Shop steward/safety rep. had left and was not replaced	None	Non-union safety reps. elected by all depts.	None	None	None	Have agreement for position but no-one fills it	Management appointed safety adviser who happens to be a trade union member	
Safety committees	None	None	Non-union safety ctts. with reps. from all depts. and all levels	Ctt. of management appointed and non-union representatives	None	None	Had been constituted but then fell into abeyance	Joint management/union safety committee	
Regular health and safety inspections	Inspections by central staff and management		Inspections by non-union safety reps.	Inspections by non-union reps.	Management audits	None	None	Occasional inspections by committee	
Other non-union forms of workforce involvement	Weekly half hour training sessions/discussions		Highly developed forms of non-union consultation and representation	Series of communication and briefing groups	None	None	Joint consultative committee	Weekly half hour training sessions/staff discussions	

the help he was receiving from his union nationally. He had no expectations of national support, though he did have some helpful contact with a local full-time official.

The other trade union safety representatives we met during the course of our case studies did not have the same independence of their management. This was shown when we were not permitted to interview them without managers being present. In one store (A) there was only a small proportion of workers in the union, and the same person was steward, safety representative and in almost every other way, the local face of the union. Perhaps not surprisingly, we found that this particular safety representative had little knowledge of her legal rights, no training to perform her role, and little evident independence from management. She had, however, taken up a number of minor matters such as loose carpets and lack of hygiene in parts of the store which local management had passed on to head office. We found a similar attitude in another branch of the same chain (B). Here, however, trade union membership was 80% of the workforce and the union steward/safety representative appeared to be a stronger and more independent spirit.

From those we met and from hearsay about other safety representatives in retail it was apparent that few of them are independently chosen by the workforce. Even less frequently do they emerge from the ranks of trade union members. They are nearly always nominated by the management and their position is legitimised through a set of procedures and responsibilities emanating from the top of the company.

Within this environment and working atmosphere we met no managers who encouraged independent workforce representation on health and safety or anything else. Independent trade union activity of any sort was described by managers as 'political' and therefore undesirable. We found no examples of independent trade union safety inspections in all our studies. Any inspections that were carried out were the responsibility, at least in part, of management appointees. It should be noted, however, that representatives argued that the involvement of management in such inspections made it easier for issues to be raised and problems solved, sometimes on the spot. The active safety representative in establishment C described how, on his joint inspections with management, he looked at electrical faults, missing stair rails, lighting and other matters, and the minutes of the safety committee revealed that he had been checking and rechecking on them. That particular safety representative told us of the problem of feeling that he was looking for 'everything and nothing' and he certainly would have welcomed some guidance and support from somewhere on this matter.

In five of the 15 stores there were apparently no inspections or audits undertaken by anyone, even though for example in stores A and B there were trade union safety representatives. In nearly all cases line managers did not imagine they had any obligation to provide facilities for workforce inspection, despite the provisions of the law.

We were led to the conclusion that within retail, independent workforce activity on health and safety matters is almost unknown in practice. This is not to say that we did not find clear evidence of concern amongst shopworkers for health and safety issues. There was also evidence of other forms of workforce involvement, even though they were nearly always management controlled. For example, in enterprises 7 and 8 there were systems for consultation, communication and training which had a significant impact on safety provision and safety awareness as well as an elaborate network of welfare facilities. Where systems of consultation and participation are located within firms where there is a clear concern for health and safety issues at top management level, a commitment to monitoring progress in safety provision, a clear designation of management responsibility at store level, and a reputation for good standards in this as in other fields of staff welfare, they can undoubtedly have a strong positive effect on safety programmes. Other systems for management controlled workforce involvement included staff meetings, briefing groups, group training sessions and suggestion boxes. Such means were quite widely established and undoubtedly allowed workers to express discontent or raise issues, including those related to health and safety.

We looked amongst our case studies, in vain, for safety committees constituted roughly along the lines envisaged by the 1977 Regulations. Unfortunately we were unable to obtain access to one department store where the safety committee was said to be of this sort. However, we did speak to the one safety representative we encountered who sat as the only trade union representative on an otherwise management appointed committee in C, a large department store. In addition we found that four of our 15 stores had safety committees which acted as a forum for discussion between management appointed representatives and managers. The sorts of issues raised and the efforts to solve them did not vary greatly with the composition of the committee. No committee was particularly notable for its lively discussion or clear influence within the company. Nonetheless, it seemed that the existence of committees, however constituted, did give some incentive to staff interest in and efforts to pursue safety matters, even though the majority of issues were fairly trivial such as worn carpets, misplaced fire extinguishers and insufficient lighting. Nonetheless, such small matters can cause or exacerbate accidents. The committee agendas and minutes also provided a means of pursuing issues and the central monitoring of such documents made it possible to assess particular issues and trends.

Within store C with the most effective trade union representative we also found one of the most apparently effective safety committees. As we found elsewhere a study of the minutes revealed numerous instances of complaints about items raised at previous meetings not being taken up. However, they also indicated a careful consideration of accident statistics within the store itself and a following up of the results of inspections into such matters as defective lighting and offensive smells. Other safety committees did not always appear so rigorous on general issues, nor so active in following them through.

Even without such committees, regular inspections and written reports can perform something of the same function providing that the results of inspections are recorded and considered by appropriate people with sufficient power and resources to take action. Table 6.10 shows that in ten of the 15 outlets studied there was some form of inspection and audit and that usually these were conducted by managers or their representatives.

Inspection and enforcement

Environmental Health Officers (EHOs) and their predecessors, Sanitary Inspectors, have long been concerned with matters of public health and hygiene. As Chapter 9 describes, their duties with respect to health and safety at work were greatly expanded in the Health and Safety at Work Act and associated Regulations, but in practice these have tended to be 'merged' with their other duties rather than be treated separately.

In contrast to the level of awareness of many people in the construction sector about Factory Inspectors, virtually all the people in retail with whom we spoke knew about their local EHOs, had encountered them, and had opinions about the way they worked. A common stereotype held by some members of the British Retail Association Health and Safety Committee and by head office safety specialists is that EHOs are petty, capricious and a menace to the procedures worked out within individual firms. Among line management at store level, however, we often found different views and a number of examples of shop managers collaborating and negotiating with EHOs to put pressure on management at a higher level.

It is not difficult to understand why, from the vantage point of the headquarters of a national chain of stores, the EHOs appear inconsistent and interfering. Any system of local enforcement is bound to have variations. EHOs have a history of enforcing regulations through formal and informal notices, orders and legal proceedings. When they first took over health and safety at work functions, the work was often carried out by young and inexperienced officers whose zeal may on occasions have exceeded their tact. Corporate safety specialists in our survey had a depressingly limited repertoire of stories to illustrate this, and the enforcement order to put a lightbulb in a shop in one London borough began to acquire for us the status of every good myth and legend. The EHOs themselves have made efforts both through their own professional organisation, and by discussion with the HSE, to ensure greater levels of uniformity in enforcement policy. Nevertheless, the myths and legends persist.

There was less hostility within the stores themselves. Local managers are well used to dealing not only with enforcement from EHOs on such matters as food hygiene but also with visits from other local bureaucrats to cover such things as fire regulations and Sunday opening. Despite cutbacks in local authority services, we found that most stores in our study had had visits from EHOs within the past twelve to eighteen months. The only exceptions were in the stores dealing in car accessories. Most store managers believe, apparently with justification, that in visiting their stores EHOs are more concerned with matters of hygiene and public health than they are with safety. Although they also pick up safety items if they become aware of them, the low level of activity and awareness of safety issues means it is unlikely that employees will bring matters to their attenton. Hence the discovery of safety problems will often depend more upon the EHO's investigative talents than on volunteered information.

We came upon a number of examples of negotiations with local EHOs about health and safety standards. It seemed that some of the early enthusiasm by EHOs to enforce regulations was being channelled into asking for changes and serving informal notices rather than on immediately trying to enforce them through enforcement notices or prosecutions. EHOs were also reported as showing increasing reluctance to take up some issues for fear of closing down shops and losing employment. This was one example of changes associated with the economic recession of recent years which may have tended to slow down the rate of improvement in health and safety standards.

The effect of recession

A number of effects of recession could be seen during our studies. In virtually all the establishments the workforce had fallen, in some cases very dramatically indeed. This was partly due to technological change with computerisation, the use of bar codes and the moving of preparation work from stores to warehouses. However, it also followed from sharp competition, especially in grocery shops, and in efforts to reduce costs to compensate for narrowing profit margins. In one chain of department stores we were told of the reduction of directly employed staff numbers by almost 40%, slightly offsetting an increase in franchising. In another chain facing financial problems, the managerial workforce was being cut and we were told that less was being spent on safety equipment. It seemed that the hard-pressed safety specialist is unlikely to be receiving increased resources in the near future.

The impact of the recession is not uniform across the retail sector. At least two or three of the more prestigious chains recorded increased profit levels in 1983 and 1984. These same firms have shown themselves less than happy with extensions in working hours including efforts to liberalise restrictions on Sunday trading. The trend to longer opening hours has nevertheless proceeded apace, especially in smaller chains and stores, and it has created obvious difficulties for the development of procedures or training in the field of health and safety. In the stores we visited there were those who worked almost all of every day, some who came only on Saturdays, and others who worked some evenings. There were also 'zero option workers' – those who were prepared to come in at short notice to cover for absences or increased demand. All such categories of workers and people were difficult to catch in any net aimed to improve safety. Such difficulties may to some extent be allayed by another possible effect of the recession on working patterns which was pointed out to us on a number of occasions – the fall in staff turnover.

Conclusion

The case studies undertaken for this study in retail indicated a wide range of procedures and attitudes. There were firms with a clear policy, a range of procedures, a developed role for specialists, mechanisms for the monitoring of performance and much else. At the opposite extreme was the shop which displayed a dusty and unread copy of the 1963 Offices, Shops and Railway Premises Act and where the manager displayed an ignorance about his legal responsibilities.

In this industry there seems no doubt that the legislation of 1974 was important in putting safety and health at work on the agenda for many – but by no means all – companies. Very little by way of formal policy and relevant practice seems to have existed before this time and significant institutional developments were made in the 1970s. A key issue is, however, the extent to which these developments have been sustained. It would seem that in many instances for managers and for those workforce representatives who have survived, issues of health and safety at work have fallen lower down the list of priorities. In companies which were relatively untouched by the legislation, little if anything has happened since 1974 to provoke greater attention or action in this area.

Two further important conclusions can be drawn from our study. One was that the external enforcement of standards through Environmental Health Officers seemed to have more impact on safety practice in many shops than any other pressure. This was partly for historical and accidental reasons and, as indicated, was not always viewed with pleasure. The second general point that clearly emerged was whatever the form of internal self regulation, workforce representation and involvement was generally limited. There were safety representatives and safety committees to be found in a few places but they were rarely independent of management or noted for their levels of activity. As elsewhere we found that the noisy controversy about the Act and the SRSCR which was heard at the time of their introduction has long since disappeared. The implementation of a safety policy was seen as a management prerogative, whatever form of consultation or discussion was involved. Where management did not regard the promulgation of safety policy as important, then it was quickly forgotten.

Our case studies also showed very clearly that the next stage in the implementation of safety standards has much to do with the general culture and organisation of individual enterprises. The policy of one company aims 'to provide the safest and healthiest working conditions possible and to prevent damage to company property'. Elsewhere, as already discussed, safety at work is bracketed with fire prevention and security. In some firms with a good reputation for safety in their stores, this is cultivated as part of a general image of hygiene and welfare. Generally speaking such firms have management structures which allow for central controls to be passed down the line, at least as far as line management. Sometimes even within well worked out management systems there is little responsibility at the level of the individual store and consequently little real effort outside the realms of general rules and regulations. In the smallest chains and stores, there is little more than the sanction of outside inspection to make a serious impact on the shopfloor.

7

Effective local self regulation: the capacity and willingness to act

Chapter 1 described how local self regulation was conceived in terms of the encouragement of systems which would create and maintain motivation and capacity to act amongst all parties in the workplace so that nationally agreed and established laws and standards would be maintained and even improved upon. In order to consider factors which are likely to contribute to or detract from the effectiveness of such a self regulatory system one must discuss the extent to which there is consensus about safety issues. Few would disagree with the simple proposition that a reduction in the number of industrial accidents is desirable, but such a reduction may entail costs or require control over individual behaviour at work, and so there exists the possibility of a trade-off between safety and other issues. Even where there is overall agreement about the goals of improved health and safety, considerable disagreements may emerge over the manner in which such goals are pursued. Even if the pursuit of safety is seen to be a shared 'objective' interest, issues of resource allocation and the inability to insulate health and safety issues from others such as bonus payments, manning levels, production continuity or work allocation are likely to generate disagreement.

However, few issues in industrial life lack the potential for conflict, particularly where they make demands on scarce resources. The important question concerns the ways in which the differences, which are almost certain to emerge over safety, are resolved. Considering unionised workplaces first, two possibilities present themselves. On the one hand, managers and unions could both recognise differences of interest over health and safety and the knock-on effects of agreements in safety in other areas, and could devise effective self regulatory systems. On the other hand, where a reasonably strong trade union forces the hand of an employer to provide resources for safety by enforceable sanctions or the use of the provisions of the legislation, then clearly consensus is absent. However, it does not necessarily follow that, *ceteris paribus*, a workplace where the latter set of factors operate is less safe than the first, since it is perfectly possible for management and unions to collude in giving a low priority to safety. A key issue is the willingness of the employers and managers, on whom the primary duty falls, to develop and implement a policy. This aspect of managerial motivation is even more important in establishments with little or no union organisation.

Beyond a general emphasis on managerial responsibility, however, one must appreciate essential differences between workplaces which will place different requirements on management, and affect the motivation to improve safety provision. Differences in technologies, materials and substances create variable hazards, that are amenable to different forms of control. Moreover in some industries, systems of management control are more sophisticated than in others, while the extent to which trade unions can direct the behaviour of their members also varies a good deal. The capacity to implement a safety policy is thus an important organisational issue which is conceptually distinct from the issue of consensus and motivation. Thus managers and unions may agree on the importance of safety, but be unable to implement an effective policy. When dealing with the factors which encourage or prevent effective self regulation, we are not simply concerned with the willingness to act, but also the capacity to do so.

The philosophy of local self regulation assumes both motivation and capacity. If either are absent on a wide scale then the viability of the philosophy is under question. If either are absent in specific industries or sectors, then the idea of universal self regulation is similarly in doubt.

This chapter describes and discusses a model of effective local self regulation for safety. It focuses on the organisational implications of self regulation in order to assess its chances of success both generally and in specific industries. At the outset, a detailed prescriptive approach to effective safety management is presented: its implications for the form and substance of workforce involvement are then discussed. The effective management of safety, and effective workforce involvement appear, despite difficulties of definition and measurement, to be much more likely under certain organisational circumstances than others.

A prescriptive approach to safety management

In a number of articles, Dawson, Poynter and Stevens have developed a prescription for effective line management and specialist organisation for safety at work (1982a, 1982b, 1983a, 1984c). This prescription was based initially on the empirical work in the chemical industry summarised in Chapter 4 and on other commentaries (see Heinrich 1959; Atherley 1975; Crutchfield 1981; Petersen 1978; HSE/12, 1977; HSE/14, 1980), and amplified in the light of the studies in the construction and retail industries reported in Chapters 5 and 6. It assumes that the general legal duties of 'reasonably practicality' enshrined in the HASAWA and more specific statutory standards and requirements which are laid down in HSC Regulations, the Factories Acts and so on, provide the basis of legally required minimum standards. Self regulation becomes crucial not then in setting minimum standards (except in those circumstances where they are held not already to exist in statute) but in determining how, if at all, the standards will be met or even improved upon.

A basic feature of local self regulation is that the jobs of line managers and supervisors are developed in such a way that standards of safety at work are incorporated in a realistic manner into sets of working objectives. It is argued that the achievement of acceptable levels of safety at work cannot simply be left to individuals, however well trained or enthusiastic. The efforts of in-house safety specialists, or workforce safety representatives, or a combination of both, are not by themselves adequate even though they are very important. The lack of an independent power base and conflicting interests mean that specialists and representatives can have significant effect only where there is strong line responsibility for safety. The assumption is not that there is a common interest between the three groups, but that unless line managers are somehow made to acknowledge their direct responsibilities, then efforts to effect changes in health and safety provision will never have lasting success. This chapter seeks to demonstrate the appropriate managerial response if self regulation is to be effective.

This issue is approached by considering both 'capacity' and 'willingness' to act as outlined above. The 'capacity' component is considered in terms of what is involved at a technical level if hazards are to be identified and controlled. Secondly, the motivation or 'willingness' component is discussed by contrasting cases when the various parties involved are strongly motivated to maintain and improve standards of health and safety, with circumstances in which the apathy which prompted so much concern from Robens and his colleagues still remains in large areas of employment.

The technical control of hazards

Self regulation requires the conscious development of strategies to identify and control hazards found in any selected workplace. *Hazards* are defined in terms of 'potential for loss or harm' and are held to be *realised* if that harm or loss occurs (Dawson, Poynter and Stevens 1982a: 96). The risk of hazard realisation is a combination of the *probability* of realisation and the severity of their *consequences* should realisation occur. Hazards originate in the interaction between the hardware of the working environment – including characteristics of materials, plant, equipment and place of work – and people in the working environment, particularly their knowledge, skills, attitudes, actions and beliefs.

The minimum requirement for an effective health and safety programme is the development and maintenance of effective technical controls for specified indigenous hazards. This involves the following sets of activities which will be briefly discussed.

The identificaton and assessment of hazards and of the need for control.

The prescription and implementation of standards, physical safeguards and administrative procedures designed to control hazards.

The maintenance, monitoring and adaptation of standards, safeguards and procedures in the light of practical experience.

(a) Hazard identification and assessment

A first step in the development of an effective health and safety programme is to identify hazards. Some, for example those associated with the operation of machinery, working at heights, handling corrosive materials, are fairly well known, but they may nevertheless be unacknowledged in some workplaces. Others, for example those which may result in ill health which takes some time to develop, are more difficult to identify. Once identified, decisions are made – whether implicitly or explicitly – about the level of risk implied and the extent to which this is acceptable. This assessment is discussed further in the section on motivation and commitment.

(b) Prescription and implementation of control

Although hazards are to be found in all workplaces the magnitude of the risks implied varies enormously. For example there is a good deal of difference between a part-time and untrained employee in a small retail shop who suffers back-strain from lifting a bulky package, and a highly trained steelfixer who falls to his death from a faulty safety harness. Whatever the range, however, most workplaces exhibit some hazards which are subject to statutory control and others which some of the participants consider to be unacceptable – whether legally, morally or operationally. The range of action available when a hazard is deemed unacceptable is shown in Figure 7.1. Two sorts of preventative actions can be considered. The first is to eliminate the risks by removing the hardware or the human contributors to the hazard. For example, automation may remove people from a toxic environment or raw materials may be changed. Even so, the newly created working environment may, in eliminating hazards, pose others in their place. For example, the introduction of robots into manufacturing processes has eliminated hazards associated with such processes as mechanical assembly, welding and furnace tending, but has presented others to those responsible for maintaining the new equipment (Jones and Dawson 1986). The second type of preventative action is to

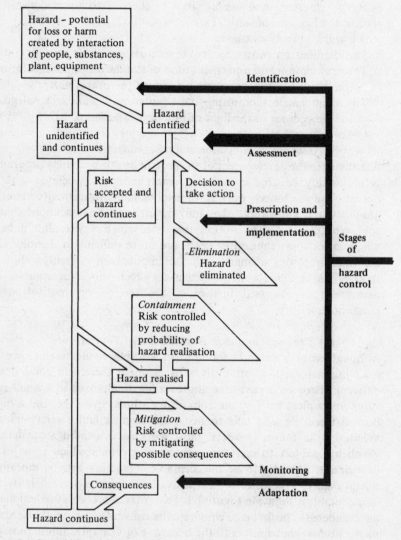

Figure 7.1 Controlling the hazard sequence.
(Source: adapted from Dawson *et al.* 1983a: 436)

contain the hazards by reducing the probability of their realisation. For example, toeboards fixed on scaffolding substantially reduce the likelihood of workers falling off, or of heavy objects falling from the scaffold onto people working below. In addition to the elimination or containment of hazards, a third sort of action can be planned which is intended to mitigate the consequences should hazards be realised. Thus if construction workers wear hard hats, the consequences of a heavy object falling on their head are likely to be less than if they were hatless.

The operational determination of local standards is clearly constrained by statutory requirements, for example to fence machinery or to limit exposure to toxic chemicals. Divergence from national standards is found on both sides. Some establishments ignore them or their attempts to achieve them fail. In these cases those concerned lay themselves open to external enforcement. Other establishments achieve significantly better than the nationally prescribed minimum standards. Effective safety management must clearly be concerned with at least achieving the minimum standards and preferably rising above them.

Once determined, the prescribed controls need to be implemented. This involves specifying responsibilities for the administrative and substantive component of hazard control, and holding people accountable for fulfilling their responsibilities. For example, ensuring that someone is designated to administer the permit-to-work system or the system for making or circulating inspection reports and having means to check that these responsibilities are fulfilled.

(c) *Maintenance, monitoring and adaptation of control standards and procedures*

Implementation is not a once and for all activity – circumstances change, the hardware and people which together give rise to the hazards change, and moreover, people's expectations, knowledge and levels of acceptance of risk, change. Systems for monitoring the results of health and safety programmes need to be established so that at least two different sorts of data are collected. First, 'outcome' data should be collected on accidents and ill health. Secondly, there is 'activity' data which can show how establishments are performing in terms of such essential aspects of safety management as inspection policy and practice and information gathering, retrieval and dissemination.

An effective approach to maintaining or improving standards of health and safety in a workplace requires, as a minimum, activity specifically relate to all aspects of technical control. Some of this technical control will be built into the design of production systems, some will be specifically required by legislation but much of it will be the result of judgements made within the workplace or elsewhere in the company about the hazards and risks involved, and the likely costs and benefits of attempts to reduce them. We return to this suggestion for monitoring activities as well as outcomes below.

Motivation and commitment

Whether hazards are identified, whether action is taken, and if so, its form, will to a large extent reflect the views, interests, power and priorities of the people involved in the decision making. These factors are likely to be influenced, but not necessarily determined, by their knowledge of their statutory obligations. Managers from different departments, specialist advisers, trade union representatives and ordinary employees may well have degrees of knowledge about statutory requirements and have different views on what constitutes an 'acceptable level of risk' and on the relative importance of alternative destinations for the scarce resources which are likely to be involved in different lines of action.

In addition to potential conflicts between groups, it is important to remember that trade-offs are also made within groups and by individuals. Safety officers have to make a judgement about which activities and projects are most important and are most likely to lead to significant improvements. Safety representatives, who are usually also concerned with other trade union activities, may need to consider the implications for working practices if a particular form of hazard control is adopted. For example, it may be proposed to designate a particularly hazardous operation as the exclusive province of specially appointed 'competent persons'. This may mean that, as only limited numbers can receive sufficient special training in this competence, other workers who had previously undertaken the work may be excluded from it. Working arrangements and manning levels may thus be changed in a way which trade union representatives regard as detrimental to their members.

Local strategies to control hazards must be understood within a broader organisational framework, as is suggested in Figure 7.2. The organisational context of competing priorities and scarce resources means that the technical control of hazards will not necessarily occur. Reliable knowledge of hazards and statutory requirements, firm commitment and motivation amongst all the parties involved – be they senior executives, line managers, specialists or trade union representatives – needs to be nurtured and sustained. Three aspects of organisation are particularly important in this respect and they will be briefly discussed.

Positive commitment.

Definitions of responsibility.

Monitoring and accountability.

(a) There is a need for *positive demonstrations of commitment* to health and safety by people involved at every level of the organisation, including those at the top. This must begin with the development of a clear and appropriate safety policy, which is implemented in such a way that senior people show themselves to be prepared to initiate and support action at all stages of technical control. Similarly workforce involvement in all aspects of technical control should be encouraged (Barrett, Brown and Janes 1980).

(b) It is essential to have *definitions of responsibility* (in job descriptions, organisation charts, general procedures and normal custom and practice) which clearly demonstrate that line managers and supervisors bear direct responsibility for the health and safety of their subordinates. This is important in moving managers from a position in which they see health and safety in terms of compliance with minimum specific standards, to a position in which it is part of their general management responsibilities. Job specifications should also give guidance on how managers and specialists are to meet their responsibilities (Cohen 1977; Cohen *et al*. 1979; Barrett, Brown and Janes 1980).

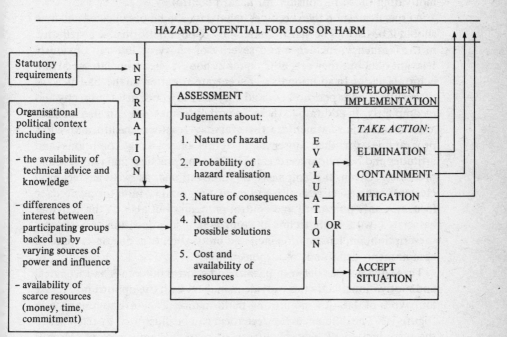

Figure 7.2 Formulating strategies to control hazards at work.
(Source: adapted from Dawson *et al*. 1983a: 437)

161

(c) A crucial aspect of an effective programme is to establish systems for *monitoring* performance and maintaining individual and departmental *accountability*. This was formally acknowledged by the HSE in 1985 when it published an occasional paper on *Monitoring Safety Performance*, which set out techniques of accident investigation and safety audits (HSE/20, 1985). Monitoring is important for two reasons. First, it can lead to the identification of problems and possibly suggest solutions. Secondly, monitoring can provide information on performance with a view to motivating employees to maintain good performance or to remedy poor performance. Difficulties arise when problem solving, performance measurement and motivation are in conflict. Since the information derived from monitoring is not neutral, but carries with it messages of success or failure, some people have suggested that monitoring information is best presented in its problem solving form and not as a basis for performance appraisal (Kletz 1981). Such an approach is unrealistic since health and safety objectives will not be achieved 'naturally', particularly when the means for their achievement compete with other priorities. Monitoring is important to solve problems, but it is also important as a basis for motivating those responsible for hazard control.

A crucial question then becomes: what data should be collected and how should it be used? The 'hazard outcomes' of poor performance as reflected in the frequency, incidence and severity of injury or loss are obviously relevant data but they are, as Chapter 2 showed, susceptible to social and cultural factors. In addition they concentrate attention on the 'bad' news of the results of poor performance and only tell the 'good' news indirectly and incompletely. In addition to these 'hazard outcomes' one can also monitor 'control outcomes' which are the everyday results of health and safety programmes (or their absence) in terms of working conditions and attitudes and behaviour as revealed in working practices and management processes. Given the emphasis on motivational as well as technical elements in an effective health and safety programme, monitoring needs to focus not only on hazard and control outcomes but also on the activities associated with both technical control (i.e. identification, assessment, prescription, implementation etc.) and motivation (e.g. demonstrations of commitment, definitions of responsibility).

These distinctions between hazard and control outcomes and technical and motivational activities provide managers with the opportunity to use four types of data for monitoring performance. They are summarised in Figure 7.3. The differences between them can be illustrated by reference to the introduction of new machinery or materials into a plant. Hazard outcome data would be limited to the details of any particular accidents or incidents which had occurred. Control outcome data would be derived from investigating the way the new machines and systems of work were being used and supervised. Data on technical control activity would be derived from investigating whether the people using the new machines and materials were aware of likely hazards and the measures to prevent or mitigate their realisation (e.g. are they aware of the dangers of working with lead, the importance and means of preventing exposure, and what to do

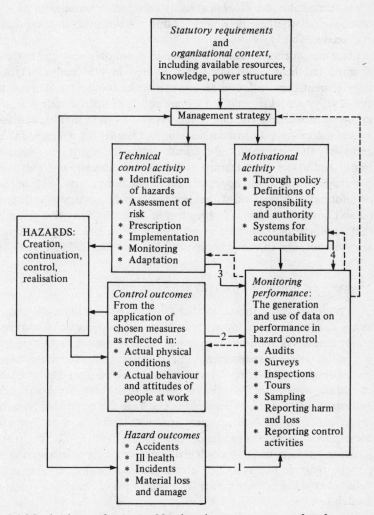

Figure 7.3 Monitoring performance. Numbered arrows: sources of performance data; dashed arrows: feedback from monitoring.
(Source: adapted from Dawson *et al.* 1982b: 792)

163

should exposure occur?); whether there was an effective procedure for 'vetting' new machinery and/or materials to identify hazards introduced by such changes and, if so, to assess their nature and significance and to determine and implement control measures. If controls are thought to be necessary, were elimination, containment and mitigation considered? If so, how and by whom was this consideration made? On the motivational side attention would be focused on examining whether decisions to develop or apply technical controls were actually reflected in managerial policy and practice and whether there were established definitions of responsibility and accountability.

Once monitoring makes data available, it will only be useful to the cause of improved health and safety if it is used in problem solving and in management appraisals and developments. Although formal management appraisal systems are usually a feature of large organisations, it is rare for safety performance to be one of the criteria. Even in small organisations, informal appraisal is often carried out, but here it is even rarer for health and safety to feature at all. But effective local self regulation requires that health and safety must feature as a factor in discussions about the past performance and future hopes of individuals and groups. Whether formal or informal, it is important that appraisals help managers to discuss the pursuit of health and safety objectives in the context of other priorities so that conflicts can be considered, plans formulated and performance assessed in terms of the four types of data summarised in Figure 7.3.

Management organisation and safety specialists

This prescriptive approach for the effective management of health and safety has implications for the role of safety specialists. An emphasis on senior executives and line management does not mean that the specialists will in time become redundant, but rather that complementary roles need to be developed. Figure 7.4 shows a matrix of activities available to specialists involved in the technical control of hazards. The horizontal axis corresponds to the stages involved in the technical control of hazards (i.e. identification, assessment, control and monitoring) and the vertical axis corresponds to different modes of operation from the highly reactive one of processing information, through giving advice and problem solving, to the highly proactive one of taking direct executive action. Examples of the different types of activity which fall within each of the cells so created are also shown.

Taking the horizontal axis of the matrix first, it seems to be relatively uncontentious that specialists, whether individually or collectively, need to become expert in all the activities associated with the control of hazards.

164

This does not mean that they have individually to know all about the identification, assessment and containment of all possible hazards, but they do need to be able to understand and articulate relevant questions and know how to seek out relevant information, whether from within their company or outside. Where more than one specialist is involved they need to appreciate their colleagues' spheres of competence and learn ways of acting collectively to form expert multi-disciplinary groups. The observations from our research suggest that whilst there is still much to be done to ensure that specialists are actually trained to cover this (top row) range of activities there is little dispute that this range of activities must form a basis for training plans. In some ways it already does. To the extent that they have considered it, employers are agreed that they 'want' people skilled in the stages of hazard control shown on the horizontal axes of Figure 7.4.

More contentious, however, are the issues raised by discussions about an approximate mix of the activities identified in the vertical axis. Empirical work suggests that safety specialists are heavily clustered in the top A row but that they must expand from this at least as far as the B2 row (of active adviser). They can sometimes function effectively in C1 (joint executive action) but it seems that they are never advised to enter C2 (unilateral executive action). The reasoning behind this is that, as has been made clear, effective health and safety programmes depend on line managers taking real responsibility for the health and safety of their employees (Dawson, Poynter and Stevens 1983a; Kletz 1982; HSE/11, 1975).

It is always ultimately up to the line manager to ensure that safe working practices are adopted, that recommended safety precautions are taken and that employees are made aware of the hazards and how best to control them. Pursuing these objectives often creates conflict with others, for example, the rate and quality of production, profitability and the stability and commitment of the workforce. These conflicting priorities have to be confronted and compromise reached. If the specialist assumes direct executive responsibility then managers may feel that they are absolved from responsibility; that they have 'passed the buck' and can get on with those things they see as more directly relevant to their management task. This would be undesirable even if specialists tended to be fairly powerful people, but given that they are frequently relatively low on power and influence in the organisation it would be a recipe for very poor self regulation.

An important question then arises; how are specialists really to influence senior executives and line managers and become a major force within an organisation, without actually assuming direct executive responsibility? What, in other words, are their sources of power and influence? It is true

Safety specialists' activities	Stage of technical control 1. Identification of hazards	2. Assessment of risk	3. Development of controls	4. Implementation of controls	5. Longer-term monitoring and adaptation
A Processing information	Keeping accident statistics Processing hazard information	Calculating accident frequencies etc. Processing information on hygiene standards	Processing equipment manufacturers' information and lists of products etc.	Processing orders for safety equipment	Comparing accident statistics over time
B Giving advice/ problem-solving					
B1 Passive adviser	Looking at work operations, on request Investigating complaints	Answering questions about severity of hazards	Commenting on available controls which have been suggested	Commenting on effectiveness on request	Investigating accidents Inspecting Providing feedback on request
B2 Active adviser	Taking initiative in looking for hazards	Lobbying for appropriate standards, control limits	Recommending controls	Identifying shortfalls and improvements	Making recommendations for update/review of systems
C Taking direct executive action					
C1 Jointly with line management	Doing joint inspections and audits	Jointly deciding on standards	Jointly drawing up codes of practice	Joint supervision and approval or disapproval to jobs	Participating in reviews of arrangements
C2 Alone	Doing own inspections and audits	Deciding unilaterally what is safe/unsafe	Issuing instructions Specifying controls to be followed	Supervising job Exercising veto Physically stopping people working	Modifying procedures etc. on own initiative

Figure 7.4 Specialist activities in the technical control of hazards. (Source: Dawson *et al.* 1984c: 258. Reprinted by permission of John Wiley and Sons Ltd)

that 'no one wants accidents or ill health' to happen, but if making things safer or healthier requires expenditure of scarce resources (such as time, money or expertise), then the specialist needs more than mere words to support his argument. Figure 7.5 summarises seven sources of power and influence for health and safety specialists.

The first is patronage – safety specialists will always tell you that it is useful to get someone important on their side; whether this is shown personally in support at key meetings or more formally through lending a name to a document. Secondly, the specialist's role in policing the control process gives some power but only within an organisation where health and safety are seen as important. There are however, as suggested earlier, some problems involved for any individual who tries to administer regulations, police activities and solve problems with the same group of people, not least because of unwillingness to share sensitive information. Other sources of power and influence can be derived through entry into coalitions – either internally, as point 3 identifies, with safety representatives and committees, or externally (point 4) with local officers of the regulatory enforcement agencies.

Point 5 of Figure 7.5 reminds us that the specialist's official position in the hierarchy as shown by such indicators as salary, grading, reporting relationships, functional position is also important in determining power and influence. The specialist needs to be independent of line management and yet have their confidence. Reporting upwards, the specialist should

---

1. Patronage of senior managerial person/group.
2. Direct role in control process.
3. Coalition formed with safety representatives and/or safety committees.
4. Maintaining strong cooperative relationships with HSE, especially Factory Inspectors.
5. Formal position in organisation.
6. Personal qualities of charm, friendliness, leadership, etc.
7. Managerial dependence on specialist expertise.

Figure 7.5 Sources of power and influence for safety specialists.

(Source: Dawson *et al*. 1984c: 262. Reprinted by permission of John Wiley and Sons Ltd)

reach someone who has the respect of senior executives on the 'direct' operating side. The specialist can effectively be an operations person, providing that he or she and the rest of the organisation are committed to establishing effective systems of hazard control. Point 6 of Figure 7.5 notes the importance of personal qualities and interpersonal skills, which can lead to increased respect and influence for specialists and which can, to an extent, be acquired through training.

Notwithstanding these six characteristics, expertise, the last source of power and influence identified in Figure 7.5, is in many ways the most important for the long-term development of health and safety programmes. However, the extent to which the expertise of specialists actually provides access to real influence within a firm is dependent both on characteristics of the specialists themselves and of the management organisation with whom they are associated. Qualifications and experience are important. However, even in an industry acknowledged to be hazardous such as chemicals, people with specialist titles are still to be found whose main qualifications are that they were recruited from the police, armed forces or the fire brigade. Other specialists have progressed through a stable but unexceptional career in operations, rising to positions of supervision with a reputation for being 'good with the men' and they have been given the pre-retirement position of safety officer. On the other hand, some specialists are graduate chemists, engineers, qualified nurses and have taken the Institute of Occupational Safety and Health courses of study and examinations. But they were by no means the rule, even in large organisations (Dawson 1986, 1987).

Even if formally qualified or well experienced, the specialists still have to gain personal credibility with line managers and the workforce. This happens to the extent that these key actors regard the specialists as supplying an important service or performing an important control function on which managers and workforce representatives depend. Dawson, Poynter and Stevens (1984c: 262) suggest that the relationship which prevails between managers and any specialist is much influenced by three interrelated factors:

1 what the specialists can offer (and whether it is available from other sources);
2 the importance of their offer to management;
3 the basis for its importance, in particular, whether imposed from 'outside' or developed 'internally'.

Using these dimensions Figure 7.6 suggests four different patterns of dependency, and hence power and influence, between 'direct' managers and 'indirect' specialists. The first and strongest is where the expert service is clearly essential to the performance of the management task. This is usually the case with maintenance specialists who keep the producton system running. The second pattern of dependancy is where the expertise can easily be shown to be important. This may be the case for industrial engineers who can demonstrate a direct contribution to cutting costs.

Thirdly, there are expert systems not directly geared to the continuation of the primary production and distribution of goods and services but which are nonetheless seen as important for control and coordination. Finance and accounting are often examples of this. In companies with improving safety performance there is a noticeable move to this type of relationship for safety specialists, as managers are considering seriously the meaning of their responsibilities for health and safety.

The fourth and weakest relationship does not derive internally but has its roots in the requirements and pressures of outside agencies. It is in this context that many specialists in health and safety actually work. To belong in this category does not necessarily imply weakness providing external regulation is strong but this is not generally the case in matters of health and safety. Certainly Inspectors would probably visit a workplace if asked to do so by a specialist but, as Chapter 9 will show, the HSE in general prefers to work through encouragement and advice rather than sanctions. On average, few workplaces are visited as often as every one, two or even three years, especially if dealt with by the Factory Inspectorate. Thus if a manager avoids serious injury or incident, specialists have difficulty in creating a role deriving from external enforcement.

The type of specialist role which develops reflects both the 'objective' characteristics of the establishment and company, and the attitudes which

---

1. Direct and obvious dependency.
   e.g. maintenance, to keep lines running; product development, to maintain market position
2. Dependency can be established.
   e.g. industrial engineering to cut production costs
3. Indirect but strong relationship because activity relevant to managerial strategies for control and coordination.
   e.g. finance, accounting, information technology
4. Required by, or thought necessary to deal with, external agencies.
   e.g. legal department to interpret and advise on legislation and Government requirements; insurance specialists to deal with insurance companies

---

Figure 7.6 Relationship between specialists and senior line managers.
(Source: Dawson *et al.* 1984c: 262. Reprinted by permission of John Wiley and Sons Ltd)

prevail. Where the technology, materials and working environment are stable and well understood, access to a good data bank on established hazards and their controls may only need to be supplemented by a part-time specialist to oversee its operations, ensure the maintenance of administrative systems and draw attention to the safety implications of process or product changes. Alternatively the use of sophisticated and changing technologies and new or toxic substances would arguably require a larger, more qualified and experienced specialist presence. The views and opinions of the managers and workforce representatives, which may be more or less tightly associated with 'objective' issues, will also affect the specialist's position. This is illustrated in Figure 7.7 which shows two dimensions. First, it identifies two extreme views of managers' on the importance of health and safety as part of their overall task. Secondly, it deals with the views of managers about whether there is significant potential for accidents and ill health within the nature of the work environment, or whether they consider health and safety problems to be mostly reducible to stupidity and carelessness. It is only where line managers regard health and safety as an important aspect of their task and take a broad socio-technical view of hazard origins and control, that

	Line management view: securing health and safety is an important part of their task	
	Yes	No
Line management view:		
There are health and safety problems deriving from physical working environment which present uncertainties and difficulties	Easy access to power based on expertise in both technical and personnel areas	Limited access to power based on expertise in technical and personnel areas
'Health and safety' problems largely derived from people's stupidity and carelessness	Access to power based on expertise in the personnel but not technical area	No access to power based on technical expertise and very limited access to power based on personnel expertise

Figure 7.7 Managerial opinions and the safety specialists' access to power based on expertise.

(Source: Dawson *et al.* 1984c: 264. Reprinted by permission of John Wiley and Sons Ltd)

specialists are well placed to perform a strong and advisory function. Figure 7.8 illustrates in summary some of the factors associated with expertise that affect a specialist's power and influence within the workplace.

Before leaving the subject of safety specialists it is important to remember that whether powerful or not, they usually only exist in the larger enterprises and establishments. Our small retail outlets and construction firms along with most other smaller establishments simply do not employ specialists directly. In some cases smaller firms may use the services of outside safety consultants or at least make use of specialist information available through trade associations and federations of employers. This, however, is by no means the norm. In the absence of specialist support, the

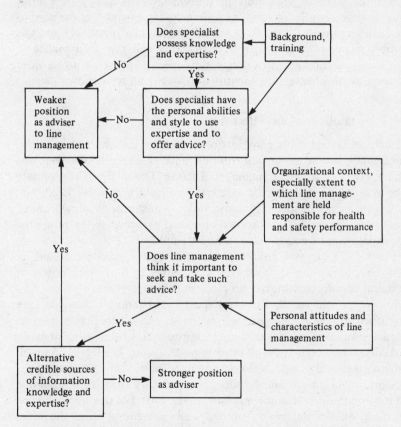

Figure 7.8 Expertise and knowledge as a source of power and influence for safety specialists in their relationship with line management.

(Source: Dawson *et al.* 1984c: 265. Reprinted by permission of John Wiley and Sons Ltd)

171

argument that ultimately safe and healthy working must depend on the motivation and capacity of line managers to act takes on even greater force.

Summary

This prescriptive approach presents a comprehensive organisational framework for safety management which is not based on a simple notion of intrinsic commitment to safety on the part of managers, but rather suggests organisational forms and activities which will secure the pursuit of safety in the context of competing demands on resources: it is not based simply on trust but arrangements for control. Although developed initially in the context of larger organisations in the chemical industry, the central elements – the key role for senior executives and line managers, the need to create a high priority for safety which will not happen 'naturally', analysis of appropriate technical controls on hazards and the maintenance of motivation and commitment amongst employees at all levels – have a wider relevance as the chapters on construction and retail have shown.

Workforce involvement and effectiveness

Robens laid considerable emphasis on workforce involvement in safety. However, on several grounds it can be argued that this involvement was seen largely as an adjunct to managerial action. This might be appropriate if the assumption of 'common interest' on health and safety is correct. Employers have the primary duty and the institutions of workforce involvement are, in this philosophy, presented as means of generating the appropriate employee attitudes to assist employers. Enforcement issues take a back seat, and collective bargaining is rejected: the idea of distributive bargaining over safety, backed either by bargaining power or the threat of enforcement, has no place in this conception.

However, not even the Robens Report could totally ignore the long established suspicion amongst trade unionists and others that employers were not always willing to take action to improve health and safety at work, especially if this conflicted with other considerations. The legislation itself rather ambiguously emphasised on one hand participative structures for workforce involvement, and on the other, statutory rights to information and inspection for workforce representatives. Part 1 of this book showed that the SRSC Regulations did not share all the assumptions of the initial Report and legislation. It is not surprising, therefore, that there is a lack of a clear and generally agreed definition of the role of safety representatives and safety committees since what would be an effective role in participation may not be effective in collective bargaining. What can be said, however, is that given the structure of decision making in British enterprises, workforce involvement through joint committees and safety representatives, even with statutory rights, can never be a substitute for line management responsibility. The question for prescription focuses then on the balance which is appropriate between participating in integrative bargaining where the parties perceive themselves as having common goals and engaging in conflict in 'zero sum' distributive bargaining, where the parties perceive themselves as having divergent goals (Walton and McKersie 1965).

The previous discussion about appropriate arrangements for monitoring safety lends support to the idea of consultative involvement and integrative bargaining as the preferred forms of workforce involvement. It is difficult to see how the provisions for monitoring and assessment could function in the context of frequent local haggling over safety or safety-related issues. Line management responsibility for safety similarly implies the avoidance of involvement of staff functions such as personnel in the resolution of local safety grievances.

Most conceptions of 'effective' safety committees rely on the views of participants and imply the achievement of successful compromise. Beaumont *et al.* (1982b) suggest that participants are more likely to judge that a committee is effective if it

  meets regularly,
  has open facility for all members to contribute items to the agenda,
  is as compact as possible,
  has a senior management member who can take decisions in committee,
  has well trained membership on both sides,
  has a safety specialist as an 'ex officio' adviser,
  has agreed balanced representation between different trade unions
    represented in a plant,
  has representation through established trade union channels,
  has a membership which sees the committee as contributing to
    improving health and safety,
  has a membership who attend regularly,
  facilitates two way flow of information between workforce and health
    and safety committee,
  (in large plants of more than 1000 employees) has a tiered structure of
    departmental and section committees coordinated by plant-wide
    committee.

However, American evidence implies that this integrative structure might not always be the most effective in pursuit of safety. Kochan, Dyer and Lipsky (1977) found a positive relationship between management's perception of safety and their attendance and contribution. However, unions tended to become involved both in integrative and distributive bargaining in committee, and Kochan, Dyer and Lipsky take the view that the law was an important external influence in promoting major safety changes. In particular,

> The main effect of the presence of the law and the threat to its enforcement has been to increase the commitment of management to deal with safety and health issues and specifically to reduce its resistance to union efforts at improving safety and health conditions (1977: 85).

Indeed, one recent writer argues that encouragement of collective bargaining over health and safety issues in the USA is one important way of overcoming the problems created by an over-stretched Office of Safety and Health Administration (OSHA). Trade unions, it is argued, will bring specific hazard knowledge and pressure to OSHA's general 'command and control' approach;

> To the extent that labour and management can be induced to negotiate health and safety rules within the context of the collective bargaining agreement, we can decentralize some aspects of the regulatory intervention mechanism almost to plant level. In theory, this should produce investments in occupational health and safety that are both more efficient and more effective than those produced by the present system alone (Bacow 1981: 58).

For all the differences in collective bargaining and the law between the USA and UK, this is an argument for self regulation of a substantially different sort than that in the Robens Report. Yet in terms of the objectives of improved safety, there are few differences.

In fact, disapproval of linking collective bargaining to health and safety in the Robens analysis is directed mainly against the sorts of distributive bargaining which would threaten to use health and safety issues in coercive action, or against the sort of collusive bargaining which allows management and unions to demote safety issues in favour of others. In terms of the actual day to day behaviour of safety representatives, it is directed against bargaining behaviour which demotes safety. By contrast, the range of 'appropriate' activities for safety representatives can be broadly summarised as follows:

(a) *Missionary:* encouraging the workforce to become more safety conscious, to give health and safety a higher priority, and facilitating the exchange of health and safety information.

(b) *Monitoring:* checking for changes in hazards, and in their controls.

(c) *Policing:* putting pressure on managers to fulfil internal and external regulations and to be more committeed and concerned.

(d) *Disciplinary:* endorsing discipline and controls over workforce to ensure safe working practices.

(e) *Communicating:* providing a channel between the workforce, safety specialists, managers and external enforcement agencies.

It is not easy to perform all these five roles adequately. In addition to the acquisition of technical knowledge, safety representatives who master all aspects of the role must acquire not only considerable personal influence with management but also influence over and independence from specific employee groups. Research on the activities of shop stewards indicates that such abilities are rare. They are likely to be found amongst the most powerful stewards who in turn are likely to manifest the greatest commitment to trade union principles (Batstone, Boraston and Frenkel 1977).

It is because of factors such as these that there has been an increasing trend in most unions to amalgamate the role of steward and safety representative. Unions have mostly been convinced that in practice the steward/safety representative is likely to be more effective in the pursuit of safety than an individual who lacks steward authority, since the activities of stewardship actually provide the resources for the performance of the representative role. The reluctance of trade unions to accept the argument that the acquisition of statutory rights in the absence of collective organisation would provide the basis for successful safety representative activity also follow. Only the 'communication' and 'monitoring' roles are guaranteed by such rights and the ability to pressurise management is substantially reduced. Consequently, it requires the assumption that wholesale trade-offs of safety issues in bargaining are likely in unionised workplaces, to sustain the argument that safety representative activity should be divorced from that of local union representation. In this sense the concerns about management and union lack of commitment to safety are symmetrical: the fear of the Robens Committee in both respects was the attraction of financial inducements to ignore safety.

In summary then, while distributive bargaining with recourse to external enforcement does not fit the self regulatory ideal, it does not follow that all forms of integrative bargaining will promote safety. The primary issue is the employers' commitment to safety. If the prescriptive model is observed then it matters less which form of worker involvement is chosen provided it does not deflect the policy from its course. If it is not, then integrative bargaining has, from the safety point of view, the wrong focus. Nevertheless the prescriptive approach to management organisation is consistent with both integrative and distributive bargaining. These mechanisms are familiar to economists. In the former case, union complaints about safety inform managers about problems which may be solved: in the terms used by the 'Harvard School' of economists, unions 'voice' grievances to rectify remediable decline in standards. In the latter case, managers experience a 'shock' effect as union threats of coercive action or recourse to enforcement propel the improvement of standards (Freeman and Medoff 1984).

Capability and the limits of self regulation

Both the capacity and the motivation of parties to pursue safety policies have been identified as essential elements in self regulation and considerable attention has been paid to motivation. However, in a number of cases there may be a problem of the *capacity* of those involved to pursue policies rather than their *willingness* to do so. Four cases are of particular interest: they all concern circumstances in which the control systems necessary for effective local self regulation may be absent.

The first case concerns non-union environments. While there is no reason to suppose that the activities of safety representatives are the only or even the primary spur to effective safety management, those workplaces which lack recognised trade unions also lack one potential force for safety improvement. In such workplaces, it falls entirely to management to inculcate safety awareness: moreover, a lack of representative structure may make it more difficult to get the message home. Policy maintenance also remains solely a management responsibility.

The second case concerns small firms. Although health and safety legislation does not seem to have had a substantial impact, there is a resistance on the part of the owners of small firms both to employment legislation and to the presence of trade unions. Scase and Goffee find the source of this resistance to external forces and regulations to lie in a concern to secure personal control over the business and a preference for informal, relatively egalitarian work practices (1980: 55–72). This preference goes along with other organisational tendencies which may inhibit effective safety management. To begin with, the costs of training and administrative provision in the area may appear excessive to small firms. The reluctance to delegate control in such enterprises also generates a reluctance to employ technical specialists, while owner-directors themselves often lack formal technical management training and feel that many managerial tasks are essentially unproductive (Bolton Committee 1971). As Goffee and Scase note, formalisation of managerial structures and responsibility are unlikely whatever the economic circumstances of the firm. In hard times, or those characterised by considerable uncertainty, formal managerial structures constitute a considerable overhead, while expansion tends to produce rather haphazard organisational forms as owners try to retain personal control (1985: 56). It is also the view of many who have been concerned with safety in smaller firms that many owners, managers and workers are simply unaware of their statutory duties, legal requirements and basic information on hazards and their control. If effective safety policy implies relevant knowledge, regular observance of procedural rules, and developed control systems, then some characteristics of small firms may inhibit good safety performance.

Certain features of Goffee and Scase's findings in the building and personal service industries are replicated in Ford's study of small retailing firms which focuses specifically on compliance with legislation. However, her findings indicate that non-compliance with regulations by small business is highly variable: higher skill levels, membership of trade or professional associations and, within the small firm category, size, were all positively related to the likelihood of compliance (Ford 1982: 46–7). Non-compliance was, in particular, associated with high levels of part-time employment and a confusion of personal with employment relationships.

The growth of different forms of work relationships in fact leads to the third case. In some sectors, particularly those characterised by the prevalence of small firms, forms of contractual arrangement have developed which not only create legal problems, but also attenuate management control systems. In particular, the growth of subcontracting and self-employment in a number of industries such as taxis, computers, domestic repairs and insurance, and most notably of all in construction, present problems for health and safety legislation.

These problems differ slightly from those experienced by other forms of legal regulation. Statutes which rely on the existence of an employment contract – such as that requiring the payment of national insurance contributions or providing protection against unfair dismissal – encounter particular difficulties (Leighton 1983). The area of health and safety is not immune from these problems (Ferguson v. John Dawson Ltd).[1] However, the 1974 Act does extend the duty imposed on the employer to ensure safety at work beyond the number of his or her employees. Section 4 of the Act imposes a further duty to provide safe premises upon 'each person who has, to any extent, control of premises or the means of access to or egress there from, other than domestic premises, made available to those not in his employment as a place of work or as a place where they use plant or substances provided for their use, or to other premises used in connection therewith' (Rideout 1979: 343). This tends to expand the older Factories Acts duties on the 'occupiers of premises'. Although it excludes responsibility for the safety of home-workers, it extends to those who maintain or repair premises (HASAWA section 4(3)), and includes all forms of 'inside contracting'.

Nonetheless, the development of subcontracting on a given site does cause substantial problems for accident prevention. The most general point to make is that employment relationships offer better prospects for the control of many aspects of employee behaviour than do other forms of contract (Williamson 1975). However, the division of responsibility between several employers on a site also generates problems of coordination and control of activities between groups: whatever the rigour of contractual specification of safety responsibility it is plausible to suggest that safety performance will be poorer under subcontracting than where there is coordination through a unitary form of responsibility and assessment. Uneven health and safety standards are likely to arise, particularly since the use of subcontracting in itself indicates something about the nature of commitment to the activity in question. Apart from the data in this volume, other recent research has drawn attention to subcontracting as a major factor in fatal injuries in the offshore oil industry (Wright 1986).

The final case does not focus on particular companies or contractual arrangements: rather it concerns reactions within all companies experiencing recession to the costs of monitoring an effective safety policy. Recession may induce companies to react in ways which affect safety directly and indirectly. The direct effect follows from any cutbacks in the resources devoted to safety issues – whether it be training, hardware provision, numbers of safety officers or representatives. The indirect effect follows from economies which on the one hand increase the number of hazards and the likelihood of their realisation or, on the other, decrease the motivation to maintain safe systems of operation. In Grunberg's example, reduced rest allowances and increased workpace were associated with a deteriorating accident rate at Talbot (Grunberg 1983). More generally, reductions in manning levels, improved flexibility of labour and a reliance on bonuses, all of which are likely responses to product market uncertainty, can lead to a decreased emphasis on safety issues.

One of the more difficult issues here is competition from firms which are not regulated in the same way. It seems unlikely that the differential costs of safety provision are the basis for strong competitive advantage or disadvantage for UK firms within the domestic market in a given industry. Nonetheless it is notable that some of the larger firms with well developed safety policies are significant amongst those calling for more enforcement of safety requirements within smaller, 'less responsible' competitors. This is now a feature of the construction industry in the UK which is reminiscent of the call of some nineteenth century factory owners who were covered by the first Factories Acts, for their extension to other premises which the owners feared would have some competitive advantage by being outside this piece of law. In terms of international competition the problem may be greater for UK firms. Overseas competitors which may not incur similar costs of safety provision may introduce competition of sufficient severity to induce UK firms to incur legal sanctions for failing their statutory duties to safeguard the health and safety of their employees, particularly if the costs of enforcement are low.

Conclusions

In summary, the detailed analysis of the requirements for effective local self regulation together with the findings of our research in the chemicals, construction and retail sectors suggest that, questions of willingness aside, there are circumstances in which the capacity of management (and of unions if they are recognised) to sustain an effective health and safety policy through self regulation may be severely limited. There is reason to suggest that these circumstances, being related to degree of unionisation, size of firm and extent of subcontracting, characterise large parts of particular industrial sectors and that the impact of the recession has been to make them more prevalent.

In such circumstances safety standards will be set primarily by enforcement, either directly through the activities of one of the Inspectorates or indirectly by the employer's calculation of likely compensation costs in the event of an accident. These standards need not necessarily be consistently below those set by self regulation. In fact, in subsequent chapters we shall argue that external enforcement is in fact *least* likely for those categories of firms which are most likely to let safety standards slip below the legal limit.

Having given consideration to developments at local level where the legislation was intended to act with greatest force, we now turn in the third part of this book to examine developments at national level.

PART 3

Developments at national level

During the 1960s, health and safety at work became a focus for discussion and concern not only in Britain but elsewhere as well. In the USA a new Occupational Health and Safety Act was passed in 1970 and an Occupational Safety and Health Administration was established (Wilson 1985; Kelman 1981). In Sweden the Arbetarskyddsverket Agency which had been established twenty years earlier was greatly expanded in funding and activity (Kelman 1981: 3–4). In Britain, as we have seen, the period of public discussion culminated in the publication of the Robens Report in 1972 and the Health and Safety at Work Act in 1974.

In the UK the primary aim of the 1974 legislation, was, within minimum statutory requirements, to secure self regulation of health and safety directly in workplaces. Employers and employees who were actually managing and working in factories and offices, together with the designers, suppliers and importers of equipment, were to be encouraged to develop policies and practices which would secure improved standards of health and safety at work. Nevertheless it was clearly understood both by the Robens Committee of Inquiry and the drafters of the legislation that these local developments would need significant institutional support at national level if they were to be successfully achieved. Two institutional developments can be identified as particularly important in establishing the national framework which, it was hoped, would facilitate the effective development of local self regulation.

The first was the establishment of the Health and Safety Commission as a tripartite institution for national policy making. Being 'tripartite' means that it was set up as a joint operation between government, trade unions and employers' representatives, independent of direct political control. In the event its constitution facilitated the participation of representatives of other interested parties as well, for example, local authorities and professional bodies. The establishment and operation of the Health and Safety Commission and its Advisory Committees are the subject of Chapter 8.

The second important national development was the formation of the Health and Safety Executive which oversees the activities of the various Inspectorates of Mines, Quarries, Alkalis,* Factories, Agriculture and Nuclear Installations. The operational activities of the Executive itself and the practices of inspection and enforcement will be the subject of Chapter 9 which considers in particular the Factory Inspectorate and Environmental Health Officers employed by local authorities.

* The Industrial Air Pollution Inspectorate (formerly the Alkali Inspectorate) was transferred to the Department of the Environment on 1 April 1987.

8

Tripartism and the Health and Safety Commission

The Health and Safety Commission

Following the recommendations of the Robens Committee, the Health and Safety Commission was established by sections 10–17 of the Health and Safety at Work Act (1974). Section 10 provides for the establishment of the HSC and its composition with a Chairman and between six to nine members, each to be appointed by the Secretary of State for Employment after consultation with organisations representing employers, employees, local authorities and professional bodies. In fact since 1974 there have been three nominees each from the TUC and CBI and two local authority representatives. The spirit of political even-handedness which is central to tripartism was reflected in the appointment by a Labour government and reappointment by a Conservative government, of William Simpson, a former General Secretary of the Foundry section of the AUEW and sometime Chairman of the Labour Party, as Chairman of the HSC.

Although there are certain provisions within the Act which set out appropriate areas of ministerial control, the HSC, as a corporate body, is established so that it can build up the expertise and status envisaged by the Robens Report and thus become 'clearly recognisable as the authoritative body responsible for safety and health at work' (Robens 1972a: para. 111).

Under sections 11–17 of the Health and Safety at Work Act 1974, the Health and Safety Commission has a general duty to do 'such things and make such arrangements as it considers appropriate for health, safety and welfare in connection with work'. More specific duties and powers are then defined, including:

the provision of research and information,
the appointment of advisory committees,
the proposing of regulations which will have the force of law,
the issuing of codes of practice which may in certain circumstances embody the force of law.

The explanation of this last duty is that where codes exist failure to comply does not of itself render the defendant liable to civil or criminal proceedings. However, where it is alleged that someone has contravened a statutory requirement and it is shown that they have failed to observe a relevant code of practice, then this can be taken as evidence of their guilt unless the court is satisfied that the defendant met their obligations in some other way. An analogy of traffic offences and contraventions of the Highway Code is often made to illustrate this point. By contrast, regulations, once made, have statutory authority. The HSC has the power to propose regulations to the Secretary of State who makes them subject to negative parliamentary approval. For the period from 1974 until January 1987 there were 159 statutory instruments (sets of Regulations and Rules) made under parts I and IV of the HASAW Act. Twenty-three approved codes of practice were issued under section 16 of the HASAW Act for the same period.

In discharging its duty to propose regulations to maintain or improve standards of health, safety and welfare established by or under the enactments specified in section 1 of the Act, the HSC has an obligation to consult interested parties, including government departments. This obligation has resulted in two main types of activity. The first has been a policy of issuing consultative documents containing recommendations and justification for regulations. In the period from its establishment to January 1987, the HSC issued 47 sets of consultative documents. Secondly, tripartite advisory and consultative committees dealing with particular hazards and industries have been formed with membership drawn from all interested parties. They can both respond to policy initiatives from government or another interested party and, perhaps more important, can have a creative role in the formation of policy and the development of practice at national, industrial and local levels.

In addition to the extensive processes of national consultation which will be discussed in detail below, the HSC has also been much influenced in proposing regulations by directives from the European Commission. For example, these have been formative in the preparation of regulations concerning the notification of hazardous installations, the classification, packaging and labelling of dangerous substances, the notification of the properties of new chemical substances and the handling of asbestos.

The operation of the HSC and its associated institutions is, at national level, another reflection of the presumption of common interest between interested parties which characterised the Robens Report. Similar approaches are found at national level in other European countries, for example Sweden (see Kelman 1981), but are in sharp contrast to practice in the USA (see for example Ashford 1976; Wilson 1985; Ives 1985).

In the USA, policy is made by OSHA which is also executively responsible for enforcement. The activities of OSHA are characterised by an 'adversarial' independence of employers and business. There is little or no prior consultation with employers, since the presumption is that they would oppose any proposals advanced simply in the cause of improved health and safety at work. No sooner are new regulations pronounced than they are normally challenged in the federal or state courts or both and, even when eventually cleared for operation, individual cases are often brought to justify why regulations need not or cannot be adhered to in specific circumstances. For example when OSHA promulgated its cancer policy relating to carcinogens in the workplace, the US Chamber of Commerce said on 5 April 1985 that the policy was 'perhaps the single most offensive, objectionable and inappropriate rule making undertaken by OSHA in its eleven year history' (quoted in Ives 1985). Ives reports that this policy was immediately challenged in several different courts.

Drawing comparative conclusions on the basis of cross-national research is beset with difficulties because of different political, social and economic conditions and different public attitudes to health, safety and risk. On the basis of available comparative work (see for example Kelman 1981; Ashford 1976; Wilson 1985; Ives 1985), one cannot conclude that an independent adversarial approach is necessarily more or less effective in terms of securing improvements in health and safety at work. It is, however, clear that an adversarial approach by a national agency must be supported by a political regime which is in favour of external regulation if it is to achieve improved standards. Under the presidency of President Carter, which believed in external regulation and that the general good was not necessarily served by the unfettered activities of the free market, OSHA was able to be a much stronger force. Both the level of fines and the frequency of inspection increased, and more regulations were made. However, OSHA's fortunes changed greatly under the presidency of President Reagan, which was in principle opposed to the idea of regulating industry for anything other than maximising profit and securing the free market.

In a political climate which opposes external regulation other than through the market, policy and practice at national level are likely to be more effective in terms of securing improvements in health and safety if the policy making process includes rather than excludes the participation of interested parties, particularly employers. How else is the policy making body going to secure the commitment and interest of those whose behaviour it wishes to influence? How else are feelings of duty and obligation to do anything other than maximise profit going to be engendered? These rhetorical questions can be followed by others. Even if some level of consensus on what is required for health and safety can be reached which moderates the unfettered quest for profit, how can policies which are formulated at national level be guaranteed implementation at local level? It is easier, as we saw in construction, to effect this national to local translation where some of the national participants, such as executives of large companies and representatives of large trade unions, are directly involved. Such arrangements are common in larger companies in industries where employers (and to a lesser extent trade unions) are well organised. But many workplaces remain untouched by deliberations at national level, and in this context one must ask what, if anything, is the effect at local level of consensual tripartite decision making at national level? These are issues to which we will return once we have looked in more detail at the activities of the Industry Advisory Committees, which it was hoped would provide a bridge in the UK between the national and local levels and be important institutions in the development of consensus about, and commitment to, improved health and safety at work.

Industry Advisory Committees

The Committee of Inquiry chaired by Lord Robens was mindful of the importance of developing arrangements at industry level which would provide a bridge between local and national levels, as well as encouraging research and the investigation of problems particular to specific industrial sectors. As one would expect, industry level activity was conceived in terms of tripartite structures which would encourage participation from all relevant parties and particularly from the trade unions and employers' associations which represented people in the industry. The Robens Report recommended the establishment of arrangements to strengthen and encourage industry-by-industry tripartite activity in health and safety, to link up voluntary and statutory activities and to facilitate cooperation between the new national authority and the various industry based institutions.

Industry level activity before the Act

In its deliberations on possible forms of self regulation at industry level, the Robens Report reviewed the wide variety of activities then current. At one extreme were 'employer-only' arrangements in which *ad hoc* meetings or review bodies were established by trade associations or groups of employers. At the other extreme were fully constituted joint trade union–employer standing committees set up under the provisions of the 1961 Factories Acts.

In between these two extremes was a variety of voluntary joint arrangements. In certain sectors of employment, occupational safety issues could be discussed through the consultation machinery of the Joint Industrial Councils. Williams estimated that some 60 industries were covered by agreements which allowed some considerations of the 'safety, health and welfare of employees' (1960: 309). However, since the main work of Joint Councils was given over to discussion of wages and conditions of employment, the scope and effectiveness of this forum varied considerably between industries. Even where consideration of occupational safety issues stood apart from those of production, the amount of time allotted for discussion was limited by the demands of other issues.

Some industries had developed voluntary joint consultation machinery dealing exclusively with health and safety, though once again there was considerable variation in its scope and effectiveness. In an attempt to standardise and extend the coverage of these voluntary committeees, the TUC and the (then) British Employers Federation issued a joint statement in 1961 which, in the words of the Chief Inspector of Factories, attempted to improve:

> liaison in those areas where steps were already being taken to deal with accident prevention in a systematic way and to encourage the setting up of safety machinery in industries where it had not previously existed (Chief Inspector of Factories Annual Report 1961: 25).

By 1963, 18 of the 25 industries approached had central safety committees and by the end of 1965, all but two of these had established such committees.

In the nationalised industries, the consultation machinery established by the various Acts of parliament imposed an obligation on management to discuss 'the promotion and encouragement of measures affecting the safety, health and welfare of persons employed' with the appropriate trade unions. Despite this formal obligation on management, Williams (1960) reports that both the machinery developed to implement it and the enthusiasm demonstrated for using it, was variable.

These approaches to some form of industry wide prevention activity, whether voluntary or statutory, can be contrasted with the method adopted in some industrial sectors falling under the jurisdiction of the Factories Acts. Under the 1961 Factories Act, the Chief Inspector of Factories or the appropriate Minister had the power to set up a Standing or Advisory Committee to monitor or review occupational safety issues in an industry or general subject area. These committees dealt exclusively with health and safety problems, and were composed of representatives of the appropriate employers and trade unions. Their difference from the committees already described was that they also contained a government representative. Such institutions were officially suggested as early as 1911 by a Departmental Committee on accidents in factories which had recommended the establishment of conferences between factory inspectors, employers and workers in each industry at national and district level. In the event a number of such Joint Advisory Committees were convened in industries covered by the Factories Acts.

In contrast to Standing Committees which met regularly to review developments in occupational safety in their industrial sector, Advisory Committees were convened for a limited time only, either to review specific problems or general arrangements in a particular industry or subject area, and to publish a report of their findings. However, as the Chief Inspector of Factories noted;

> amongst its recommendations, such a committee usually
> suggests the creation of a Joint Standing Committee to observe
> the effect of its recommendations and keep up to date with
> progress and development (Chief Inspector of Factories Annual
> Report 1954: 34).

National Joint Committees of these types were potentially a much more effective form of prevention activity than the voluntary machinery discussed earlier. Not only were they a forum for the continuous monitoring of occupational safety arrangements in a particular industry, but the addition of a government representative to those of employers and trade unions gave their intermittent reports and recommendations an added weight and authority. In some cases the suggested codes of practice or recommendations were ignored by both employers and the government of the day, but as Williams concluded, after reviewing the work of such committees:

> Joint Standing Committees have a strong role to play in
> accident prevention; their activities have an authoritative basis
> since they involve the practical knowledge and experience of
> both sides in industry together with the specialised knowledge
> of the Factory Department . : . a characteristic of these
> committees is that they are constituted for continuous work: it
> is implied that they will constantly review the conditions in the
> trade or industry so that the prevention measures may
> regularly be brought to the most effective level. The importance
> of this role cannot be overestimated and it offers the unions an

188

excellent opportunity in their activities to improve standards (Williams 1960: 304–5).

Given the concerns of the Robens Committee, it is perhaps not surprising that the work of the Standing Committees should provide a potent example of what might be achieved at industry level. The Committee was looking for an organisational form which would cement and encourage the cooperation of employers and trade unions, establish closer links and liaison between the Inspectorate and industry and, if its proposals on the future framework of legislation were adopted, provide a forum for the production of regulations, standards and codes of practice. Moreover, the structure of Industry Committees would act as a half-way house between the new national authority and the workplace, making consultation easier and more effective. Finally a structure of such Industry Committees would not prejudice existing voluntary arrangements or inhibit the activities of voluntary associations. The Robens Report thus opted for a structure of Subject and Industry Advisory Committees, composed of representatives of management and trade unions. We now turn to a description of this structure, and a review of the work and performance of Advisory Committees.

The Advisory Committee Structure

Once established, the HSC identified Advisory Committees as 'one of the most effective ways of putting into practice the underlying philosophy behind the Health and Safety at Work Act – the involvement of all concerned in the reduction of occupational hazards'. The Committees were to be of two broad types; Subject Advisory Committees dealing with hazards common to a variety of industries, occupations and the general public, and Industry Committees dealing with specific problems within a given industry.

Subject Committees were to 'provide a blanket cover of advisory services ranging through the whole spectrum of our [HSC] responsibilities' with membership to reflect both 'the composition of the Commission' and expertise 'in the appropriate disciplines'. From the start it was clear that the Commission wished to emphasise the practical utilisation of any recommendations which might be made. Thus the HSC stressed that membership reflecting the representative character of the Commission would enable it 'to make recommendations in the full knowledge of their implications for industry' and whilst each Committee 'should include a few highly esteemed experts ... the main weight of expert representation and also the technical deliberations would be within sub-committees appointed by the main committee' (HSC/9, 1974).

189

Three major Subject Advisory Committees were set up in the Commission's first year; toxic substances, dangerous substances and medical matters. The terms of reference of each Committee were very similar; to consider and advise the Commission on risks and problems associated with the relevant subject area. By 1987, four more Subject Committees had been established to cover dangerous pathogens, genetic manipulation, nuclear installations and the safe transport of radioactive materials. Working groups were also set up to examine particular problems. For example the HSC established an Asbestos Manufacturing Industry Working Group which together with CONIAC's Asbestos Working Party has produced guidance and other publicity material, as well as providing important inputs into the Asbestos (Prohibitions) Regulations, 1986 and the HSE guidance Note EH10 1984, which set out new control limits and guidance on air sampling and asbestos removal.

Industry Advisory Committees (IACs) were established on similar lines to the SACs, though their membership and terms of reference were somewhat narrower. Membership of IACs was to:

> reflect the representative character of the Commission and
> include representatives of the main organisations concerned,
> with assessors from Government Departments; minor interests
> should be represented only when they have a real contribution
> to make (HSC/9, 1974: 3).

The size and constitution of the IACs was to be decided upon after the CBI and the TUC had consulted appropriate member firms and unions. For their part, the HSC considered it essential that 'committees should be set up with the full agreement of both sides of the industry concerned' (HSC/1, 1978: 29).

Committee size was the subject of some negotiation. The HSC wished to limit the size of the major Subject Committees to a dozen members, which was also the preferred size of the Industry Committees. In practice, however, the size of each Committee is determined by the number of groups seeking representation. Thus for example the Railways Committee with three trade unions organising in the industry is the smallest, with 10 members, whilst the Health Services Committee is the largest with 26 members. All Committees have equal employer and trade union representation and are chaired by the Area Inspector of the appropriate National Industry Group of the Health and Safety Executive.

All IACs have similar terms of reference. For the majority, these are to consider and advise the HSC on: 'the protection of people at work from the hazards to health and safety arising from their occupations within the industry and the protection of the public from related hazards arising from such activities', and any 'other associated matters referred to them by the Commission or Executive' (HSC/9, 1974: 3). IACs, like the Subject Committees discussed earlier, are able to appoint their own subcommittees to consider particular aspects of subjects within their terms of reference. By 1985 the HSC reported that eleven IACs had been established, with a twelfth, for the wool textile and carpet industry, being in the process of creation out of an old Standing Joint Committee.

The role of the IACs

The Commission's first report set out in some detail the role and functions of the future IAC structure. The Consultative Document identified some 18 industries for which the Commission hoped to establish an advisory committee and the Report expressed a desire to develop committees in 'some twenty major industries', and to 'create more in the light of experience and as resources permit' (HSC/1, 1976: 61). IACs were seen as being both necessary for the development of national and local self regulation and an expression, in themselves, of the self regulatory process in action.

One of their primary functions was to bridge the gap between the more remote HSC and activity in the workplace, a link necessary for the self regulatory process envisaged by the Robens Report:

> The establishment of our commission arose from the decision
> to involve both sides of industry and local authorities in the
> development of solutions to particular problems. At the level of
> the workplace, the Act also provides a mechanism for joint
> consultation. We were conscious however that the available
> communication machinery might prove too remote to provide
> the ready feedback ... we decided that we required ... an
> advisory structure which would reflect the interests concerned
> (HSC/1, 1976: 9).

But in providing this link, the Committees simultaneously secured 'the effective participation of employers organisations and unions in the creation of safe systems work', the process at the very heart of the 'Robens Philosophy' (HSC/1, 1976: 59).

The form and terms of reference for the Advisory Committee structure reflected ideas of participation and consultation found in the Robens Report and its recommendations about the respective balance of statutory law, codes of practice and self regulation. Whilst the IACs were to 'provide a forum for continuous discussion between interested parties and to make expert advice available', they were to be more than a mechanism for the transmission of information between the various parts of the self regulatory machine. They were also to be 'an addition to, not a substitute for, our arrangements for general consultation', and to 'play an important part in the formulation of legislative proposals'.

The IACs were also seen to be important in terms of another aspect of the Robens analysis. In seeking to dispel the apathy which was felt to underly many industrial accidents, the Report pointed to the need to change the prevailing attitudes, to encourage interest and activity in the subject of occupational health and safety. Accordingly the HSC looked to the IACs 'for the major effort in developing positive attitudes from shop floor to senior management' (HSC/1, 1976: 59).

Thus the Advisory Committee structure was to provide for both consultation and participation at a national level which was seen as an important basis for local self regulation. As part of a wider consultative process and by virtue of the closer links between industry and expert opinion, their deliberations, reports and proposals would be better informed and, especially when legislation was considered, aware of the 'implications for industry'. IACs in particular were to provide a continuous and permanent forum for joint consultation between both sides of industry and would, by both example and work, provide the impetus for the change in attitudes necessary for effective self regulation. The HSC attached the 'highest importance to the effective working of industry advisory committees' (HSC/1, 1976: 61).

It is impossible to describe in anything but the briefest detail the work of the separate Advisory Committees. The cumulative body of research undertaken and subjects scrutinised is large. Rather than attempt a wide ranging assessment of their work, this section will examine one particular committee, the Construction Industry Advisory Committee, in order to illustrate the range of tasks undertaken.

The Construction Industry Advisory Committee

The Construction Industry Advisory Committee (CONIAC), one of the first to be established, was convened in 1978. Since a Joint Advisory Committee of the type discussed earlier was established in 1955, a certain degree of industry level collaboration between employers, trade unions and the Inspectorate had already been achieved. CONIAC's work therefore began by considering the reports on safety in demolition, steel erection and scaffolding prepared by the Joint Advisory Committee as well as identifying a number of other problems and processes requiring special attention. Amongst these, particular emphasis was placed on research into health and safety in construction and the coordination between this and the planned five year programme of the HSC; the wearing of safety helmets; the accuracy and quality of accident statistics in construction; prevailing attitudes towards safety in construction and ways of encouraging increased awareness of health and safety problems, especially in small and medium-sized firms. In order to study these particular problems in detail, the Committee convened four separate working parties, each containing one CBI and TUC member and chaired by HSE staff. CONIAC itself contained six CBI nominees, senior managers in large construction firms, and six TUC nominees, full-time officials from the appropriate unions recognised in the industry. The committee was chaired by the Director of the Construction National Industry Group, a Deputy Chief Inspector of Factories, and HSE staff acted as its secretariat.

The Committee later established four standing subcommittees to deal with the subjects of training, research, statistics and attitudes, and established further working parties to examine, amongst other things, the problems of specialist advice and safety officers, the provision of protective clothing, the wider issues of environmental health, multi-contractor sites, the use of asbestos and noise levels in the industry.

As a result of this work, the Committee has published a number of reports setting out its findings and giving guidance on a variety of topics. CONIAC's work on the provision and content of safety policies resulted in the publication of a guidance leaflet, 'Safety Policies', which was 'the first such document to be published under an IAC banner. More than 35,000 copies have been distributed to employer organisations, trades unions and individual firms' (HSE/7, 1982: 98). Other recent publications stem from the work of the standing subcommittee on statistics, guidance on the collection and use of accident information and the working party on advisory services.

CONIAC's work on the use and provision of safety helmets spilled over into the industry's industrial relations machinery. In August 1981, following the recommendations of CONIAC and the publication of an HSE discussion document, the wearing of safety helmets was introduced as one of the National Rules governing terms and conditions of service throughout the building and civil engineering industries. However, this did not have the desired effect and in 1985, after a symposium on head protection and on the advice of CONIAC, the HSC decided there was a need for regulations on the supply and use of safety helmets on construction sites and a consultative document was published.

The attitudes working party was initially responsible for the idea of the Site Safe 83 campaign which was discussed in Chapter 5. The principal aim

193

of the campaign was to

> bring about a permanent change in attitudes to safety by creating a greater awareness of the hazards and precautions which can control them, and by preaching the message that the remedies lie in the hands of everyone who works in, and with, the industry – from client to architect and engineer, from labourer to chairman, from multi-national contractor to self-employed roofer (HSE/7, 1982: 99).

In order to effect this change in attitudes, the Inspectors in the National Industry Groups coordinated a wide variety of activities including the distribution of leaflets, newsletters, promotional materials and a Site Safe Pack outlining the scope and consequences of the industry's safety problem. Seminars, talks, discussion groups, exhibitions, etc. were arranged to spread the work and involve even the smallest companies in the industry. Thus, according to the HSE, the campaign saw

> the growing involvement and active participation of many companies, trades unions, federations, safety organisations and insurance and professional interests in the preparation of information and guidance material and the development of programmes to promote the aims of the campaign (HSE/7, 1982: 91).

We have seen however that the statistics on the combined rate of fatal and major accidents in the construction industry show that the campaign was not successful in reducing the likelihood of serious injury. Nonetheless the HSE and CONIAC determined to try to maintain the momentum generated in the campaign. Thus the HSE construction group continued to issue its twice yearly 'Site Safe News' and in June 1987 CONIAC launched a booklet of general importance to the industry. Entitled 'Managing Health and Safety in Construction: Principles and Application to Main Contractor/Subcontractor Projects', the booklet deals with the responsibilities of all main participants including clients, architects and subcontractors as well as main contractors, and provides advice on how to draw up safe systems of work on construction sites. The discussion in Chapter 5 illustrated the importance of these considerations in any attempt to improve standards of safety in the construction industry.

There can be little doubt that the activities described above have proved CONIAC to be more than a 'talking shop', which has aimed to fulfil the range of functions originally envisaged by the HSC. It has produced and coordinated the research necessary for the publication of guidance notes, provided literature giving advice on legal compliance, acted as a forum for joint consultation and, in the work of the standing committee on attitudes and the Site Safe campaign, attempted to encourage greater safety consciousness throughout the industry, paying special attention to medium-sized and small firms.

An evaluation of this work depends, as always, on the criteria adopted. The Committee has without doubt attempted to do all that has been asked of it by the HSC, extending the scope and content of subjects discussed at industry level far beyond that of the previous Joint Advisory Committee. Criticisms of CONIAC relate not to the content of the work undertaken, but more to its effectiveness in reaching the darker corners of the industry it is designed to serve, for example, in the scope of the consultation undertaken.

Membership of CONIAC on the employers' side is drawn from the larger firms in the industry and their representatives are aware of the difficulties of influencing smaller firms. The Site Safe 83 campaign was aimed particularly at these smaller firms but the HSE admitted that 'the message may not be getting through to the smaller end of the industry nor even to site level in the case of some larger contractors who have senior management commitment to the campaign' (HSE/7, 1982: 95). Some would argue that this reflects the fact that attempts to change attitudes to safety in the Site Safe campaign actually ignored the very conditions which allowed them to breed (Glendon and Hale 1983). Attempts to change behaviour, for example by encouraging the wearing of safety helmets, have largely been unsuccessful, despite this specific example being written into the working rules covering the terms and conditions of employment within the industry. The increase in the combined incidence rate for fatal and major accidents in the industry since Site Safe year, discussed in Chapters 2 and 5, does suggest that although significant efforts have been directed at the problem of construction safety at national level, their impact at site level is limited.

It is notable that the terms of reference and composition of CONIAC, together with those of other national advisory institutions, have encouraged exclusion of controversial issues from their agendas. They are more concerned with issuing model procedures of guidance on best practice and their pronouncements are generally couched in as non-controversial terms as possible. For example, CONIAC has not considered issues associated with the appointment of safety representatives, the level of fines or the staffing levels of the Inspectorate even though these are topics which the pages of union journals show to be issues of great interest to trade union representatives.

For the present such matters fall outside the terms of reference of the Committees and are the concern of other bodies such as the HSE, the HSC, the government, or national industrial relations institutions. For example, the appointment of safety representatives is the subject of a Working Rule negotiated through the normal industrial relations machinery regulating the industry's terms and conditions of service, and thus issues relating to safety representatives would properly be raised in this forum rather than in CONIAC.

Nonetheless other IACs have concerned themselves with some of those more controversial issues. For example, the Rubber IAC expressed some concern about levels of HSE staffing and aspects of HSC policy. Accordingly this IAC asked the chair of HSC to report on those areas of concern at the IAC meeting in June 1987.[1]

The contribution of CONIAC and other IACs

Judged against their general aims and terms of reference, IACs have been successful. They have improved consultation between both sides of industry and between industry itself and the Inspectorate and they have been central to the process of establishing regulations and codes of practice. Drawing attention to the fact that it has over 100 representatives in Subject and Industry Advisory Committees, the TUC attached 'particular importance' to the participation of these representatives, welcomed 'the greatly extended opportunities' to influence the scope and content of new proposals they offered unions and argued that they

> provided an opportunity for unions to promote new initiatives to protect their members in particular industries and services (House of Commons 1982: 33).

The CBI, though a little more grudging in its enthusiasm for the new machinery, admitted that

> a number of gaps have been filled and systems have been strengthened by the creation of Industry Advisory Committees (House of Commons 1982: 3).

It noted 'with satisfaction' the establishment of National Industry Groups (NIGs), drew attention to the fact that joint consultation had been 'fostered' in the IACs, NIGs and other similar structures and offered the opinion that

> The IACs set up by the Commission have played a useful part in guiding and overseeing training on a tripartite basis (House of Commons 1982: 7–8).

The HSC itself has stressed the importance of the Advisory Committee structure. When asked to consider the value of the Advisory Committee structure during Sir Leo Pliatzky's examination of non-governmental bodies, the Commission reported that the work of the Advisory Committees was very important and

> one of the most cost effective ways of putting into practice the underlying philosophy behind the HSW Act ... they encourage participation in the improvement of health and safety at work, enable us to draw on the expertise and advice available on both sides of industry and elsewhere and can give particular hazards or the problems of particular industries, closer and more detailed attention than we could ourselves. We have no doubt that policies worked out in this way ... are much more likely to be more realistic and to be implemented in practice at the workplace than those developed by officials alone (HSC Report 1979–80: p. 8, para. 38).

The Advisory Committee structure has generally been well received by those bodies participating in it. In particular the CBI and TUC defended it against criticism of the scope of its consultation and its speed in reaching and issuing recommendations (House of Commons 1982). However, both the TUC and the HSC have regretted that a shortage of resources in both their institutions is one factor in curbing the expansion of the structure. The original plan, to set up Advisory Committees in the 20 industries first mentioned in the consultative document, has not yet been achieved and the TUC have complained that they have 'a list from the TUC unions in various industries who want to have an industry advisory committee ...' (House of Commons 1982: 55).

HSC policy at present is to 'build on existing joint consultation arrangements wherever possible (HSC/3, 1983: 16). In consequence, priority is given to the upgrading of Joint Standing Committees into fully constituted Industry Advisory Committees. For example an IAC in the cotton industry has been established to replace the old Standing Committee. This policy of upgrading undoubtedly widens the scope of consultation and the potential for action at industry level. But some groups of employers prefer to stay with the older institutions. For example, the Chemical Industries Association (CIA) have argued that

> The chemical industry does not currently have an IAC and in view of the good liaison between HSC and CISHEC [Chemical Industries Safety Health and Environmental Council] on one hand and the existence of the NJAC [National Joint Advisory

197

Council] on the other, there would seem to be no strong case for a statutory chemical IAC (House of Comons 1982: 18).

However the Chief Inspector of Factories Report 1985 comments that although CISHEC functions with representation from CIA, observer status for HSE and includes input from the NJAC (a joint trade union–employer body), it is not a truly tripartite body and thus the full benefits of such discussions are not available.

It is impossible to assess whether the attitude of employers has hindered the development of the Advisory Committee structure. Whilst the opposition of the CIA is an example of employers' traditional distaste for replacing voluntary arrangements with formally constituted committees, it is possible that opposition in other industrial sectors is motivated by a desire to keep the unions at 'arms length'. Occasionally too some trade unions are reluctant to disturb established machinery like CISHEC and NJAC.

Recent trends in HSC activity

The preference for proceeding through consultation and consensus rather than through diktat and imposition has been a major influence on the HSC since its inception. In recent years this characteristic has, if anything, been stressed with even more clarity and commitment than it was in 1974. In its Plan of Work, 1985–86, the task of the HSC together with the HSE, was identified as establishing and maintaining 'an acceptable pattern of behaviour in others'. Its aims are

(a) to stimulate and guide the efforts of industry to achieve higher standards of health and safety at a cost that is realistic
(b) to protect both people at work and the public, who may be affected by risks arising from work activities and keep them properly informed about the risks and the protective measures adopted (HSC/8, 1985: 2).

The plan proceeds to emphasise that the HSC and HSE must work through consultation and encouragement, and that these can be pursued by using a variety of routes of which investigation and enforcement are but two. The Commission is intent on trying to establish the 'right climate' in which it is hoped the various parties will then be motivated to act in accordance with the self regulatory spirit of the Act. Thus in commenting on the rise in fatal accidents in agriculture the HSC Report (1984–85) emphasises that there is a need for the industry to develop

> a more positive attitude to safety. The inspectorate will
> continue with its efforts to encourage and ensure safe practices,
> but the onus lies properly with industry itself (HSC/4, 1985:
> 14).

The HSC comments in its Plan of Work 1985–86 that while it has found it to be feasible to issue general regulations, approved codes and guidance notes underpinned by section 2 of the Act, it nonetheless has found that the 'drafting of codes that give guidance in sufficiently specific terms without an effect that binds industry too closely to particular solutions is a considerable technical challenge' (HSC/8, 1985: 16). Experience has shown that it needs a good deal of time and goodwill to convey the necessary information and secure consensus. This reserve accounts in part for the emphasis which the HSC now gives in some circumstances to providing guidance and advice backed solely by the general provisions of the HASAW Act rather than specific regulations. The HSC reports that it expects to put comparatively less time into making regulations and policy and more into their implementation and evaluation in the future (HSC/8, 1985: 18). Evaluation will proceed within the assumption that, as earlier, firms have scarce resources and have to consider 'the costs' of any action and whether it be 'required' or 'advised'.

Coupled with a decreasing emphasis on specific regulations, comes a greater emphasis on the benefits which can accrue from collaboration with those involved in setting standards, notably the British Standards Institute. 'We regard standard making as an economical and effective route to safety and health and intend to continue to make a major contribution to the development of the British standards system' (HSC/8, 1985: 17). Elsewhere we find another justification for the virtues of 'adequate industrial standards' for products not only as defining safety requirements but also as contributing generally (to industry through) the quality and competitiveness of British goods (HSC/2, 1982: para. 6).

Recent suggestions from the HSC show that it has looked beyond the British Standards Institute to other 'outsiders' who could be the 'prime mover' in initiatives which could amongst other things, secure improvements in health and safety standards. In reviewing their work in the ten years since HASAWA, the HSC identified two important potential collaborators in this context; insurance companies and the safety departments of large companies. On insurance companies they comment that 'their natural interest in maintaining a downward trend in accidents and, much more potent, their fear of future claims on risks that cannot easily be estimated, raised the question of whether their role could be expanded under statute, either in support of, or in replacement of present activity by others' (HSC/8, 1985: para. 263). The argument is developed by a proposal for discussion that the HSC could husband its scarce resources and fulfil its role as a 'facilitator and information giver' (HSC/8, 1985: para. 257) by encouraging, and then as it were informally licensing, internal systems of 'health and safety assurance' within large enterprises.[2] It is suggested that enterprises would qualify for entry into a health and safety assurance scheme if the following conditions applied:

(a) the employer had a comprehensive health and safety policy;
(b) the organisational arrangements were acceptable and the management was competent;
(c) appropriate resources were available for health and safety;
(d) there was securely established specialist health and safety expertise in-house;
(e) there was active trade union involvement in safety and health with positive employee commitment and relevant institutions;
(f) the enterprise had a satisfactory recent record in relation to accidents and ill-health;
(g) the arrangements were fully acceptable both to the employer and the employee representatives concerned (HSC/8, 1985: para. 270).

The HSE under such a scheme would have a role in investigating particular kinds of circumstance, like major incidents or those attracting public concern, and would have to be informed of new technical developments or particular problems. Apart from this, most workplaces would be left, within the law, to operate their own systems. Such autonomy would, the HSC argued, be a 'natural inducement' to firms to 'maintain satisfactory safety and health conditions and to utilise and develop existing institutions within the firm for that purpose' (HSC/8, 1985: para. 270). The arrangements would also help to economise on scarce inspection resources. However, questions remain – as we have shown – concerning the capacity and willingness to support such systems at workplace level.

This specific proposal and other aspects of the general thrust of the HSC Plan of Work were strongly opposed by some trade unions, particularly those which are notable for their concern for and investment in health and safety: ASTMS, NALGO, BFU, GMBATU and the union (IPCS) which represents the field force of HSE Inspectors. A resolution at the 1986 TUC Congress expressed grave concern about the poor performance of much of British industry in matters of health and safety at work; it also deplored the decreasing resources for the HSE and called for stronger and extended action by the HSC and HSE. The resolution emphasised the need for more effective consultation between the General Council and affiliated unions.

Prompted by these debates the TUC General Council was instructed by its 1986 Congress to prepare a ten year plan for health and safety. As part of this process the General Council prepared a draft statement for discussion entitled 'The Way Forward' (November 1986) and the GMBATU prepared its own 'charter' under the title 'Hazards at Work' (GMBATU 1987). The draft TUC statement condemns the proposals contained in Chapter 6 of the HSC's Plan of Work (HSC/8) as an unacceptable departure from a commitment to regular inspection by an independent enforcement authority.

Evaluating the HSC

A review of the activities of the HSC by the House of Commons Employment Committee in 1982 noted the success of the tripartite venture, welcoming 'the consensus between employers and unions which has developed since the passing of the Health and Safety at Work Act and the Establishment of the Commission' (House of Commons 1982: v). This consensus emerged in the evidence of both the CBI and TUC. The CBI had commended the 'constructive tripartite structure' of the HSC and its achievement in building 'effective consensus and an increased commitment from both sides of industry to an extensive programme of legislation'. They acknowledged that the HSC had 'helped to make the legislation more practicable and more easily understandable', had 'taken the party politics out of health and safety', had 'permitted cooler examination of the facts behind proposals', and had 'taken some of the emotion out of issues', for example manual handling, major hazards, the carriage of dangerous goods (1982: 4).

The TUC, for its part, took the view that the HSC 'provides an effective structure within which health and safety arrangements and systems can be developed in Britain'; it further endorsed the Robens principle that 'arrangements for the control of occupational risks must be evolved by, and must be acceptable to, those who create such risks and those who have to work with them' (1982: 31). In verbal evidence, the TUC representatives refused the Committee's invitation to identify industries which had failed to comply with the Act, drawing the remark eventually from the Chair that 'you put up a far better defence for the employers than they managed themselves' (1982: 50–1, 57).

The two sides did not agree on everything. The main sources of disagreement were on resources and costs. The TUC was worried about the decline in resource provision both by recession-hit employers and by the government in the funding of the Inspectorate (see Chapter 9). The CBI drew some ire from members of the Committee with the proposal that 'The HSC must recognise that industry's capacity to produce wealth, provide employment and compete effectively in overseas markets are priorities just as vital as the maintenance of good health and safety standards'. The basis of good regulation was, they argued, cost-benefit analysis (1982: 2, 36).

The Employment Committee itself was not as uncritical as the protagonists. The HSC came in for criticism of its pace and volume of work, its public profile and lack of 'flair and vigour' in communications. The Committee were further concerned that consensus on legislation 'might have been at the expense of reasonable expedition or progress in controversial areas' (1982: v). Nonetheless for all the reservations expressed, the tripartite structure was endorsed by the Employment Committee and agreed, by the major interests concerned, to be an appropriate regulatory framework.

Several reasons can be advanced for this agreement. One factor may be that criticism by participants would involve admission of a degree of contributary failure. Protection of the institution also involves protection of influential positions. Both the TUC and CBI achieve a leadership and influence role in the HSC – 'the most corporatist body in Britain' (Wilson 1985: 113) – with respect to their constituents which they do not achieve in many other areas. The CBI in particular acts both as a lobby and as a target for lobbying activity in the HSC, but in few other decision making arenas.

Wilson (1985) found the TUC's satisfaction with the HSC more surprising than that of the CBI. To judge from their comments in the verbal evidence, members of the House of Commons Employment Committee were also perplexed. After all, the main criticism of the HSC was the protracted period it took to reach decisions on regulations, and in this case the failure to reach agreement is not neutral, since 'it gives advantage to employers and disadvantage to employees in equal measure' (Wilson 1985: 114). Moreover, in emphasising consensual decision making, the structure gives each party the opportunity to attempt to veto proposals. On the other hand consensus is seen as important since it is assumed that external enforcement of safety standards alone is not a feasible strategy for safety at work. It can also be argued that long periods of consultation give employers time to adjust to and accept higher standards than they would have accepted initially. By the same token, however, it does mean that the unions and expert advisers may also be persuaded to accept lower standards.

Two further factors underpin the TUC's commitment. The first is that the HSC is, with NEDC and the Manpower Services Commission, one of the few remaining tripartite arrangements in a climate generally inimical to them.[3] Although the government showed no sign in the early 1980s of abolishing the HSC, the TUC may have felt that overt criticism of the sort that can be heard in certain parts of the trade union movement would not improve its chances of survival.

Finally, there is the insulation of HSC activities from the courts. The HSC regulations have gone unchallenged in parliament or the courts. In presenting evidence to the Employment Committee the Chairman linked this to the length of consultation periods. Consequently the TUC or its constituent unions have not had to fight battles with the judiciary, as they have in other spheres of labour legislation recently.

However, one cannot assume that support from the trade unions will continue regardless of shifts in central policy. Pressures for the redirection of policy away from deregulation were clearly in evidence in the debates within the trade union movement which were prompted by the publication of the HSC's Plan of Work 1985–86 and culminated in the critical resolutions passed at the 1986 TUC. Nonetheless, the prevailing view is that whilst campaigns for change are important, support will still continue for the existing national structure, as the best available in the present political and legal context.

Contrasting the consensual basis of health and safety policy in the UK with more combative relations between the parties in the USA, Wilson suggests that with the exception of a small but important number of officials of individual unions, both employers and unions are satisfied with the procedures of the HSC: 'safety and health at work has by and large been taken out of politics as a general issue' (1985: 30). In any event challenge in the courts is much more likely in the US where regulations are made by an independent Agency with no obligation or inclination to consult, than in the UK where regulations are made on the recommendations of the tripartite Commission by the Secretary of State subject to parliament.

There is a view that as Britain is now required to ensure harmonisation with EEC regulations, there are pressures which will move the orientation of the British system more in the direction of the US model. Regulations which arise from EEC activities are thought to be less likely to secure the commitment and support of important representatives of employers.

Pressures in the opposite direction, to take the HSC further away from the US model and to reinforce commitment to proceedings with due regard to the interests of employers as well as employees, have come from successive Conservative governments supported by the Scrutiny Report by Lord Rayner (HSC/19, 1984). In 1979, the then Secretary of State for Employment explicitly required the HSC to take into account the economic consequences of new regulations. The argument advanced here was that the worst problems of industrial safety had been overcome and therefore that further improvements needed to be justified in terms of a quantification of their costs and benefits. The application of a cost-benefit approach in this context is thus directed towards assessing the effects of future regulations, not towards a reappraisal of the costs of regulations already made. The issue of cost-benefit analysis is one of the subjects given further consideration in the concluding chapter of this book.

The opinion of the Conservative government since 1979 is that industry in the UK has had too much regulation. This is said to apply particularly to small businesses. An official statement of this view is contained in the 1985 White Paper, 'Lifting the Burden'. It proposed, among a number of other measures affecting both the HSC and the Inspectorates, that one of the Commissioners be designated to represent 'the interests of small business' (Cmnd 9571, 1985: 23). This reflects the government's more general view that the burden of regulation 'is that much greater on small businesses where the owner/manager is wholly responsible for all aspects of the business and the people he or she employs' (Cmnd 9571, 1985: 2). It is reinforced by proposals to raise the threshold of the requirement on employers to prepare a written safety policy from 5 to 20 employees and to give specific training to Inspectors to increase their awareness of small firms' interests (Cmnd 9571, 1985: 23).

A subsequent White Paper 'Building Businesses ... Not Barriers (Cmnd 9794, 1986) outlined progress on the 'Lifting the Burden' package and reported progress on 'Safety Assurance Schemes'. Significantly it also made proposals for systematically reviewing existing regulations as well as scrutinising future proposals.

The impact of these proposals on the safety standards and the practice of inspection particularly in small firms will be discussed further in Chapters 9 and 10. In this chapter we should note their relevance for the structure of the HSC. One of the premises of tripartism has been the assumption that the represented interest groups have the ability to present the views of, and to communicate decisions to, all employers and employees. We have seen in the case studies that small firms tend to fall outside the ambit of local self regulation and enforcement; the White Paper suggestions imply that they have fallen outside the scope of tripartism in that they now require special attention. To the extent that there are more interest groups, for example employees in workplaces without recognised unions or the self-employed, who could be given a voice on the HSC, its coverage of industry and influence over safety standards might be enhanced, but this would be likely to be at the expense of the current rapprochement between the TUC and CBI.

Summary and conclusions

The HSC's activities of collecting and disseminating information and making policy, regulations and guidance are all interlinked and imbued with the spirit of consultation and the hope of consensus. Even the greatest optimists who sat on, or gave evidence to, the Robens Committee had to admit that at local level, given the scarcity of resources, there would sometimes be conflict over what to do and how to do it, if one were to secure acceptable levels of health and safety in the workplace. However, the hope was that at the national institutional level, through providing information, advice and guidance, and establishing forums for discussion and extensive consultation with interested parties, the HSC could stimulate and nurture consensus which would then have an impact, both substantively in terms of specific regulations and procedurally in terms of patterns of behaviour between and within interested parties at local level. Never in its reports does the HSC suggest that there are ever fundamental reasons for a lack of agreement on safety policy and practice between the main interested parties.

The Commission and the Executive both freely adopt the CBI's language of the applicability of 'cost-benefit' analysis to aspects of health and safety provision without addressing the issue of whether, if the costs are borne more by one party and the benefits more by another, it is difficult to 'arrive' at a simple judgement of the utility and desirability of implementing certain proposals. This approach raises two important questions. First, can consensus be established at national level and, if so, has this actually happened and to what effect? Secondly, what is the impact of national developments on local activities?

In answer to the first question it seems that a general level of consensus can be achieved at national level. This facilitates the pronouncement of regulations which, unlike in the USA, have the support of important sectors of industry and which certainly have a positive influence upon the conduct of some employers and employees. The 'price' of this achievement is fairly slow progress with securing agreement on codes of practice, regulations and policy, and a lack of specificity in some regulations which eventually are given statutory authority.

An alternative to this consensual approach is furnished by the 'adversarial' independence of OSHA in the USA. However, this appears to be less successful in terms of influencing behaviour of those involved in industry except possibly where the prevailing political climate is strongly in favour of regulation as it was in the USA under President Carter. In the USA of President Reagan or the UK of Mrs Thatcher where there is a strong movement away from regulation in all areas of industrial life, there is very little chance that an adversarial approach at national level can achieve more than a consensual approach. On the contrary it seems that in terms of actually influencing behaviour so as to reduce accidents and improve standards overall, the consensual approach is likely to be more successful in a climate of deregulation. Those who suggest that either the substantive or procedural aspects of national policy making for health and safety at work can be kept separate from wider political issues are, in our view, misguided, whatever the political stance. Whether, to oversimplify, in favour or against external regulation, the political climate will have a profound effect upon the operation of national institutions for health and safety.

On the second question, concerning the impact of national developments on local activities, conclusions must also be tentative. The example of CONIAC and the local activities of construction firms are relevant here. There is a significant relationship between the activities and declarations of CONIAC and the activities and policies of larger firms which is secured through common membership and a shared concern for the public image and social responsibility of the industry. However, many smaller firms are more or less untouched by CONIAC and, it seems, will only begin to be more responsive within the present framework of law if required to be so through the terms and conditions of contracts between clients, main contractors and subcontractors and/or through tough enforcement by Inspectors.

The tripartite structure at national level can only be as good as its various parts, although the hope is clearly that, through interaction, the collectivity will assume increased strength and sense of purpose. Nevertheless, the good intentions of the parties at national level can only be translated into good safety practice by endorsement of their objectives within particular workplaces. The role of inspection and enforcement becomes of paramount importance where such endorsement is lacking, and it is to this aspect of safety at work which we now turn.

9

Inspectors and enforcers: regulation and compliance

One of the fundamental aspects of efforts to enforce legal control over conditions of work in Britain has long been to secure the observance of laws and regulations through the efforts of specially appointed public officials. With a history of more than a century and a half, the Factory Inspectors have firmly established a strong and particular tradition in dealing with health and safety at work which is central to any understanding of its regulation. The Environmental Health Officers, who took over some of the work of enforcing standards of health and safety at work as a result of the OSRP Act 1963 and the 1974 HASAWA, also have a long history of enforcing health standards and a major role in securing safe working conditions.

This chapter is devoted to a discussion of the origins and developments of these methods of inspection and enforcement and their effect on current practices and likely future trends. It is divided into four sections. The first deals with the history and philosophy of the Factory Inspectorate and Environmental Health Officers. Two sections then follow on the present structure and practice of inspection and enforcement as established by the 1974 Act and subsequent Regulations. The concluding section deals with issues in enforcement policy and, in particular, with debates about appropriate degrees of centralisation and the extent to which compliance with the law can and should be secured through evaluation and guidance and the use of punitive sanctions.

Inspection and enforcement before 1974

The Factory Inspectorate

The appointment of the first Factory Inspectors under the provisions of the 1833 Factory Act was a clear indication that whatever faith nineteenth-century legislators might place in the laws of political economy and the operation of the market, they still found it necessary to rely on an element

207

of state regulation and collectivism (MacDonagh 1958; Taylor 1972: 42; Bartrip, 1979: 2). Factory Inspectors have always loomed large in accounts of nineteenth-century social reform. They have been described as 'perhaps the most important innovation in British labour legislation', and have been seen as precursors of a general administrative system, even as models to be emulated around the world (Wedderburn 1971: 239; Djang 1942).

A wide range of Inspectors of other sorts dealing with matters ranging from educational standards to atmospheric pollution have been noticed and studied (Rhodes 1981; Richardson, Ogus and Burrows 1982; Hawkins 1984). A supporting role in this drama of administrative development has been attributed to Inspectors of Nuisance and Sanitary Inspectors, appointed locally as a result of legislation from 1848 to 1871, and the precursors of modern Environmental Health Officers. Gradually their role in dealing with matters of public health and hygiene increased until in the 1970s they were given particular responsibilities for health and safety at work (Johnson 1983; Martin 1978; Paulus 1974; Hutter 1984).

A good deal of recent analysis of the various Inspectorates has been concerned to explain the limitations on the strict and continuous enforcement of the laws and regulations for which they are responsible. Inspectors of every sort have always engaged in a wide range of activities short of wielding the full majesty of the law. They have always negotiated in some way with those subject to legal regulation and tried to persuade people of the principles and practices that would help them to avoid coming into conflict with the law. This was inevitable during the early period of the Factory Inspectorate in the mid nineteenth century, when Inspectors had to enforce the length of a working day they could not ceaselessly monitor and regulate the employment of women and children when they could not always expect to obtain full information.

There were limits also on what they were able to do when they were drawn into issues related to safety at work, most notably the fencing of machinery (Hale 1978: 90; Bartrip 1979). Efforts to secure safety were never seen as the continual enforcement of a set of fixed regulations, although a different impression has sometimes been gained as a result of the attention given to Leonard Horner, the first Inspector of the Lancashire district. He was a 'passionate innovator' who actively enforced the law and campaigned publicly and privately to change it. He won praise from Karl Marx in *Das Kapital* for his 'invaluable service to the English working class' and from trade union leaders for his 'administration of the laws made for the protection of our wives and children' (Martin 1969: 432; Lyell 1890: II, 371). Horner's interventionist style took on this historical reputation precisely because it was unusual amongst his contemporaries and successors. Much more typical was the statement of one of his fellow

Inspectors that they should be 'refraining from all angry discussion and altercation' (Thomas 1948: 259; Hale 1978: 106).

From the earliest days individual Inspectors could never be in a position consistently to enforce all the laws and regulations that parliament had made. In the first place, they had large numbers of places to inspect, though by no means as many as a modern Inspector; they were also frustrated by the leniency of those on judicial benches. Furthermore, manufacturers soon found that they themselves could affect the impact of legislation so as to make it a good deal less onerous for them. Thus few employers were greatly inconvenienced when laws were introduced to bring about the fencing of machinery in the 1850s (Bartrip and Fenn 1980: 95; Bartrip 1979: 44). In the generation that succeeded Leonard Horner, Inspectors explicitly acknowledged this change. Thus Alexander Redgrave told the 1876 Commission on Factory and Workshop Acts that he considered it 'erroneous' to aim for 'strict compliance' with the law. The aim of the Inspectors should be 'to *explain* the law' and then to 'do everything we possibly could to *induce* [all classes] to obey the law'. In the opinion of the most influential Inspector since Horner, 'a prosecution should be the very last thing we should take up' (Bartrip 1985; Bartrip and Fenn 1980: 98; Carson 1979: 52; Hale 1978: 38).

Each generation since the appointment of Alexander Redgrave as Chief Inspector in 1878 has re-emphasised the view that the laws and regulations which they were called upon to enforce were not susceptible of continuing and unremitting enforcement. Thus in 1920 an internal report said that 'what may be called the police duties of the inspectors are becoming less and less important'. The 1932 Annual Report of the Chief Inspector of Factories spoke once again of 'advice', 'rather than compulsion'. During the Second World War administrative scientist William Robson described the Inspector as 'a humane public official who achieves most by winning the confidence of the employees and the good-will of the employers'. During that same period, this same official was thought to have become 'less of an inspector, more of an investigator and administrator' (Rhodes 1981: 67; Hale 1978: 39; Djang 1942: 16, 204). By the 1960s this view of the functioning of the Inspectors had become so commonplace that when their daily routines were opened to outsiders the same distinct emphasis on conciliation, persuasion and education was found, and the same reluctance to prosecute or punish (Carson 1970b; Law Commission 1970).

There has been some debate about the reasons underlying the development of this style of enforcement. There have been those who have argued that the limited use of legal sanctions was a result of the success of private entrepreneurs over humanitarian lawmakers. For others the pattern of enforcement has to be seen as a function of the organisation of the Inspectorate and the technical methods available to enforce standards which make it difficult for them to arrive at comprehensive coverage or to secure large numbers of convictions. Their failure to prosecute very often was simply an example of 'cost-effective enforcement techniques' (Carson 1979: 37; Bartrip and Fenn 1980: 101; Carson 1980; Bartrip and Fenn 1983: 202). For others, the pattern of enforcement reflects the nature of compliance and transgression which in turn are affected by technical and resource considerations. For example Veljanovski (1981) argues that an analogy between safety offences and many other criminal offences is ill conceived. This is because the offence is rarely a positive act but a failure to comply, and also because it is rarely a discrete but more often a continuing event. Furthermore, it is perpetrated in organisations where responsibility is often diffuse and where, if transgression occurs and an Inspector visits, then both the enforcer and offender know each other. Hawkins (1984) in similar vein argues that where deviance is categorical, a penal response is triggered. However, when deviance is continuing, repetitive or episodic, that is a 'state of affairs' or 'a set of problems' then enforcement cannot be of a 'once for all variety' but must depend in part on an incremental approach in which a relationship is created between enforcer and miscreant in an attempt to 'educate' to better performance. The validity of these various arguments both as a basis for descriptive analysis and policy making will be the subject of discussion in the last section of this chapter.

For whatever reason, a pattern was established where breaches of the law were often undetected and where they were detected, prosecution and punishment did not always follow. The Inspectors only went to the courts in cases of flagrant and persistent breaches of safety regulations, or where serious accidents were the result of manifest negligence. In a study carried out in 1969 by the Law Commission it was found that the Inspectorate only generally instituted proceedings where they considered the firm was seriously at fault. Even in the days before 1974 when Factory Inspectors had to deal mainly with more specific regulations, they regarded themselves more as educators and publicists than as enforcers or prosecutors (Law Commission 1970; Carson 1970a, 1970b; Djang 1942).

Thus attitudes to enforcement by Factory Inspectors have shown a striking continuity amidst many variations in political and social circumstances over many decades. This is not to say that the role and organisation of the Inspectorate has remained unchanged. After some pressure from the Trades Union Congress and elsewhere dating from 1878, 'workmen inspectors' were first appointed in 1893. In the same year the first women Inspectors were appointed against the publicly stated objections of the Chief Inspector, and women have remained part of the Inspectorate ever since (HSE/17, 1983: 18–20). Until the 1890s it was predominantly an employment Inspectorate, and thereafter there was a 'steady transformation into a safety inspectorate'. Only in the 1930s were there actually more prosecutions on safety than other matters (Hale 1978: 94; Rhodes 1981: 67). As a result of this, and developments in industrial processes and techniques, the Inspectors became increasingly concerned with scientific and technical matters. The particularly complex regulations which came with the 1937 Factory Act hastened this process, and the 1944 Annual Report of the Chief Inspector said that for the future Inspectors 'the technical and advice side of their work will become more and more important' (Hale 1978: 143). However, there always remained something of the gentleman or (occasionally) lady amateur about the Factory Inspector; as late as 1974 only 60% of Inspectors had technical qualifications, though many steps have since been made to develop every possible technical skill.

Together with increasing emphasis on the technical matters came moves to establish a more systematic administration. In 1929 a departmental committee, while resisting pressure to increase the numbers of the Inspectors or their use of sanctions, nevertheless set out for the first time details of the criteria and timing of their visits (Henderson 1929). In 1940 the new Minister of Labour, Ernest Bevin, took the Inspectorate out from its historic place in the Home Office 'where it was in danger of being identified with police, prisons and the control of vice', and placed it in an expanded Ministry of Labour where it became associated with employment policy more generally and even with overall government intervention in the economy (Bullock 1967: 78).

The emphasis upon self regulation which had always been implicit in enforcement practices also became more apparent. As early as 1911 a departmental committee reported on the need to ensure that those occupying factory premises should be persuaded to take 'constant daily care' in carrying out a number of precautions. The Inspectorate took an interest in the 'Safety First' movement which developed as a result of concern for industrial conditions during the First World War, and advocated better management techniques and forms of self regulation. In 1922 Chief Inspector Bellhouse thought they could 'bring to the notice of employers the good results which have followed from efficient organisations'. However, such efforts were not always crowned with success. 'Progress in the establishment of safety organisations', it was discovered in 1926, had in fact been 'disappointingly slow'. By 1931 Chief Inspector Sir Duncan Wilson had grown somewhat sanguine about efforts to encourage safety committees and came to the view that 'the scope of an inspector's activities in this direction is inevitably limited'. He was also unhappy with the tendency to replace joint organisation with safety officers who were part of management, since this created the danger of seeing 'safety conditions as matters for the management, and that any suggestions from the workers might be looked on as unwarranted interference'. A generation later in 1961, the Chief Inspector was still bemoaning the fact that 'too many firms have no safety organisation whatsoever' (Rhodes 1981: 68–9, 71; Hale 1978: 139–40).

By the time health and safety at work once again because a major issue for public discussion in the 1960s the role of the Inspectorate had been clearly established. One survey of the reports of the HM Chief Inspectors of Factories in the century before the 1974 Act found them 'biased towards an optimistic view of the inspectorate and the importance of their role' (Renton 1975). By 1970 there is no doubt that the Inspectorate had developed a reputation for professional expertise and understanding which derived less from their scientific and technical qualifications than from their reputation as patrician administrators stretching back over many generations. They were firmly of the view that they were educators rather than policemen and this is a theme which runs through the Robens Report and the legislation. The evidence presented to the Committee by the Department of Employment emphasised that the Inspectors 'as a matter of policy' had 'in recent years spent more time in giving advice' and had initiated prosecutions 'only in relatively rare cases, e.g. of flagrant or persistent transgression'. Hence the view of the Department of Employment and the Inspectorate – that 'the future development of legislation' would be 'more in measures designed to influence attitudes than to detailed regulation of particular hazards and conditions' (Robens 1972b: 174, 210).

Not all the evidence to the Robens Committee supported this view. For example, the TUC evidence disputed the view that 'the purpose of prosecution is simply to punish for past failure to comply', arguing that 'the inspectorate must necessarily rely on the threat of prosecution as the only means of securing compliance with the law' (Robens 1972b: 686). Others also supported this view. For example, W. H. Thompson, a solicitor with widespread experience of litigation on compensation for accidents, expressed a point of view very different from that accepted, presented and subsequently introduced into legislation:

> In theory the Factories Act is enforced by the Factory
> Inspectorate. In practice the Act is not enforced at all.…
> Undoubtedly if the Factories Act was enforced the number of
> industrial injuries would be substantially reduced (Robens
> 1972b: 660–1).

According to Thompson the problem with the earlier legislation was not so much that it was too complicated, but that no serious effort was made to enforce it. He argued that despite many similar problems about tracking down offenders, nobody would advocate dealing with 'careless, reckless and dangerous driving' by education and the punishment of only the most persistent offenders. For all the difficulties in detection there was no dispute that every effort should be made to pursue all dangerous drivers.

> Why is there no similar provision in respect of industrial hazards? Are not many industrial accidents – probably most of them – caused by the negligence of persons in control of industrial enterprises? Does anyone doubt that? Why is there one law for motorists and another for employers? (Robens 1972b: 659).

In response to the Robens Report itself Thompson argued that there was a fault in logic in saying that breaches in the regulations were not the cause of unsafe working practices when so little effort was made to enforce these regulations.

Apart from disputing the uncritical attitude that Robens took to the Inspectorate and its arguments, there was also some questioning of the Inspectorate's crucial argument that only one-fifth of reportable accidents resulted from breaches of regulations and that the majority could be laid at the door of 'apathy'. The National Institute of Industrial Psychology study has figures that could have occasioned a very different conclusion (Woolf 1973; Powell *et al.* 1971). Other accident analysis also challenged this view (Nichols and Armstrong 1973), and lawyers engaged in the discussion during that period were also dubious of the Inspectorate's assumption

> that, as a general rule, all employers are prepared, even anxious to meet their legal obligations with respect to the safety, health and welfare of their employees (Fitzgerald and Hadden 1970).

Environmental Health Officers

Environmental Health Officers have only taken on extensive functions in relation to health and safety at work in recent times. Nonetheless the origins of their work and activites can be traced back to some of the same reforming impulses as those that produced the Factory Inspectors. The movement for sanitary reform in the 1830s and 1840s could not be represented as having the same mass basis as did that for factory reform. It did, however, have a famous champion in Edwin Chadwick, a bible in his

1842 *Inquiry into the Sanitary Conditions of the Labouring Population of Great Britain*, and an impetus to success in the fears of the middle class about the spread of disease. The 1848 Public Health Act allowed the setting up of local boards who employed Inspectors of Nuisance, whose numbers and functions expanded with the reorganisation of local government in the 1870s and 1880s (Martin 1978: 34f). These officers, who preferred to be called Sanitary Inspectors, expanded their functions in later years to cover many more aspects of food, hygiene and drugs, as well as housing and health conditions more generally. In the 1950s they took on the title of Public Health Inspectors. In the 1960s they first became qualified through a range of professional diplomas and degrees, and in the 1970s they began to emphasise the further expansion of their field of activity through the use of the term Environmental Health Officer. They also acquired new enforcement functions with respect to sanitary provisions and general aspects of hygiene in all factories. They had exercised some specific duties with respect to working conditions in the dwindling numbers of 'workshops', that is manufacturing premises which did not use mechanical power. However, with the 1963 Offices, Shops and Railway Premises Act, local authority Inspectors were given a clear responsibility for working conditions in the workplaces covered by this legislation. The Health and Safety (Enforcing Authority) Regulations 1977 gave EHOs enforcement responsibilities for the relevant statutory provisions in an additional range of premises, although certain provisions for health and safety legislation still give specific powers exclusively to HSE Inspectors.[1]

With expanded concerns for working conditions in specific premises, more EHOs had to be trained and appointed and departments reorganised during the same time that there was a major upheaval in the organisation of local government and the health and welfare services. The changes affected not only the geographical areas covered by various administrative units, but also brought new forms of corporate management, with integrated environmental health departments being established under local government Chief Officers. This led to a good deal of stress among Environmental Health Officers, culminating in new programmes for their education, and in much discussion about their morale, workload, role and attitudes (Page 1975).

Local authority Environmental Health Officers came to deal with health and safety at work from quite a different starting point from Factory Inspectors. For one thing, they had a good deal more difficulty in establishing their own status and importance. Edwin Chadwick was worried in 1885 that they were 'paid like journeymen and mechanics' (quoted by Page 1975: 19). A century later complaints were still to be heard within the profession about their relative pay and status in comparison to other inspectors. Other differences concern their style of work. Before the 1974 Act, EHOs were seldom neutral arbiters whose role was to advise and explain. They were much more like local officials sent in to enforce regulations. They had little experience of discussing matters with representatives of the workforce, or arbitrating in disputes (Martin 1978: 104, 189). Their history was one of attempting to improve conditions by frequent visits, measurement and enforcement. In principle at least they believed it possible to decide whether offences were being committed by the application of clearly defined criteria, even precise measurements. On this basis they used powers, unlike the Factory Inspectors before 1974, to issue 'orders' to stop unhealthy practices. Environmental Health Officers thus came in the 1970s to the issue of health and safety at work with attitudes and procedures which had developed in a different context from the various groups of Inspectors who after 1974 came under the direct ambit of the Health and Safety Executive. Some of the resulting variations have been seen in the case studies described earlier in the book.

The structures of inspection and enforcement since 1974

The Health and Safety Executive

The Health and Safety Executive was created on 1 January 1975 as in effect the operational arm of the Health and Safety Commission. It has three members, including the Director General, appointed in accordance with section 10(5) of the HASAW Act. The detailed provisions governing the Executive are given in schedule 2 of the 1974 Act. The Robens Committee had recommended a merger of the existing Inspectorates for factories, mines, quarries, explosives, nuclear installations, alkali works and agriculture in order to achieve greater coordination, operational efficiency and collective scientific and technical expertise. In the event one of these Inspectorates remained outside the structure initially with all agricultural matters being the responsibility of the Minister for Agriculture. However, the Employment Protection Act 1975, section 116, provided that those responsibilities should be transferred to the Executive and Commission. The Alkali Inspectorate was subsequently renamed the Industrial Air Pollution Inspectorate and transferred from the HSE to the Department of Environment on 1 April 1987.

Although they were merged, the different Inspectorates still retained their own functional lines of authority headed by their own 'HM Chief Inspector'. This is illustrated in Figure 9.1 showing the organisation chart of the Commission and Executive. Attempts have been made to increase coordination on policy and inspections across the various Inspectorates and disciplines. Three developments illustrate this move. First, the two main field Inspectorates, Factories and Agriculture, have been linked under the same divisional head. Secondly, the Deputy Director General has since 1985 assumed personal charge of a newly created Technical, Scientific and Medical group which includes most of the specialist resources. Thirdly, the Board of Chief Inspectors has been replaced by the

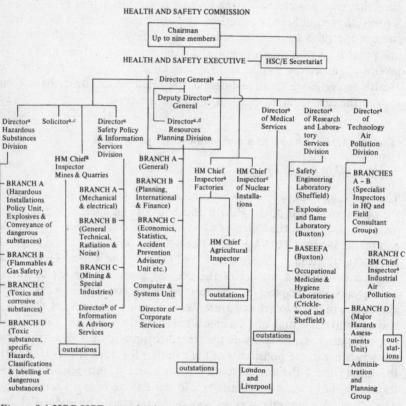

Figure 9.1 HSC-HSE organisation chart (as at January 1987).

[a] Members of the management board of HSE.

[b] Has direct functional responsibility to the Chairman of HSC and the Director General of HSE.

[c] Has direct functional responsibilities to the Chairman of HSC.

[d] The third member of the executive is not always the Director, Resources and Planning; it may be one of the other directors.

(Source: personal communication from HSE, 1986, 1987)

field operations group of the Management Board, which, unlike its predecessor, includes the heads of the specialist support divisions.

Another change is that whereas it used to be regarded as a positive benefit to have a clear separation of the policy making Commission from the operational Executive, a common secretariat has now been established and the heads of the HSE Policy divisions together with the three person Executive meet regularly and informally with the Chairman of the HSC in the Chairman's Policy Group. The HSC Report 1984–85 comments that 'While preserving the constitutional relationship between HSC and HSE', the secretariat allows 'an important central overview of matters of common interest, such as forward planning of legislation and greater flexibility in the use of staff and facilities'. Elsewhere in the Report the development is commended because it will allow the work of the HSE to be 'kept under central review' (HSC/4, 1985: 23, 25).

The Health and Safety Commission and Executive had a total permanent staff of 3701 on 1 April 1986. As Table 9.1 shows this represents a rise over the past three years but is less than the number employed between 1977 and 1982. The peak time for staff resources was 1979, with 4169 staff in post. Decline in staff numbers has been particularly marked in the HMFI. The total staff of the HSE declined by 10.0 % from 1981 to 1986 whereas the number of Factory Inspectors in HMFI declined by 20 % from 1980 to 1986.

The Factory Inspectorate, the largest within the HSE, was reorganised in 1977. Instead of 126 regional and district offices, 21 area offices were established with up to 30 Inspectors in each office. Eighteen of the area offices were headed by an Area Director, two by Senior Area Directors, and one by a Deputy Chief Inspector of Factories (Drake and Wright 1983: 489). Each area office had groups of Inspectors dealing with those industries which were heavily represented in the area, a number of generic multi-industry groups, a construction team, and a 'new entrant' or 'services' team dealing with those workplaces which became subject to health and safety legislation for the first time in 1974. By 1986 these new entrant groups were being merged with other current activity.

As well as organising by industry on a local basis, the HSE also initiated arrangements of National Industry Groups (NIGs). They were first set up in 1976. There are now NIGs to cover 24 industrial activities: namely, asbestos, drinks and brewing, ceramics, chemicals, cotton, construction, defence and disciplined services, docks, food and packaging, foundries, engineering, education, hospitals, local authorities and entertainment, paper and board, plastics and leather, printing, public utilities, rubber, shipbuilding, steel-making, wool, wire, rope and woodworking. Where possible NIGs are located in area offices near appropriate industrial

217

Table 9.1 *HSE staff, 1977–86*

	Total staff of HSE[a]	Numbers of Inspectors in HSE[a]	Factory Inspectors in HSE as a whole[b]	Factory Inspectors in HMFI[b]	Factory Inspectors in HMFI (field only)[b]
1977	3917	1353	N/A	N/A	N/A
1978	4104	1390	695	642	619
1979	4169	1424	742	688	656
1980	4110	1435	759	702	664
1981	3883	1404	735	682	638
1982	3712	1323	678	620	594
1983	3593	1276	654	589	563
1984	3563	1242	627	564[c]	539
1985	3616	1266	652	589[c]	559
1986	3701	1250	623	560	540
Decrease 1980–86	10.0%	12.9%	17.9%	20.2%	18.7%

[a] Permanent staff in post at April 1 (HSE Communication 1986).

[b] Parliamentary Questions, Hansard Written Answers, November 6, 1986.

[c] The Fieldforce of factory inspectors was reported to be 566 at the end of 1984 and 552, at the end of 1985. Clearly numbers vary depending on date of count. The HMFI has a planning target of 600 field inspectors. (HSE/6, p3).

concentrations. Where possible they work in parallel with an IAC. The purposes of a NIG have been specified as follows:

(a) to collect information in respect of an industry and distribute it to inspectors and the industry;
(b) to stimulate discussion and raise standards of health and safety;
(c) to ensure more uniform standards of enforcement in relation to the industry;
(d) to act as a link between the industry, its trade association and unions and HSE (HSE/6, 1986: 24).

In a further attempt to foster high technical standards, the HSE has also established seven field consultant groups (FCGs) distributed around the country. They are staffed by multi-disciplinary teams of specialist inspectors, and each has a laboratory fully equipped for the analysis of dust, gases, vapours etc. The focus of this book on accident experience and safety in the workplace means that this discussion of the HSE can only make passing reference to work undertaken in relation to other issues such as toxic hazards, major hazards and the safety of gas appliances and leisure equipment.

Liaison with local authorities

It has been noted that local authorities have inspecting and enforcing powers through the Health and Safety (Enforcing Authority) Regulations 1977. The original idea was to make local authorities responsible for all non-industrial premises but it proved difficult to divide the activities of businesses into industrial and non-industrial categories. Furthermore financial considerations meant local authorities were limited in the extent to which they could expand their establishments of EHOs or train new recruits. In the event, the local authorities took sole charge of all health and safety legislation which applied in premises whose *main* activities were not those of a factory, but fell into the following groups:[2]

1 The sale or storage of goods for retail or wholesale distribution other than:
   (a) on premises controlled or occupied by a railway undertaking;
   (b) in warehouses or other premises controlled or occupied by the owners, trustees or conservators of a dock, wharf or quay;
   (c) at container depots;

    (d) water and sewage and their by-products;
    (e) natural and town gas;
    (f) solid fuel or other minerals at any mine or quarry or at premises controlled from a mine or quarry;
    (g) petroleum spirit in premises where motor vehicles are maintained or repaired by way of trade;
    (h) wholesale distribution of flammable, toxic, oxidizing, corrosive or explosive substances or petroleum spirit.
2 Office activities.
3 Catering services.
4 Consumer services and launderettes.
5 The provision of residential accommodation.
(Drake and Wright 1983: 55–6; communication from HSE 1986).

Thus there was an attempt to avoid any premises being subject to health and safety inspection by both local authorities and the HSE, although there inevitably remain some areas of overlap.

Various institutions have been set up in an attempt to secure coordination between the HSE and local authorities. There is a national HSE/local authority committee with the acronym HELA which discusses matters of mutual interest, attempts to promote common applications of technical standards and issues guidance to local authority inspectors with a view to achieving an increasingly consistent approach. HELA has three functional subcommittees:

1 Standards of compliance with HASAWA.
2 Training of inspectors.
3 Enforcement and accident statistics (HSC/3, 1983: 34).

In 1983 the HSE established a Local Authority Unit staffed by HSE Inspectors and one Principal Environmental Health Officer on secondment. This acts as a national focal point for technical advice and issues guidance to Inspectors, employers and employees in the local authority sector. One of its particular concerns has been the promotion in local authority inspection sectors of a 'central approach' to senior managers in firms which have premises in several different local authority areas.[3] In effect, the purpose is not only to standardise the activities of EHOs between local authorities but also to make the health and safety activities of EHOs more like those of the Factory Inspectorate. Such standardisation even if wholly desirable is, however, not easily achieved. There is a lot of variation in the structures and policies of local authorities themselves as well as differences between EHOs and Factory Inspectors. EHOs operate with different traditions and views of enforcement founded on their long experience as guardians of public health and hygiene.They tend to visit more frequently and to have more visibility in the workplace. Their different approach to inspection and enforcement has been a subject for criticism from employers for many years (see Robens 1972a: 72). It will be discussed further in the concluding section of this chapter.

An EHO was also seconded in 1984 to work with the HSEs 'Accident Prevention Advisory Unit'. Locally each HSE area officer has a nominated Inspector as the liaison point with local authorities. This Inspector is regarded as particularly important in providing access for EHOs to the specialist technical services and expertise of the HSE.

Inspectors' powers

The powers vested in Inspectors, tribunals and courts are a critical aspect of inspection and enforcement. They were also subject to significant changes in the 1974 Act when 'sweeping' summary powers were conferred on Inspectors. They are 'summary' in that they can be exercised without recourse to the courts but the way they have been used can be questioned in the courts. They include powers to enter premises with such equipment as is required to take samples, measurements and photographs, to examine articles or substances and to ensure that they are available for use as evidence, to require answers to questions from people whom an Inspector has cause to believe have relevant information and to require copies of documents. Under section 25, the Inspector also has powers to seize or render harmless an article or substance which there is reasonable cause to believe to be a cause of imminent danger or serious personal injury. Under section 28(8) HSE Inspectors are required to supply certain information on health, safety and welfare matters to workers or their representatives.

The Robens Committee had been concerned about what they saw as the inflexibility of criminal prosecution and the then limited powers of direction given to Inspectors. Accordingly they recommended 'non-judicial administrative techniques for ensuring compliance with minimum standards of safety and health at work' (paragraph 265). Thus in 1974 for the first time HSE Inspectors had powers to issue improvement and prohibition notices, as EHOs and Mines Inspectors had been empowered for some time. Thus, if an Inspector believes someone is contravening a statutory provision, an improvement notice can be served giving details of that opinion and requiring that the contravention be remedied within a specified period. The Inspector is then in a sense 'turning a blind eye' to any previous and present contraventions whilst requiring the culprit to improve activities or conditions so that a contravention no longer takes

221

place. The improvement notice may or may not give details of what remedial steps are to be taken.

Section 22 of the 1974 Act confers on Inspectors the power to serve a prohibition notice which can require that an activity be discontinued if the Inspector is of the opinion that its continuance involves a risk of serious personal injury. Such notices can be issued with immediate effect or at the end of a specific period. Unlike the improvement notice, where only contravention of statutory requirement is required, prohibition notices are tied to 'serious personal injury' whether or not associated with a contravention of a relevant statutory provision. A notice can also be applied in respect of a prospective risk such as a piece of equipment which has been installed but not yet used. As with improvement notices, prohibition notices may specify measures to be taken which may refer to an approved code of practice and/or provide a choice between remedies. Any time limits imposed under either form of notice may be modified by the Inspector unless an appeal is pending. Appeals against the serving of both sorts of notices or their terms are heard by industrial tribunals who may affirm or cancel the appeal, or modify the terms of the notice such as the time limit or specific requirements.

The effect of an appeal against an improvement notice is to suspend its operation until the appeal is completed or withdrawn. However, the operation of a prohibition notice is only suspended on appeal if on the application of the appeal the tribunal so directs.[4] Tribunals may appoint assessors to assist the hearing of these appeals, but in the event they rarely make use of this facility.

Criminal sanctions

Although the Robens Committee stated that enforcement through extensive use of legal sanctions 'runs counter to our philosophy' (1972: para. 255), they did recommend prosecutions for offences of a flagrant, wilful or reckless nature. They also recommended an increase in maximum fines with higher penalties for repeated offences, and that individuals as well as corporate bodies should be liable for prosecution. Section 33 created 15 categories of offence under the 1974 Act. The more grave are indictable, that is triable by judge and jury in the Crown Court, others are 'triable summarily' by magistrates. Defendents may opt for trial by jury, but if the decision is left to the courts then the factors affecting the decision are the gravity of the offence, the adequacy of the powers held by the summary court and the record of the accused and his or her responsiveness to advice. Under the Criminal Law Act 1977 most offences are 'triable either way'. Section 33 is framed so that most of the offences render the offender liable:

- (a) On summary conviction to a fine not exceeding £400 (increased to £1000 from July 1978 and to £2000 from May 1984) or
- (b) On conviction on indictment –
    - (i) to imprisonment not exceeding two years, or a fine, or both, for the offence specified in Section 33 (4),
    - (ii) to a fine.

(Drake and Wright 1983: 163)

Furthermore, under the Powers of the Criminal Courts Act 1973, sections 35–8, courts have a power to make a compensation order requiring a convicted person to pay compensation for any personal loss, injury or damage resulting from the offence. A magistrates court may not award more than £1000 compensation in such a case (increased by £400 under the Criminal Law Act 1977, s60(1)). Criminal proceedings are of course separate from any civil proceedings which may be brought for damage, loss or injury.

The practice of inspection and enforcement since 1974

As a result of the considerable changes made in the structure of inspection and enforcement following the 1974 Act, a new administrative machinery was established, new powers were determined and criminal sanctions were increased. What trends can we discern in the way these new arrangements have worked in practice and what has been their effect on inspection and enforcement policy?

Tables 9.2, 9.3 and 9.4 summarise some of the inspection and enforcement activity by HSE and local authority Inspectors since the passage of the Act. The number of visits by HSE Inspectors has declined markedly since 1976. This reflects a fall, since 1979, in the number of HSE Inspectors. Table 9.1 showed that whereas the total staff of the HSE had fallen by 10.0% for the period 1981–86, the figure for field Factory Inspectors for the same period is 18.7%. Taking the period 1980–86 we find a decline of 20.2% in Factory Inspectors in HMFI. Further evidence of a more general reduction in the resources of the Factory Inspectorate was given in a written answer to a Parliamentary Question in 1985 when it was revealed that in the London area the number of Factory Inspectors had dropped from 85 to 74 between 1977 and 1985.[5]

The number of local authority staff employed on health and safety at work enforcement is difficult to determine exactly because the data are supplied to HSE on a voluntary basis. Table 9.5 shows details of the data on staff resources supplied voluntarily for the period 1976–85. This suggests that the numbers of Inspectors has been fairly stable over the period. However, the estimated total hours spent by staff on health and safety duties appears to have declined from 1 528 000 hours in 409 authorities in 1981 to 1 484 000 hours in 413 authorities in 1985.[6]

The fall in the number of visits is also linked to a number of policy changes such as the strengthening of a priority system such that 'less risky' and 'more responsible' establishments are likely to be visited even less frequently than before. Fears have been expressed however that standards deteriorate as visits become less frequent.[7] It must now seem to belong to aspirations of a very distant age when the TUC reminded Robens that the ILO in 1961 had recommended that workplaces should be inspected at least annually. At that time the Inspectors went to factories on average once every four years (Robens 1972a: 684–5). In 1982 it was reported that the inspection average stood at one visit in seven years (House of Commons 1982: 92).

The number of accidents or incidents investigated has also continued to decline from 18.8 thousand in 1982 to 11.4 thousand in 1984, a decline of 34% (HSC/4, 1985). The HSC claims this is largely accounted for by the changes in the industrial injury benefit system from 1983 which have reduced the flow of information to the HSE about some injuries[8] (HSC/4, 1985: 28). But it must also reflect the fall in the number of Inspectors.

Table 9.2 also shows the number of notices issued by HSE, HSC agencies and local authority Inspectors since the Act. The number of HSE notices is low in relation to the number of visits, but has not shown the same tendency to decline; the 'notices per visit' ratio has thus tended to increase. Figures for the number of local authority visits over the whole period are not available, but those available for the period 1977–84 suggest a fairly stable picture with 529 000 visits being made by 413 local authorities in 1985.

In contrast to the stability of the HSE figures, Table 9.2 shows a rise in the number of local authority notices concerned with safety and health at work, but this time from a low base.[9] In the 1980s, statistics collected from approximately 409 local authorities show an average of 18.1 enforcement notices concerned with safety and health at work per local authority per year. Informal notices are, however, more widely used by EHOs with 106 000 reported by 374 local authorites in 1984 (i.e. over 280 per annum per local authority).[10]

Where notices were issued, they tended to be accepted. Table 9.2 reveals the very low number of appeals against all forms of notice; the bracketed figures reveal that the success rate of appeals is even lower. In reviewing

Table 9.2 *HSE, HSC agencies and local authority visits and enforcement notices, 1973–85*

	Visits		All notices related to health and safety at work[a]		
	HSE and HSC agencies[b] (thousands)	Local authority[c] (thousands)	HSE and HSC agencies (thousands)	Local authority[c] (thousands)	Appeals against all notices[d] (successful)
1973	503.7	—	—	—	—
1974	452.8	—	—	—	—
1975	481.0	N/A	6.6	1.0	30[f] (0)[f]
1976	450.7	N/A	7.2	2.8	52 (1)
1977	N/A	534.7	8.9	3.5	77 (8)
1978	N/A	536.3	10.1	5.6	104 (9)
1979	285.0	554.3	9.9	7.3	100 (6)
1980	285.0	548.3	8.6	7.2	89 (4)
1981	267.0	619.2	8.0	7.5	196 (8)
1982	258.0	571.8	7.7	8.6	220 (11)
1983	248.0	511.8	8.6	7.5	96 (6)
1984	245.0	555.9	8.8	7.2	121 (11)
1985	246.0p	529.0[e]	8.0	6.5[e]	120 (10)

[a] Drawn from HSE Statistics 1981–82 and 1983, 1984/85 (draft).
[b] Drawn from HSE Statistics 1976 for 1973–76; from HSC Annual Reports 1979–84; 1985/86 (draft).
[c] Based on voluntary returns from Local Authorities. Out of a possible total of 461 the figures related to 409 in 1981, 414 in 1982, 374 in 1983, 409 in 1984, 413 in 1985, average of 420–430 in 1977–1980.
[d] Drawn from HSE Statistics 1977, p7; 1980, p10; 1981–82, p14, 1984/85 (draft).
[e] Health and Safety in Local Authority Enforced Premises 1985 Report.
[f] Excluding local authorities.
Source: HSE.

their achievements since 1974, the HSC comment that 'the new tools for enforcement, particularly improvement and prohibition notices, have been accepted in industry' (HSC/8, 1985).

Table 9.3 shows the compliance rate for notices issued by the Factory Inspectorate between 1975 and 1985. In no year did this fall below 92%. Further figures show that this compliance was maintained over longer periods of time than that indicated by an immediate response.[11] Taking just the notices issued by HMFI, Table 9.4 shows an overall decline in all HMFI notices, accounted for by a significant decline in improvement but not prohibition notices.

Table 9.3 *Compliance with improvement notices issued by HMFI, 1975–80 and 1981–85*

		Number complied with	
Year	Number of notices issued	Number	%
1975	4567	4232	93
1976	3901	3617	93
1977	4415	4134	94
1978	4952	4681	95
1979	4720	4491	95
1980	2922	2802	96
Total 1975–80	25477	23957	94
1981[a]	3919	3742	95
1982[a]	3629	3358	93
1983[a]	3185	2934	92
1984[a]	3048	2899	95
1985p[a]	2459	2338	96
Total 1981–85	16240	15271	93

[a] These figures relate to notices issued where result is known as at November 1986. The difference between these figures and those in Table 9.4 is between total notices issued and total for which result is known.
Sources: HSE/18 1985, p. 26, for 1975–80; communication from HSE, November 1986, for 1981–85

Table 9.4 *Improvement and prohibition notices issued by HMFI, 1982–85*

Type of notice	1981	1982	1983	1984	1985p
Improvement	4035	3800	3405	3322	2993
Deferred prohibition	182	173	176	175	181
Immediate prohibition	1085	1298	1497	1630	1481
Total notices	5302	5271	5078	5127	4655

Sources: HSE/6, 1985: Table 5, p. 10 for 1982–85; communication from HSE, November 1986, for 1981.

Table 9.5 *Local authority staff resources employed on HASAWA enforcement, 1976–85*

Year	Number of Inspectors appointed under section 19 of the HASAWA[a]	Estimated total hours spent by all staff on HSW duties (thousands)[a]
1976	5046	N/A
1977	5129	N/A
1978	5412	N/A
1979	5151	N/A
1980	5355	1586
1981	5082	1528
1982	5231	1451
1983	4924	1383
1984	5100	1484
1985	5210	N/A

[a] Number of returns on which data are based:

1976–80:	average 420–430
1981	409
1982	414
1983	374
1984	409
1985	413

Source: personal communication from HSE, August 1987.

We know that the HSE has a preference for achieving changes through education and advice rather than through enforcement and prosecution. However, within the latter category there is no doubt that both the HSE and local authorities have a preference for the use of enforcement notices rather than prosecution. It will be recalled that the power for HMFI to serve notices was granted through the HASAWA 1974. In the period 1974–85, the HMFI served a total of 41 717 improvement notices, thereby taking action to improve safety standards which would not have been possible before 1974.

Table 9.6 summarises the prosecution activities of the various Inspectorates; Table 9.7 gives the same information for two of the industries which have been considered in detail in this book: chemicals and construction. The numbers of prosecutions undertaken by HSE Inspectorates overall has fallen from 2091 in 1973 to 1269 in 1984. The number of prosecutions in chemicals did not show the same tendency to

Table 9.6 *Prosecution activity by Inspectorates, 1973–85*

	HSE Inspectorates[a] and HSC agencies		Local authority[a,b] Inspectorates		Average[c] fines at 1975 prices
	No.	Conviction rate (%)	No.	Conviction rate (%)	
1973	2091	N/A	123	(91)	N/A
1974	1998	N/A	120	(96)	N/A
1975	1588	N/A	78	(90)	75
1976	1327	(92)	106	(89)	77.3
1977	1623	(90)	97	(96)	76.7
1978	1671	(91)	335	(88)	87.2
1979	1373	(92)	211	(84)	112.8
1980	1443	(92)	307	(90)	90.1
1981	1260	(91)	291	(86)	97.4
1982	1427	(92)	296	(86)	109.4
1983	1366	(89)	261	(82)	107.3
1984	1269	(90)	283	(90)	N/A
1985	1265p	(88)	257	(91)	

[a] 1973–82 from HSE Statistics (1982–82), p. 14; 1983 from HSE Statistics (1983) p. 16; 1984 from HSC Annual Report 1984–85. Amendments and additions in personal communication from HSE, November 1986.
[b] Based on voluntary returns from local authorities. Out of a possible total of 461, the figures relate to 409 in 1981, 414 in 1982, 374 in 1983, 409 in 1984, 413 in 1985.
[c] From HSE Statistics 1975–83, based on all prosecutions completed in Factories Acts premises during year, average for all offences, deflated by December 1975 RPI (retail price index).
Source: HSE.

decline until 1985. The number in construction, which is notable for its recent poor safety record, has actually increased from 1981 to 1985, although the 1985 figure is somewhat less than the peak figure for 1982. The number of prosecutions by local authorities shows no simple trend, but is generally higher in the 1980s than in the 1970s with 283 prosecutions being reported in 1984. With an approximate average of 290 prosecutions concerned with safety and health at work completed each year by approximately 409 local authorities the average is 0.7 prosecutions per authority per year.

The figures for conviction rates in Tables 9.6 and 9.7 indicate that both HSE and local authorities enjoy a higher conviction rate in the small

Table 9.7 *Prosecution activity by HMFI in the construction and chemical and allied industries, 1981–85p*

	Year hearing completed				
	1981	1982	1983	1984	1985p
Chemical and allied industry					
Informations laid and results recorded	48	39	53	50	25
Convictions obtained	45	39	47	43	21
Conviction rate (%)	94	100	89	86	84
Average penalty per conviction (£)	198	664	275	407	615
Construction industry					
Information laid and results recorded	585	823	721	657	684
Convictions obtained	531	734	651	590	567
Conviction rate (%)	99	89	91	90	84
Average penalty per conviction (£)	218	219	261	344	420

p = provisional.
Source: personal communication from HSE, November 1986.

number of prosecutions actually brought. Not all of the prosecutions are brought directly under HASAWA. Many are still brought under the Factories Acts or the OSRP Act. Where prosecutions are brought under HASAWA, they are overwhelmingly section 2 'general duties' issues. These appear to outnumber all other categories (Drake and Wright 1983: 165).

The HSC Annual Report (HSC/4, 1985) suggests that the fall in HSE prosecutions is largely accounted for in terms of a reduction in prosecutions by the Factory Inspectorate – whose activities account for the majority (90%) of the total. In commenting on the fall the HSE says it

reflects no change in policy, which continued to be, in broad terms to prosecute where flagrant and repeated breaches of the law occur. It should be recognised however, that formal enforcement methods such as prosecutions and notices account for only a very small part of the Inspectorate's efforts in seeking to ensure industry's compliance with health and safety requirements. Guidance, advice and persuasion continue to account for the great majority of all Inspectorate's compliance activities, as is clear from a comparison of the number of visits made annually with the total number of prosecutions and notices arising from those visits (HSC/4, 1985: 28).

Tables 9.6 and 9.7 indicate the low level of average fines imposed following successful prosecutions. The amounts in Table 9.6 are in 1975 prices, and although there has been an increase in the real level of fines since 1975, the amounts are small. The amounts given in Table 9.5 are the real sums involved. The fines imposed fall well short of the maxima. The maximum fine until 1977 was £400; the 1976 average was £89. Thereafter until 1984 (when it was increased to £2000) the maximum has been £1000; the 1983 average was £252, the 1984 average £329 and the 1985 average £474.

The relatively low level of fines has always been a cause for concern. For example a resolution carried by the Trade Union Congress in 1977 deplored it and concluded 'despite the provisions within the Act for stringent penalties, the average level of fines levied in the first year of operation was £75' (TUC 1977 Report: 421). This state of affairs prompted a comment in the House of Commons Debate on Health and Safety at Work February 1984 from Mr Don Dixon, MP for Jarrow, that 'on the day on which the National Graphical Association was fined £50 000 [for contempt of court in an industrial relations case] two employers were fined, on average £1000 each as four people had been killed due to neglect. That was ridiculously low.'[12]

The statistics of what the HSC calls 'compliance activities' do not, then, reveal a great surge of activity during the period 1981–85 when we know the statistics on accident trends show decreasing performance. Indeed the effects of recession and a strengthening of the HSC and HSE resolve to work through guidance and advice rather than through legal sanctions, are reflected in a reduction of prosecutions by HSE Inspectors. In evaluating inspection and enforcement activity, however, one must remember what has always been the view of the Inspectorate – supported by the Robens Report and firmly enshrined in HSC policy – that legal action is only to be taken in the last resort. Thus one would not expect the 1974 Act itself nor the recent rise in the combined rates for major and fatal accidents in construction and manufacturing to have caused a fundamental change in the way the inspectorate operates.

An important dimension to 'educating and advising' is the provision of information to people at work other than employers. Under section 28(8) of the HASAWA, Inspectors are required to supply certain information on health, safety and welfare matters to workers or their representatives. This applies particularly to factual information about hazards identified during visits and information about action which Inspectors have taken or propose to take. The HSC gave guidance to enforcing authorities on the provision of information by Inspectors and other staff to employees or their representatives in 1979. This guidance makes it clear that the primary duty to provide employees with information about hazards at work rests with employers and that the role of Inspectors is to ensure that employers carry out that duty, supplement the information with additional material and respond to requests for advice.

There has recently been concern within the trade union movement about the lack of willingness of members of the HSE to provide information directly to safety representatives.[13] However, the HSE maintains that its policy is unchanged and that its Inspectors will continue to respect the requirements of section 28(8) in the correct and most helpful way. The HSE has always maintained that one of the underlying principles of inspection policy is that contact is made with both management and employee representatives during visits and that matters arising from visits should be discussed wherever practicable with employee representatives at the time. Subsequently, for the record and to avoid misunderstandings, certain matters may be confirmed in writing.[14]

A strategy based on education, advice and discussions, not simply with employers or their representatives, but also with members of the workforce or their representatives, does of course place heavy demands on HSE resources. These demands must be seen in the context of the 1980s when the theme of the scarcity and depletion of their own resources has been a subject for comment in all the HSC and HSE reports. In the face of the first cuts in 1981 the HSC was stoical, but fearful that fewer Inspectors would mean fewer prosecutions (HSC/2, 1982: 26). In their Plan of Work for 1985–86, the HSC (HSC/8, 1985) reported without comment that it must be subject to public expenditure scrutiny with, at best, level funding for the next four years. It accepted that it must consider how to use its resources most 'efficiently and effectively for indispensable objectives' and reported that in making judgements about how to achieve its final output of 'greater industrial health and safety and greater satisfaction as to its being achieved' it must decide on its balance of 'intermediate outputs' which are, in its opinion, substitutes for each other. For example, 'the existence of effective guidance will influence safety and so indirectly reduce the need for investigation of incidents; and it may directly reduce the flow of inquiries with which our field force has to deal and help standardise and guide their efforts' (HSC/8, 1985: paras. 37, 45). It did, however, reserve the right 'either because the tasks we face demand it, or because we find we cannot absorb a real reduction when stability was intended, to seek an increase in resources' (HSC/8, 1985: para. 39).

Any concern the HSC may have about reduced resources are not expressed in terms of the dangers involved in completing fewer inspections. Whilst the HSC Report 1984–85 says it has a priority to keep 'enough inspectors in the field' it claims that 'with improved efficiency and the introduction of a system of hazard ranking we believe we have sufficient resources to carry out our essential responsibilities at the present time'. They promise to keep the situation 'under review' because their Inspectors are taking on extra duties, for example, licensing of companies for asbestos work and the investigation of domestic gas incidents. The HSC and HSE are, however, worried about the effects of cuts on non-inspection work:

> If as a result of reduced activity on our part, as for example,
> through failure to produce standards, guidance, certification or
> advice that industry constantly seeks from us, the whole system
> became less effective ... that would be a false economy
> (HSC/8, 1985: para. 52).

It can easily be argued that an educative policy is in fact more labour intensive for the HSE than a strict enforcement policy since effective education and guidance has been shown in other areas to depend on the development of relationships of mutual trust between Inspectors and their subjects (Hawkins 1984).

In order to evaluate the impact of diminishing resources, it is necessary to look more closely at the practice of inspection. Despite their different approaches to enforcement, both the HSE and the local authority Inspectors are subject to serious resource constraints.

The Factory Inspectorate develops a five year rolling programme of inspection work aimed primarily at planning and evaluating factory visits. The HM Chief Inspector of Factories Annual Report (1985) indicated that national guidelines are issued by FI headquarters on the allocation of available time, although these may be altered for particular localities through discussion with Area Directors. The programme for 1985–86 shown in Table 9.8 indicates 27.5% for basic inspection and 29% for reactive work in response to complaints, accidents, dangerous occurrences and court work. This, one must remember, is a statement of intent rather than of fact but it does indicate a considerable shift from 1980, when the Inspectorate's field force was said to spend 53.8% of its time on basic inspection and 14.9% on reactive inspections (ILO 1982: 24). Furthermore, practice may vary between different parts of the field force since it may be recalled from Chapter 5 that the Construction Inspectors of HMFI estimated that in 1987–88 they would spend 40% on basic

Table 9.8 *HMFI planned inspection programme: 12 April 1985 – 31 March 1986*

Basic routine inspection	27.5%
Unplanned/reactive work of which:	29.0%
Accident investigation	10.0%
Complaints investigation	6.0%
Legal work	2.5%
Follow up visits	4.0%
Other reactive work	6.5%
Special initiatives	11.0%
NIG/NRG	7.5%
HASAWA section 6	5.0%
Special projects national	3.0%
Special projects local	2.5%
Other work	14.5%

Source: HSE/6, 1985: Figure 8, page 34.

inspections and 47% on reactive work. Since the reactive work is, in effect, compulsory, a rise in the number of accidents and complaints, or a rise in other 'non-inspection' work, or a fall in the number of Inspectors will affect the programme of basic inspection.

This can cause severe problems, since, in the words of a senior Inspector we interviewed, 'it [i.e. a cut in basic inspection] strikes at the heart of the Inspector's educative role'. The example of resource cutbacks in the London area of the Construction Inspectorate is a case in point. In 1981, the Inspectorate had 11 Inspectors available for the London area; by 1984, this had reduced to 7, and the level of reactive work had not dropped. In discussions with those involved we were told that this led to doubts about whether there were sufficient staff even to deal with reactive work, let alone to undertake a properly planned programme of basic inspection.

To the extent that Inspectors deal only with transgressions or complaints, their educative role in accident prevention is reduced. Moreover, such an emphasis may change both the quality and the nature of enforcement. Carson (1970b) noted that the Factory Inspectorate's knowledge of offences was gained largely through routine, proactive inspection rather than through reactive work: lack of such experience would act to the detriment of enforcement activity. Hutter goes further to suggest, on the basis of an analysis of the HSC and local authority Inspectorates, that

> if regulatory agencies were to place their greatest efforts towards reactive strategies, to the detriment of proactive strategies, then ... they would become more removed and remote from those they control (Hutter 1986: 127).

One response to the problem of decreasing resources is to 'target' basic inspections around known hazards or workplaces where standards are felt to be slack and to leave these workplaces which are judged 'exemplary' in their health and safety record almost entirely to self regulation under the broad oversight of some sort of 'licensing arrangements' with the Inspectorate. Chapter 5 (p. 124) has already shown how the increasing concern of the HSE about poor standards of safety in construction was manifest in an inspection blitz on all construction sites in particular locations in 1987, first in Sheffield and Humberside and subsequently in London. In a few days hundreds of sites were visited and many notices served.

The HSE may also develop a targetting system for particular establishments as well as particular industries or areas of work. A valuable aid in the progress of targetting establishments is the HSE computerised information system with the acronym, SHIELD, initiated in 1981. This system is intended to provide a database of all factories, including newly established workplaces, concerning type of activity, substances used, number of workers, number of accidents, notified occupational diseases, dates of inspection and a hazard rating compiled by the Inspector on the last visit. In parts of the Factory Inspectorate, the rating is based on the Inspector's assessment of general standards, hazard potential and managerial competence. A similar system operates within certain local authorities (ILO 1982; 43). Factory Inspectors specialising in construction base their rating on the action taken, i.e. improvement or prohibition notice, rather than overall assessment.

The system, consisting of a series of area minicomputers, with national data held on a central minicomputer, offers the prospect of a nationwide database on hazards, compliance and enforcement which could be used to plan the system of basic inspection. Problematic workplaces could be isolated, and more frequent inspection could play an educative role. Unfortunately, at least initially, there appear to have been several problems with this information system. Some are merely technical, relating to the coding and classification of information. However, others indicate that the resourcing problem frustrates its own solution. For the database to work, a systematic programme of basic inspection is necessary to establish a set of hazard ratings; such a programme has in many areas been frustrated, while the training necessary to use the system as a guide does not appear to have been given. This problem was noted by the ILO team which evaluated the Inspectorates (1982). From our own interviews it was clear that the quality of information fed back from Inspectors varied enormously, several busy field Inspectors regarding the extra form as just one more unwelcome imposition.

Finally, there is the problem of data collection. That relating to accident statistics themselves has already been noted. However, in some industries, notably construction, it is difficult to compile a list, especially of smaller firms. Those firms most likely to warrant inspection are thus least likely to appear on the guiding database.

The ILO study team concluded that 'in several of the workplaces we visited, especially among the smaller ones, we felt that it was not enough for the factory inspector merely to give advice. In our opinion, improvement and prohibition notices should be issued more often' (ILO 1982: 71). This raises issues of enforcement policy to which we now turn.

Issues in enforcement policy

Two important issues have recurred in this account of the development, structure and practice of the HSE and local authority Inspectorates. The first concerns the extent to which the policy and practice of inspection and enforcement can and should be centralised. The second concerns the philosophy behind regulation and the extent to which compliance with legal standards can and should be secured through guidance, advice and education on the one hand and strict enforcement and punitive sanctions on the other. Both of these issues have been phrased in terms of 'can' and 'should', since it is important to distinguish between descriptive and prescriptive analysis. In public pronouncements by the institutions concerned and in some of the literature commenting on policy and practice these two levels of analysis are merged. The aim of this analysis is to focus on the descriptive level whilst at the same time making some general prescriptive remarks. These will be taken up again in the final chapter.

The issue of centralisation

Since the mid nineteenth century, when local authority Inspectors had enforcing responsibility for sanitary arrangements in all factories and specific responsibilities for conditions in non-mechanically powered

235

workshops, the issue of whether enforcement was best achieved through local or central organisation or some combination of the two has been raised repeatedly. However, it was only in 1964, when the OSRP Act gave specific duties to EHOs to inspect and enforce working conditions in these 'non-industrial' workplaces that it became a subject for extensive public discussion.

The Gowers Committee (1949: cmnd 7664) had decided, largely on practical and resource grounds, that EHOs should be responsible for non-industrial workplaces. Fears were expressed at the time about variable standards between individual local authorities and the Factory Inspectorate and various arrangements such as a requirement on local authorities to submit an annual report to a central department, direct central supervisions, ministerial appointment and dismissal of Inspectors through regional or central officers and default powers, were all considered.[15]

It took fourteen years for the Gowers Report to be reflected in legislation, largely because of Conservative backbench and constituency opposition to the idea of regulating working conditions in offices and fears about the cost burdens of regulation on small firms. In the event local authority inspection and enforcement was established, but there was a requirement that each authority should submit an annual report. Ministers were also given powers to secure more uniform enforcement if they judged it necessary by making regulations and by appointing officers to investigate how local authority Inspectors were discharging their duties and to give them advice.

The central–local relationship after 1963 was characterised more by advice and collaboration than direction. This occasioned more disquiet which was shown when, to considerable surprise, the Redcliffe Maud Commission on Local Government (1967) considered evidence on the substantial variation in practice between local authority enforcement agencies and received recommendations that the local workplace functions of EHOs should be transferred to a central body. Their Report endorsed the existing arrangements but proposed stronger default powers for ministers to require local authorities to improve their performance in specific ways (or else risk a central takeover) and to prescribe minimum qualifications and experience for Inspectors. Before action could be taken, however, this debate became subsumed into the considerations of the Robens Committee.

Once again the same arguments were rehearsed but generally there was a feeling that the *status quo* should be retained. The Factory Inspectorate was seen as relatively small and highly trained, concentrating on the more dangerous premises and processes, whilst the EHOs retained their local concerns with offices and shops. In fact, the 1974 Act gave greater autonomy to local authorities in matters of health and safety. Whereas under the OSRP Act local authorities had a duty both to enforce and to appoint inspectors, the regulations under the HASAWA required them to make 'adequate arrangements for enforcement' and to appoint as many Inspectors 'with suitable qualifications' as they thought necessary. Local authorities are required to carry out responsibilities in accordance with guidance from the HSC, and in the event of their defaulting on these responsibilities, the Secretary of State can only require them to improve their performance following a report from the HSC (HASAWA s18(4)6).

The HSC maintains a general overview of the work of local authorities in enforcing the HASAW Act and has instituted formal liaison arrangements at national level, through HELA and at local level through liaison officers. HELA issues guidance notes to local authorities, many of which are specific and technical; for example on control limits for exposure to specific hazardous substances. However, those that deal with the practice of enforcement are couched in general terms. For example, the guidance on enforcement policy and methods of inspection states that 'local authorities should review their philosophy and practices and base their inspection programmes on systems of priorities relative to the seriousness of the risks'.[16]

Nothing more specific is given, and indeed the note goes on to state that 'the unique local knowledge of the local authority will put it in a position to identify priorities and change its programmes of inspection accordingly'. With the move towards 'targetting inspection', general guidance on priority planning for local authorities is now being prepared. The HSC receives annual reports on the work of EHOs in respect of health and safety at work and from time to time it also requests reports on specific topics. For example, in 1984–85 they investigated the two topics of commercially used sunbeds and occupational noise. The HSC coordinates replies and through HELA considers whether and what advice and guidance should be given. The Institution of Environmental Health Officers also issues a range of guidance notes aimed to secure greater uniformity of enforcement.

Thus at the formal descriptive level there is an established local Inspectorate for one set of workplaces which coexists with, and to an extent is informally coordinated by, a central institution which has direct control over all other Inspectorates with responsibility for health and safety at work.

Over recent years, however, the issue of centralisation and standardisation has faded in importance. Each of the Inspectorates has a particular view of the other although there are signs that these are changing. Factory Inspectors still consider EHOs to be relatively less professional and expert, more inclined to visit, to place orders and to bring prosecutions in circumstances where the Factory Inspector would be less inclined to act. Even so, EHOs do not conform to a punitive model of enforcement; they too exercise considerable discretion over when and how to act and the available figures do not suggest a more active prosecution policy in matters of safety at work. From the other point of view, EHOs have been critical that Factory Inspectors are often less zealous and locally knowledgeable than they are. Generally, however, EHOs develop their own particular forms of enforcement activity depending on local circumstances, including the nature of local political control (Hutter 1984).

There are discussions at the time of writing about whether the role of EHOs should be extended to cover enforcement in some of the so-called 'new entrant' areas. The HSC reports that this possible extension, together with existing resource constraints, has meant that some authorities are reviewing their enforcement priorities. 'A number already based their programme on well developed priority systems; others reported plans for the introduction of computer based priority scoring systems to assist their work' (HSC/4, 1985: 22).

Changes are certainly taking place and the more obvious differences between EHOs and HSE Inspectors are lessening. The effects of centralised political control, not only through the implementation of the more professional standards of the HSE, but also through the limitations in resources available to local authorities, together with the availability of central computerised information systems may yet achieve an integration of styles and procedures which a century of reports and rhetoric has failed previously to achieve.

The issue of compliance

Many studies of regulation and inspection draw a strong distinction between a remedial, conciliatory style of enforcement with an associated compliance strategy and an accusatory style of enforcement associated with a sanctioning strategy (Black 1976; Veljanovski 1981; Hawkins 1984; Hutter 1984). The issues discussed in this chapter have made it clear that the HSE Inspectors and to a lesser, but still significant, extent EHOs operate at the compliance end of the continuum, where it is said it is quite possible 'to conceive of the law being enforced even though the formal apparatus of prosecutions is hardly ever used' (Hawkins 1984: xiv). Certainly there are examples of Inspectorates throughout the world that work with little compulsion of any sort, as is the case with those who cope with the powerful interests who run open cast mining industry in the United States (Shover *et al.* 1986). However, generally speaking, it is thought that inspectors in the United States need to use the law to a greater extent than for example in Sweden where there is a good deal more consensus in the political culture, and all those concerned are prepared to seek agreement without recourse to external constraint (Wilson 1985; Kelman 1981: 117–87).

Within the administrative culture in Britain, a strong conventional wisdom has developed that the 'informal-educative' approach is most appropriate to the enforcement of health and safety at work. Every author considering the subject has noted the reluctance of the Factory Inspectorate to prosecute, and within the Inspectorate, the power to prosecute is severely limited by formal rules (Carson 1970b; Wilson 1985). Nonetheless people actually subject to hazards, especially if they take more than a passing interest in preventing them, invariably believe that the legislation consists of a set of rules which Inspectors are called upon to enforce. The same phenomenon – an assumption that rules are to be enforced – has been noted among employers (Rhodes 1981: 85). No amount of explanation or discussion will shift the common-sense view that rules exist to be enforced and that it is insufficient to get employers or workers simply to examine their own consciences and act justly, or even to calculate the costs and benefits of safety provision.

One of the few surveys of the attitudes of Factory Inspectors themselves indicates that despite generations of discussion about the importance of advice and guidance and the lack of a policing role, enforcement is still given very high priority. Shortly after the passing of the 1974 Act, 44% of Inspectors still gave enforcement of the law as their chief overall objective – more than any other such statement as 'improving standards' (33%) and giving 'advice on solutions' (22%). When asked about priority tasks in relation to enforcement, 47% put factory visits on top, and various other forms of visits such as accident investigation were given priority by a further 38%, a mere 15% chose 'getting the message over' (Hale 1978:276). This survey provides a rare but illuminating glimpse of the attitudes of the 'enforcers'. It is also interesting to note that, in a study of EHOs, regional variations were found in that enforcement through sanctions appears to be more widely used in urban areas where agreed values can be less easily assumed than elsewhere (Hutter 1984: 85, 96, 187 and 263).

There are those who argue that criminality has nothing whatever to do with any form of economic regulation (Kadish 1963). Many of this persuasion take such a view on the basis of the belief that the market should be left to regulate all industrial and economic activity (Weidenbaum 1981). In practice, an element of legal sanction and enforcement always remains, however attenuated. Apart from those described in the case studies in this volume, and the evidence on the attitudes of Inspectors themselves, it seems likely that people expect there to be regulations of some kind that are enforced.

Studies of groups of 'law enforcers' as diverse as the police, Factory Inspectors, prison officers and regional water inspectors, suggest means whereby one can understand the way enforcement is carried out and compliance achieved. One can look, as Hawkins (1984) suggests, at the following factors:

(a) The strength of consensus in social and moral values which underly relevant sections of the law.
(b) The relationship of powerful vested interests to the law and its enforcement.
(c) The assumed motivation of the culprit and the identification of a victim.
(d) The nature of the deviance, in terms of whether it is a discrete act or a continuous problem.
(e) The terms of reference and organisation of enforcement agents, the resources at their disposal and the nature of the sanctions they can exert.

Much of the preceding discussion has been concerned with the fifth point and it has been shown that the formal arrangements for inspection and enforcement for Factory Inspectors and EHOs strongly support an educative compliance rather than a punitive enforcement strategy. It therefore remains to consider the first four points in respect of the law relating to health and safety at work.

(a) Social and moral values

Where there is strong consensus that a particular activity is morally wrong and a culprit can be identified, there is little difficulty in adopting a strong punitive enforcement strategy in which every effort is made to apprehend, punish and deter the culprit and deter others from following his or her example. 'Where deviance has a categorical, unproblematic quality, a penal response is triggered.' However, when the authority of the enforcer is 'not secured on a perceived moral and political consensus about the ills they seek to control', the issue of enforcement is not so clearcut (Hawkins 1984: 6, 13).

In matters of health and safety at work, it falls to a great extent on the HSC and HSE to use their discretion to determine what really constitute activities worthy of prosecution and what activities represent satisfactory compliance with the law, particularly given the relatively open phraseology of 'reasonable practicability' used in HASAWA. These powers are exercised through the HSC proposing regulations and the HSE developing enforcement policies and influencing the activities of their field forces. The idea behind this arrangement is that as the policies and regulations are made through tripartite arrangements for extensive consultation and consensual decision making, the results will embody a strong consensual force. While, as we have shown, there may be strong consensus within the HSC this may not be an adequate reflection of reality in many enterprises and workplaces.

(b) Powerful vested interests

Where powerful vested interests are likely to be harmed by the enforcement of the law, then, *ceteris paribus*, strict enforcement will be more difficult. Indeed, there are those who argue that a general tendency exists for regulatory agencies to be captured by those they are empowered to regulate (Bernstein 1955; Wilson 1985: 24). This is particularly the case where the vested interests are legally recognised and are seen to contribute to the 'national interest' as in the case of industrial firms. In contrast while the vested interests of illegal drug producers and dealers may be harmed by laws against drug abuse, their opposition cannot be voiced or their defence developed 'in open court' as it were, although they can, of course, use other informal and covert means of bringing pressure to bear on the law makers and enforcers. With health and safety at work however, the vested interests of employers and trade unions are not only legally represented but are also important participants in the policy making body. One of the justifications for this is that they share a 'common interest' to improve standards of safety and health. This may be true at a general level, but there are many times when the interests of health and safety are accorded low priority in the face of competing or contradictory pressures from employers, managers and trade unions.

The existence of strong legally constituted vested interests does of course have a significant effect upon value concensus. In the case of safety at work, the employers can justify their position not simply in terms of their own interests but in terms of the economic well being of the nation. Hence the Conservative Secretary of State for Employment in 1979 instructed the HSC to take economic factors into account in the making of regulations, an instruction which the Commission promised to honour in 1981. This approach, based in cost-benefit analysis, received short shrift when presented by the CBI to the House of Commons Employment Committee in 1982, but it is being given serious consideration by the HSC and HSE. One of the major problems appears to be practical; the lack of available personnel at the HSE who can produce reliable cost-benefit analyses to support or reject any specific regulation on economic grounds (Heywood 1985).

(*c*) *Motivation, intentionality and the identity of culprit and victim*
Where illegal acts are intentionally directed against the person or property of an identifiable group or individual there is often strong support for the apprehension, punishment and deterence of the culprit. However, where there is doubt about the intentionality of the act or an illegal act has not actually resulted in injury, loss or damage to an identifiable victim, then there is likely to be less strong support for the apprehension, punishment and deterrence of the culprit (or potential culprits). [17] The first condition can be illustrated by the case where someone is throwing a ball across a children's playground which results in serious injury to a child. A crucial question in terms of public opinion is likely to be whether the culprit actually intended the harm to the child or whether it was 'unintended'. An illustration of the second condition is where an unsafe scaffold is used on a building site, but no loss or damage results. It is worth noting that the HSE and EHOs are both more likely to take formal action after an 'accident' has occurred particularly if someone has been harmed and 'blame' or responsibility can be apportioned to the defendants.

(*d*) *Nature of the deviant act*
Where deviant acts are clearly identified with particular times and places and the existence of both a culprit and a victim is clear, then punitive enforcement activity often follows. Sometimes the existence of a culprit and/or a victim is difficult to establish and transgressions of the law are continuing or episodic and so represent a 'problematic state of affairs'. Evidence of a continuing problem rather than clearly defined deviant acts sometimes prompts the development of a continuous relationship between the law enforcer and the law breaker as the route by which compliance with the law is eventually to be achieved.

Conclusion

From the evidence presented in this book it is clear that the social context of enforcement and compliance in respect of legislation concerning safety and health at work predisposes the Inspectorate to an educative and informal negotiating strategy for compliance rather than a punitive strategy for enforcement. Contradictory views have been expressed and the debate has not ceased (Rhodes 1981). However, arguments for a stronger enforcement policy are rarely seriously considered, particularly as the HSC and HSE are now even stronger in their emphasis on compliance through advice and guidance and institutionalised self regulation. Recent proposals in this area include schemes of 'health and safety assurance' (HSC/8, 1985). Formal legal action is only taken in a small minority of instances of law breaking and is usually the 'last resort' for flagrant and persistent offenders

242

who have occasioned some clearly identifiable harm or damage to other people. Just as Hawkins (1984) concludes when he considers data on pollution prosecutions, so some may conclude on health and safety prosecutions that they are interesting as a description of organisational behaviour, useless as an index of the scale of the problem.

In the main, Inspectors are reluctant to take cases to court. To do so will consume precious time and resources. The matter of securing compliance will pass from their hands to those of the courts who may then, on a verdict of guilty, invoke very small penalties. This is not altogether surprising since the magistrate or judge will be considering individual acts of omission or commission rather than the history of non-cooperation and law breaking which is likely to have preceded the case in hand.

An educative informal compliance strategy for safety and health at work is thus certainly an accurate description of 'what is'. Whether the strategy is as it 'should be' is another matter. We must caution against the view that either punitive enforcement or negotiated compliance is always better. Strategies must be evaluated in terms of their achievements in securing the objects of the law, and here we have a problem for we have no comparative data on the achievement of compliance under a strict enforcement strategy. In any case, as shown in Chapter 2, there are difficultes in monitoring the effects of a single factor in a complex process.

We do know from the evidence contained in this book that at a time when greater emphasis is being put on educating and advising for compliance, economic recession and industrial reorganisation are associated with increasing serious accident levels, decreasing enforcement activity and declining emphasis on safety. Our discussion of the foundations of different strategies shows that the reasons underlying their development lie far deeper than the whim of any particular political party or the immediate persuasions of members of the HSC and HSE.

Some are content with the present strategy, others are not. Rhodes contends that the HSC 'cannot assume, for example, that an extreme reluctance to prosecute will go unchallenged' (1981: 71). This is particularly pertinent at a time when accident rates are once again rising. However, those who wish to reverse this trend must recognise that change will not be achieved simply by focusing attention on the law makers and the inspectorate. Rather one must look at the structure and ideology of the social and economic context of safety regulation. In a sense it was because the Robens analysis was founded on what are now shown to be assumptions of common interest which are limited in their application, that we have both the system and the outcomes observable today. It is then appropriate to return, with the benefit of our analysis, to these assumptions in the final chapter.

10

Conclusion: the future of
self regulation

There are four main sections in this final chapter. The first provides a summary of the main arguments and findings of the book. The second moves on to assess the future for the national system of self regulation in terms of changes in the legislative and regulatory climate since 1980. The third looks at three specific issues which affect safety at work: the impact of recession, changes in trade union organisation and membership, and changes to industrial structure. The final section examines the limits of the philosophy of self regulation and offers some suggestions for future policy on the basis of the conclusions presented.

Summary

The framework of health and safety legislation has been broadly stable since the passage of HASAWA in 1974. Subsequent regulations, including the Safety Representatives and Safety Committee Regulations in 1977, have amplified and enhanced rather than fundamentally changed the statutory approach established by the Act.

The Act itself was a radical departure. It sought to prevent accidents and to provide a common framework based on general duties and a more unified system of enforcement and inspection. It sought to create conditions which would enable the Robens principle of 'self regulation' to flourish. Both the Robens Report and the Act are concerned to establish that the primary responsibility for improved safety will lie with employers and workers themselves, with a residual, though important, role for the external enforcement activities of the Inspectorates in maintaining minimum statutory requirements and providing advice and guidance on their achievement. The Act thus lays duties, linked to the idea of 'reasonable practicability', on employers, suppliers, manufacturers and designers of equipment, the self-employed and employees.

244

The Robens conception of self regulation attributed considerable importance to the need for workforce involvement not least because the Committee considered there to be a greater natural 'identity of interest' between employers and workers over the issue of safety than in other matters at the workplace. As a result, the Committee favoured the development of consultative – but not bargaining – mechanisms to facilitate the involvement of employees in safety at work. As it turned out, the statutory framework has departed from the original Robens ideal, which was also essentially that of the 1974 Act, in two ways. The first, which dates from amendments to the Act made by the Employment Protection Act in 1975, is that safety representatives, who enjoyed certain rights under the Act, could only be appointed by recognised trade unions. The second, which dates from the passage of the SRSCR in 1977, as enhanced by subsequent case law, is that such representatives attract 'intermediate' rights similar to those established for trade union representatives in other contexts.

Given the many changes since 1979 to other statutes concerned with industrial relations, one might say that the framework of the Act has emerged relatively unscathed. However, at least from the perspective of the Robens Committee, any overlap between safety and industrial relations issues was to be seen as undesirable. For one thing, it raised the possibility that safety issues might be 'bargained away'. There was also the fear that invariable standards of safety provision might not operate as such across unionised and non-unionised firms and industries. In fact, there are substantial variations both in accident incidence rates across industries and in the development of safety organisation, although it is not easy to relate any part of such variance to the operation of statute.

In seeking to assess the impact of the legislation, Chapters 2 and 3 dealt with two sets of data. The first concerned the accident incidence rate. The second set was information on the growth at workplace level of institutions for safety provision, such as particular management policies and practices, safety committees and safety representatives. For both sets of data, methodological problems arose in the attempt to assess legislative impact.

The first is that of attribution, and this particularly affects the study of accident statistics. It is not possible to attribute any decline in the accident rate in a direct way to the operation of the legislation because of the many other factors which might at the same time affect accident rates. Nor is it possible to assume, for example, that all safety committees were established as a consequence of the Act. Moreover, the two sorts of data interact. The establishment of safety committees improves the level of accident reporting, hence the development of the institutional framework may, paradoxically, be associated with a rise in the reported incidence rate.

Analysis of the statistics is further complicated by two problems. First, the substantial but uneven under-reporting, which appears to have varied over time and across industrial sectors. This is related to the second problem, namely that the requirement to report accidents and the categories of reportable accidents have both varied. Since the passage of the 1974 Act, the series has been interrupted three times. One must therefore be cautious in interpreting the interrupted series. Exercising such caution by focusing on the more reliable series of fatal and major accidents, one can say that the improvement seen after the passage of the Act did not continue into the 1980s at least as far as manufacturing and construction are concerned. For the period 1981–85 there was a 31% increase in the combined rates of fatal and major accidents in manufacturing and a 45% increase in construction. The rate of increase appears to be particularly high in industries where pay is low and productivity is increasing most rapidly.

In a study of self regulation at local level three aspects of the institutional framework required examination; the development of safety policies, management organisation, including the appointment of safety specialists, and the development of safety committees and networks of representatives. The available evidence documenting these issues indicates growth in all three aspects following the passage of both the Act and the SRSCR. Safety policies, the publication of which is a statutory requirement for most employers, are often in existence, but there is great variation in their content and the degree to which their terms are observed. Safety specialists are employed in most sectors, usually by larger firms, but their expertise and authority are, again, extremely variable. Similarly, the institutions of workforce involvement have developed unevenly. Sectors characterised by a preponderance of large firms, stable employment and a high level of trade union organisation are also characterised by the proliferation of these safety institutions. By contrast, such institutions are less frequently in evidence in sectors with a higher proportion of small, non-union firms, or those which are characterised by unstable employment.

The chemical industry cases in Chapter 4 document the impact of the Act in the first type of industry, characterised by oligopoly, stable employment and relatively high risks. The data show considerable variety across firms in the nature of safety provisions, in relevant expertise and knowledge and in institutions for workforce involvement. Generally speaking, the chemical industry cases were characterised by well developed safety organisation, if not by effective workforce involvement. From the cases it emerged that the most important ingredient in effective self regulation of safety at work is the role and commitment of line managers. Without such commitment, formal provisions such as the writing of a safety policy or the establishment of a safety committee need have no positive effect on the level of risk.

Data on two other sectors in which effective safety management is likely to be more difficult have also been presented. Chapter 5 dealt with construction, Chapter 6 with retail. The construction industry for 1980–85 has a worsening safety record. It is an industry characterised by a growth in subcontracting, an expansion in the number of small firms and the volume of the work that they do, and by a decline in the level of trade union membership. The size issue is important, not least because it relates directly to the likelihood of external enforcement; small sites are less likely to be inspected than large ones.

The willingness, at least on the part of the larger firms, to ensure safe sites does not appear in doubt. Campaigns such as Site Safe 1983, the devotion of resources to safety matters, and the employment of safety specialists testifies to this; the sector also has a lively Industry Advisory Committee. However, the evidence from our cases is that workforce involvement is almost completely absent. Moreover, whatever the commitment of the large firms in the industry, there are major problems of safety management where subcontracting, self-employment and a proliferation of small sites are concerned. In many parts of the sector, agreements made on safety by management and unions cannot be enforced. On many large sites, because of the complexity of subcontractual relationships, managerial controls are weak or absent. Many small sites escape the notice of the Inspectorate altogether, yet small sites are known from the accident statistics to be disproportionately hazardous. In an inherently hazardous sector, changes to industrial structure are affecting accident incidence rates.

Retailing, although by contrast a low risk sector, shares several of the features of construction. The industry is dominated by large multiples, but many employees work either for small firms or in small establishments. Trade union organisation in the sector is weak, pay is low, conditions are often poor and many employees work part time. In addition, there appears to be some movement towards the franchising of operations. Accident rates in the sector fell between 1975 and 1980 but have shown no further improvement since.

Across our sample of retail cases, safety provision varied substantially. Once more there was a noticeable size effect, with better provisions in larger organisations, but even here substantial variance in the nature and effectiveness of provisions was noted. Many firms employed specialists, but it was not clear in some cases either where they fitted into the managerial hierarchy or what powers they had to affect line management commitment. Workforce involvement through safety representatives and safety

247

committees was not encouraged. In some of the larger enterprises there were well developed consultative and participative schemes which encouraged non-union workforce involvement in a variety of workplace matters. Safety was generally a relatively minor issue in these schemes which concentrated on such things as training, security, quality of service and customer contact. Nonetheless, albeit almost incidentally, such schemes did provide a means for non-union workforce involvement in safety matters. Involvement of the workforce through safety training was in many cases hampered by the prevalence of part-time employment.

In all sectors, the contrast between the commitment of large firms to safety provision and the practice of many smaller ones was pronounced. Where managerial willingness or capacity to ensure safe workplaces was absent, trade union organisation was generally too weak to exert pressure for change. This implies a need for greater external enforcement.

The case study material supported some general observations about what is necessary for successful local self regulation and these were discussed in detail in Chapter 7. From all three industries, it emerged that the most important ingredient is the role, commitment and accountability of senior executives and line managers. Without this, formal provisions such as the establishment of a safety committee need have no positive effect on the level of risk.

This finding is of significance not least because, whereas the Act and SRSCR spell out in some detail the sorts of institutions and powers needed to be made available for workforce involvement, they do not specify the form of management organisation and resource provision which are required to fulfil the duty of 'reasonable practicability'. The legislation is silent on this issue, presumably on the assumption that a basic element in local self regulation lies in the responsibility of managers not only to operate but also to devise the necessary mechanisms for the regulation of health and safety.

Nevertheless, the question of the appropriate arrangements for safety management is of considerable interest. It is possible to spell out the necessary features of effective safety practice in terms of management activity in hazard identification, the prescription and implementation of controls, and the monitoring and adaptation of strategies for control. The key elements of effective safety management are the recognition that accident prevention and hazard control require the allocation of scarce resources of time, money and expertise, and that consequently there needs to be real line management responsibility for safety at work. Acceptable levels of safety at work cannot be achieved simply through the activities of specialist functions, but only by the incorporation of safety standards into

248

general management objectives. From this perspective, the institutions of workforce involvement are secondary to managerial organisation in the specific sense that they depend for their effectiveness on management commitment which in turn relies on management accountability.

If this model of effective local self regulation is an accurate picture of the necessary requirements, then important questions arise concerning both the willingness and the capacity of companies to adopt it. Willingness is likely to be affected by the costs to the employer of accidents versus the cost of safety provision, the likelihood of prosecution under the Act for safety shortcomings and the strength of the requirement to demonstrate to employees, customers or the public at large that the workplace is safe. Capacity is likely to be influenced by the resources available for safety provision, the nature of workplace hazards and the ability to exert controls over line managers and employees in the interests of safety. In chemicals, although the resources required for safety provision are often considerable and the hazards are often intractable, many firms devote substantial resources to effective safety management because of the costs of certain types of accident and the public concern about chemical safety; in addition, the organisation of many chemical firms facilitates line management accountability. In other sectors, both willingness and capacity are likely to be lower because of the lack of external pressures and the lack of resources. In such sectors, the limits of self regulation are most obvious.

The Act's intent was to reduce dependence on external enforcement, except in the last resort, in favour of local self regulation. However, it acknowledged the need for policy and standards to be set nationally and for a more unified system of external enforcement even if the hope was that such a system would become less important over the years. The HASAWA 1974 provided for national institutions to deal with policy making and enforcement by establishing the tripartite HSC and a more unified system of inspection and enforcement under the aegis of the HSE. These are the subjects of Chapters 8 and 9. Both sets of institutions have developed distinctive characteristics.

The HSC has continued to operate in a remarkably consensual way during a period when many other tripartite institutions have disappeared. Indeed, its participants have largely been content with the organisation despite the relatively slow procedures for the production of regulations and codes of practice and the increasing emphasis given to the idea of cost-benefit analysis as a basis for policy development. The deliberations of the House of Commons Employment Committee in 1982 revealed that this contentment was not shared by all Members of Parliament and the debates at TUC Annual Conferences in 1985 and 1986 showed that parts of the trade union movement were becoming increasingly alarmed by the tendency for the HSC apparently to support deregulation in health and safety matters.

In spite of these misgivings about the recent operation of the tripartite institution in the UK, international comparisons have failed to produce evidence that any other system of national policy making is likely to be more effective, particularly if it is operating within a political framework which is biased against, rather than for, 'more regulation'.

The tripartite national structure can, however, only be effective if its policies and advice are acted upon at local level. Evidence on the construction and retail sectors shows several cases where the deliberations at national level which resulted in decisions made by consensus were not translated into good safety practice. Once again, where endorsement of good intent is lacking, the role of inspection and enforcement becomes important.

Although their role was modified by the HASAW Act 1974, and new powers were settled upon them, the Factory Inspectorate had already established a strong tradition in dealing with health and safety at work prior to their incorporation within the HSE. This tradition has emphasised the importance of exhortation, education and advice in dealings with employers, rather than a reliance on prosecution and punishment as a routine response to identified breaches of the law. Since the passage of the Act, this method of operation has been maintained; the number of prosecutions taken by HSE inspectors having fallen since 1974 despite the increase in the number of workplaces covered after the passage of the Act. The level of fines remains relatively low.

The EHOs employed by local authorities operate according to a rather different tradition, and certainly with a wider remit since they act in respect of public health and hygiene as well as workplace health and safety. They inspect premises more frequently, have a higher visibility in workplaces and use their own system of informal notices quite extensively. 'Over zealousness' has been a criticism of local authority inspectors by employers for at least the last two decades, as has the unevenness of application of enforcement powers between local authority areas. Efforts at greater consistency may reduce at least some of the latter complaints about lack of uniformity in the near future.

The two sets of Inspectors have faced the same major problem in the last five years, namely depletion of resources. The number of HSE Inspectors and of factory visits have both dropped since the late 1970s. The programme of basic inspection which is the backbone of the advisory and educational role has been particularly vulnerable. Despite the adoption of computer technology to collate information on hazards and visits and to generate a database to guide selective inspection, the frequency of inspection has dropped substantially so that in 1982 it was reported that, on average, premises were inspected by HMFI approximately once every seven years. The changes to reporting arrangements noted in Chapter 2 have also caused additional problems for the Inspectors in their attempts to deploy their scarce resources in the most effective way. It is particularly disturbing that the prospect of external enforcement, particularly in construction, and the development of the institutions of self regulation both seem least likely in similar sets of circumstances.

Overall, our data and analysis point both to general and specific problems with the self regulatory framework for safety at work. The general point concerns the extent to which self regulation of safety can be expected to flourish in the future. We pointed out in the opening chapter that the legislative and political climate of the 1970s affected the form of self regulation. Chapter 8 gave further consideration to the inevitable links between national policies for health and safety and different political climates. It seems therefore, appropriate to ask about the operation of the legislative framework in the changed climate of the 1980s and this is the subject of the next section.

The legal and political context, 1980–86

Chapter 1 suggested that the 1974 Act and ensuing Regulations shared several features with legislation passed during the 'Social Contract' period, in that they include regulatory, intermediate and auxiliary provisions. Questions therefore arise concerning the effect on health and safety legislation of other legislative changes since 1979 which have substantially modified the labour law of the 'Social Contract' period. We also suggested that the period since 1980 has been characterised by a political preference for 'market regulation' rather than for external, joint or tripartite regulation, and that this is likely to affect the tripartite system operative in the safety area. In this section, we shall look at specific legal and general regulatory changes in the 1980s and assess their impact on the operation of health and safety legislation.

Although no changes have been made to the HASAWA or SRSCR themselves, changes to other individual or collective rights in the 1980 and 1982 Employment Acts are relevant to our discussions of self regulation. It will be recalled that the current legislation is drafted in such a way as to ensure that the coverage of safety representatives supported by statutory rights cannot exceed that of trade union recognition. Restrictions on the spread of trade unionism are currently restrictions on the scope of safety representation. From 1975 to 1979, the Employment Protection Act 1975 gave legislative assistance to the growth of trade union membership by allowing unions seeking recognition to refer the issue to ACAS for conciliation, enquiry and recommendation. However, the 1980 Employment Act repealed these provisions, and offered some discouragement to the extension of recognition by discouraging 'union labour only' contracts. Section 12 of the Act makes void any term in the contract for the supply of goods and services requiring the use of unionised labour, section 13 makes void any similar term requiring recognition, negotiation or consultation with a union and section 14 removes immunity from unions seeking to pressure employers to breach sections 12 or 13.

Together, these provisions are likely to exert a restrictive effect on the growth of union coverage and therefore of safety representation in industries where subcontracting is common. Since we have suggested that these industries are in any event likely to experience difficulties in developing self regulatory institutions and practices, this set of changes is a further blow to the establishment of good safety standards.

It is debatable whether changes to individual rights are likely to assist improved safety, particularly in small firms. Since 1979, the qualifying period for making unfair dismissal applications has been extended. In 1979 the initial extension was from six months to one year of continuous employment. Section 8 of the 1982 Act laid down a qualifying period of two years for such dismissal protection for workers in firms with fewer than 20 employees and allowed the introduction of clauses waiving employee rights in this area into any fixed term contract of one year or more. Subsequently, the qualifying period has been extended to two years for all employees, except in cases of dismissal for automatically unfair reasons. The 1980 Act (s6) also requires tribunals to take the employer's size and resources into account in deciding cases of unfair dismissal, including safety related dismissals, and removes from the employer the full burden of proof of 'reasonable' action.

The cumulative effect of these changes in industries such as construction and retail may have been substantial. Particularly in the former industry, a high percentage of employees work in firms of fewer than 20 employees, on sites of less than two years duration without union representation and in environments of considerable hazard and contractual complexity. Safety representation is rare, and individuals who refuse to operate unsafe equipment or to work on unduly hazardous operations have no statutory protection against dismissal or action short of it. Employers are hit by recession and firms tend to be small; the extent of liability for particular operations may be unclear. In addition, the likelihood of inspection has decreased.

Given the considerable changes to other statutes concerned with terms and conditions of employment since 1979, the legislative framework for health and safety has been quite stable. However, the reliance on individual rights and intermediate rights related to trade union activity, which was the preferred method of securing safety representation rights in the 1970s, looks less satisfactory when individual rights are being reduced and auxiliary legislation has almost disappeared from the statute books.

These legislative changes both indicate and reinforce a more general change during the 1980s in the preferred method of regulating industry in general and management–union relations in particular. Whereas the tripartite HSC was not unusual in the 1970s tripartism has generally retreated in the face of a political impetus for 'free market' regulation. Through deregulation and privatisation, the Conservative governments of the 1980s tried to retreat from direct involvement in the regulation of industry and, in some cases, to dissolve the older regulatory bodies. The HSC is, in this sense, a survivor of a previous era. Nevertheless, as we have seen, it is one which has had strong support from its industrial participants, and one which international comparisons suggest may be the most effective at the national level. One might conclude from this that safety remains an area in which more consensus is possible than elsewhere. This seems a reasonable conclusion for the national level. The problem is, however, that policy, developed through national consensus, cannot presume local consensus or effective implementation. Furthermore, even at the national level there is some evidence that the views of the parties are changing. We shall look in the turn at the views of employers, government and unions.

The current view of employers generally on the provision of resources for safety is perhaps best typified in the CBI presentation to the House of Commons Employment Committee in 1982, in which it was stressed that the benefits of devoting resources to improved safety at work needed to be traded off against the costs involved. These costs were seen to include the possibility of job loss in the face of international competition. Although the House of Commons Employment Committee in 1982 was uneasy about this approach, the idea that employers would – formally or informally – utilise cost-benefit analysis in decisions to devote resources to health and safety is by no means new. Indeed, the definition of 'reasonable practicability' in law has contained the idea of cost-benefit analysis for some time. The original definition dates from the judgement in Edwards vs. National Coal Board (1949), discussed in Chapter 1.

There is a problem with this approach in periods of recession. The level of risk may not be affected by recession but the propensity of workers to endure it may be much affected. The costs to the business of meeting a particular safety provision, i.e. the 'sacrifice', will depend on solvency and market conditions. The very standard of 'reasonable practicability' if defined simply in terms of the employers' cost-benefit equation is inevitably affected by recession.

The employers' concern about safety costs has fed through to that of government. In the UK, this link was seen when the (then) Secretary of State for Employment made his instruction to the HSC in 1979 to consider the economic implications of new regulations. It is worth noting that the cost-benefit exercise conducted by the HSC pursuant to such an instruction would need to be different from that of the employer. The assessment of risk might be similar but the valuation of costs might differ. The HSC might, for example, calculate the costs of protection on a different basis from the employer where employment of more safety staff, previously unemployed, is required. The calculation from the point of view of the wider society is in fact far more complex and beyond the scope of current resources. As one informed commentator has noted 'In reality, the HSE cannot identify all the effects of a proposed regulation and it cannot value these effects with any precision' (Heywood 1985: 27).

Nevertheless, the scrutiny of the HSE carried out on behalf of the Conservative government by Lord Rayner has reinforced the recommendation that economic implications of new regulations be considered at all stages of policy formulation, primarily to assist cost-benefit estimation, while recognising that 'there are other criteria, apart from those of costs and benefits, on which the merits of health and safety policies are judged' (HSE/19, 1985: 17). The concern here was explicitly less to reduce the level of safety provision and more to assess the additional burden of costs. Hence the focus was rather more on the economic consequences of new regulations than on the enduring cost of the general duty of reasonable practicability. It is a concern based upon the view that the worst problems of industrial safety have been overcome:

> Until recently the general judgement of ministers and society
> was that more effective health and safety controls were needed
> and specific quantification of their costs and benefits
> unnecessary. But as the obvious grosser risks are progressively
> eliminated, the need to justify further improvements is
> intensified (HSE/19, 1985: 1).

It is, of course, a moot point as to whether the change in the views or in the identity of ministers has been more significant in this area. It is in any event a particularly contentious view to hold while the major accident rate is certainly not falling overall and is in some industries clearly rising.

Moreover, the analysis of the costs and benefits of new regulations is distinct from an analysis of the costs of enforcing existing ones. It is possible to argue the need for economic justification of further improvements while simultaneously arguing that the 'grosser risks' have not been eliminated due to non-compliance with older standards. In this respect, the cuts to the manpower and resources of the Inspectorate since 1979 may have in the long term a much more severe effect on the occupational accident rate than the requirement to provide economic justification for new regulations. Indeed since 'under current conditions no additional manpower resources can be provided', the view was taken by the Rayner scrutineers that new regulations actually distract the HSE from the enforcement of existing ones (HSE/19, 1985: 16). The main problem is thus set up by the initial decision to cut resources.

This decision may not seem important where the logic for the statutory system is self regulation with only a residual role for inspection. However, as we have seen, cuts in manpower affect those elements of HSE activity which best support the capacity and willingness of employers to observe the general duty, namely education and advice. Such education and advice has recently become more scarce when economic circumstances are eroding the capacity of employers themselves to devote resources to the problem of safety.

We have already seen that small firms pose a particular problem in this regard. They are least able to devote resources to safety provision, have a high accident rate in certain industries, and are less likely to experience enforcement. Where recession further undermines their safety capacity, the unacceptable choice may be presented between firm closure or the maintenance of an unsafe workplace.

The current approach to the squaring of this particular circle has been presented in two White Papers, 'Lifting the Burden' (Cmnd 9571, 1985) and 'Building Businesses . . . Not Barriers' (Cmnd 9794, 1986). As part of a set of measures to reduce the regulatory burden, particularly on small firms, the first White Paper suggested the raising of safety policy thresholds, a range of mechanisms to ensure that the HSE and HSC take account of small firms' interests and 'making clearer to employers that they have the right to question inspectors' decisions and showing them how this can be done' (p. 23). The second White Paper outlined progress on the 'Lifting the Burden' package, indicating a range of items which applied to small firms, for example the lifting of the threshold on written safety policies and increasing Inspectors' awareness of the requirements of small businesses. For the first time it also proposed a systematic reviewing of existing regulations in order to identify where the 'burdens' really lay. In addition, the Paper reported progress on 'safety assurance schemes', and examined the suggestion that all inspection responsibilities should fall on the Factory Inspectorate, rather than local authorities (p. 38).

255

Both White Papers explicitly locate safety enforcement in the category of a 'burden on business', hence the review not only of new regulations but also of 'outdated legislation'. Moreover, in dealing with a wide range of issues concerned not only with employment but also with government's entire relationship to business, they illustrate the extent to which, still, the approach to safety issues is defined by wider political preference.

The political movement towards deregulation finds many apologists in the USA (see for example Breyer 1982). Weidenbaum (1981) argues that regulation imposes too great a burden on industry which works to the detriment of all parties in terms of higher taxes, higher prices, job losses, bankruptcy and restrictions on big business so that their resources are diverted from their main and socially most desirable tasks of production, distribution and sale of goods and services. Little attention is paid to the costs of a rising accident rate, or to the issue of where these costs are most likely to fall.

Other commentators have indicated that the effective operation of a deregulated market for health and safety at work is dependent on freedom of information so that all parties have access to expert knowledge (Stone 1982). The argument here is that if employers are to be free to make their judgement on the costs and benefits of any particular action then employees must surely have the same right to make their own judgement about their participation. In order to make such a judgement, employees need access to the same information about hazards at work as their employers. For the 'market' to operate in favour of health and safety, employees who did not wish to work in conditions they judge to be unsafe or otherwise hazardous, would need either to have the right to refuse work or to have access to alternative equal employment. When unemployment rates are high, and trade union power is declining, the idea of market regulation of health and safety through employees' actions of this short seems to be a little unrealistic.

Implicit in the deregulation approach is a view of current inspection and enforcement practice as the imposition of a cost burden on business which can and ought to be reduced. This is not, of course, necessarily true given the advisory and educative bias of the HSC and HSE. Moreover, the costs of any compliance may be less than the costs of accidents experienced in the absence of inspection and enforcement, even where the calculation focused on the cost to the employer rather than on the costs to society as a whole. This is because accidents and ill health do actually impose considerable costs upon employers. For example, there are the direct costs of stoppages of work, lost management and labour time and compensation payments, as well as the indirect costs of lowering morale and recruitment problems. These are important considerations quite apart from any fines or other penalties imposed by the courts or the enforcement officers. When the costs are considered from the point of view of the wider society, then one must also include health service costs, disability pensions and other benefits which may accrue to the victims. However, whatever the arguments for the future our evidence from the past is that the 'burden' of inspection and enforcement on small firms is light, that inspection of small firms, particularly in construction is infrequent, and that safety standards are low. Indeed, one of the Health and Safety Commissioners was reported in 1987 as saying that employees in small firms were significantly more likely to be seriously injured at work than their counterparts in larger establishments.[1]

One way to deal with the trade-off between safety and cost is to remove regulation. Another is to offer assistance to those who must comply. In this case, the alternative to 'lifting' the burden would be to spread it more broadly. Small firms, particularly in high risk industries, could be targetted for selective inspection and enforcement, and financial or tax benefits provided to encourage compliance. We shall return to this in the final section.

Following outcry in sectors of the trade union movement against the proposals for deregulation implied in the HSC Plan of Work 1985–86 (HSC/8, 1985), the TUC was charged to develop its own ten year plan for health and safety. The Annual Congress also called for an increase in the number of prosecutions, contributed a paper on deregulation and small firms and committed itself to campaigning for 'a general expansion of resources available to the Health and Safety Inspectorate'.[2]

There are thus differences developing among the participants in the HSC. This is despite the comparative harmony which has been noted in comparison with the situation in other countries (Wilson 1985: 122). It is possible that differences might jeopardise the national self regulatory system in future, since the preference for market regulation stands directly at odds with the preference for increased joint regulation stated by the TUC. However, there may also be reasons why all parties should continue to participate, and indeed few criticisms focus directly on the HSC as an institution. For the unions, the HSC remains one of the few tripartite forums through which views can be expressed. For employers, particularly large employers, it provides a public platform to demonstrate their safety commitment. For the government, there simply seems no reason to abolish it, nor any clear view of what might replace it.

Whatever the outcome of present deliberations there is no doubt that current economic and legislative trends do restrict the full coverage of the self regulatory framework. Small employers and non-union workers are not only not represented by the CBI and TUC respectively but are, by the 'Lifting the Burden' philosophy, encouraged to fall outside the regulatory framework altogether.

Specific issues affecting self regulation

Recession

We have seen that recession influences safety standards in several ways. More straitened economic circumstances generate increased competition for financial resources within organisations and may encourage economies in specialist roles. Pressures arise to contain labour costs and to increase labour productivity: there is reason to associate both with rising accident incidence rates. Changes to labour flexibility, or to the balance of full-time, part-time and temporary employment, also appear to have an effect on the level of accidents. They may also alter the extent or nature of supervision which, we have argued, is vital to self regulation.

These pressures operate on the employer. Others may operate on the government, for example in the temptation to economise on inspection resources. Still more pressures are felt by individuals, who may in slack labour markets be prepared either to accept risky working conditions in employment, to take risks in order to increase pay, or to tolerate unsafe conditions through fear of discipline or dismissal.

The latter point raises questions about the role of unions in safeguarding employees during recession. Particularly where employers put forward cost-benefit arguments about safety measures which might affect jobs, unions are unlikely to give priority to the safety argument. Moreover, in industries where large scale job loss has occurred, unions may find it difficult to establish or preserve networks of safety representatives. Unions which have suffered resource depletion may also find it difficult to train and support safety representative networks.

The contribution of recession to the observed reduction in trade union density since 1979 is debatable, but to the extent that the number of employers with recognised trade unions is reduced, the scope for the development of safety institutions enjoying the full measure of statutory support is similarly curtailed. As we have noted, measures which exert a negative effect on the level of trade unionism may well have a negative effect on the standard of industrial safety.

Empirically, we have found the impact of recession on safety standards to be pervasive rather than direct. Managers would not necessarily make direct choices between cost and safety in a different way in recessionary conditions, nor would unions be more likely to 'sell' safety for gain. Rather, the infrastructure which supports effective safety management appears slowly to disintegrate. Managers are pressed by other priorities; often reorganisation blurs safety responsibilities. Union organisation may not disappear, but safety representative and safety committee activity declines. Overall the activities necessary for the maintenance of a safe workplace are eroded.

Trade union organisation

We have made the point that, legislatively speaking, union recognition and safety representation are coterminous. The decline of union organisation in the early 1980s was thus fairly straightforwardly associated with a deterioration in safety representation. However, the association of union organisation with safety was politically contingent – a product of the labour relations climate in the 1970s – rather than part of the analysis which supported the philosophy of self regulation. For Robens, there was no necessary association.

The logic may be rather different in the late 1980s, primarily because, even if not Robens' chosen instrument, unions have *de facto* become the prime instrument of workforce involvement. The experience of over a decade of safety representation, training and activity has resulted in a level of expertise in hazard identification and knowledge of the law within trade unions which did not exist in 1974. Without making any principled statements about trade unionism as the appropriate vehicle for workforce safety representation, one can still say that union recognition might well improve safety standards in many firms where they are now low.

Nevertheless, the association of union membership with safety improvement is difficult to establish. Table 10.1 uses the most recent available data to compare incidence rate changes with union membership changes. To the many *caveats* given in Chapter 2 concerning accident statistics, one must add several more concerning those on union membership. In particular, changes in union density, which are not available for the whole period, would be a better indicator than simple membership changes. Having said that, however, there seem to be two rather different patterns. Falls in membership and a rising accident rate are associated in the manufacturing and construction industries. Elsewhere the pattern is more complex.

Survey evidence (Daniel and Millward 1983; Millward and Stevens 1986) illustrates that trade unions have continued, throughout the recession, to retain some form of safety representation, and also some involvement in joint procedures for regulating safety. This has occurred across all sectors, although in private services approximately one-third of establishments had no representation in 1984 (Millward and Stevens 1986: 147–51). Despite membership loss, union densities in traditionally organised sectors have remained high. We thus have continued organisation and representation, combined with rising accident rates in some sectors. However, our case studies suggest that some of the 'formal' representation picked up in these surveys may in effect be 'dead' in practice with safety representative positions unfilled and safety committees moribund. The general conclusion must be that, in practice, union

Table 10.1 *Union membership trends and accident rates trends, 1981–84*

Sector	SIC	Percentage change in union membership 1982–84[a]	Percentage change in incidence rate 1981–84[b]
Agriculture, forestry and fishing	0	0	+60
Energy and water supply	1	− 37	−42.2
Mineral extraction	2	− 18	+29.2
Metal goods	3	−20.5	+ 19.3
Other manufacturing	4	− 0.7	+36.4
Construction	5	− 4.5	+50.9
Distribution etc.	6	− 5.7	− 1.4
Transport and communication	7	− 7.4	0
Banking etc.	8	+ 2.0	+ 15.4
National, local govt. and education	9	+ 5.9	− 2.7

Source: [a] DE.
[b] HSE. Figures are for fatal and major accidents, reclassified according to 1970 SIC.

organisation alone is not, under current legislation, an adequate safeguard of worker safety. Other factors are at work, notably management provision and external enforcement.

Industrial structure

We have laid emphasis on the importance of access to relevant knowledge about hazards and means for their containment and on the capacity and willingness of senior executives and managers to act on this knowledge to improve safety. Our contention is that clear responsibilities and systems of accountability for safety are necessary ingredients of successful safety policies. Certain types of organisational structure are implicit requirements of such policies: a certain level of formality and control, the necessary resources, and the environmental stability to plan improvements.

Although it did not emerge from the data we analysed in Chapter 2, our conclusion from the case studies was that a fragmented industrial structure makes safety very difficult to manage. Two of our sectors, construction and retailing, had a very high proportion of small firms, and often complex subcontracting relationships between them. The consequences in terms of incidence rates were very different primarily due to vast differences in the underlying levels of risk. However, we found that the same failures to observe routine safety precautions arose from lack of knowledge, lack of concern and lack of resources within individual firms to tackle problems as they arose. In both sectors, the gap between standards in large and small firms was considerable.

In 1987, the HSC was becoming increasingly concerned about the safety performance of small firms. One of the Commissioners was quoted as referring to evidence to the effect that

> people in firms with less than 100 employees run up to 50 % higher risk of serious injuries than those working in larger establishments.[3]

In response to this trend, the HSE published a new free leaflet '500 dead' which it distributed particularly to small firms seeking to remind them of basic legal requirements, the need for them to register with the Factory Inspectorate or local authority and encouraging them to seek advice from local experts and Inspectors. Establishments which do not register with an enforcing authority will of course escape inspection altogether unless or until a serious health or safety problem brings it to public attention. The Annual Report of the Chief Inspector of Factories notes that there is a 'high failure rate to notify industrial activity as required by Section 137 of the Factories Act' (HSE/6, 1986: 19). It seems a reasonable assumption that such failure to notify activity is particularly characteristic of small firms.

Overall, there is said to have been substantial growth in the numbers of small firms in recent years. In manufacturing, the percentage of employees employed in enterprises of fewer than 100 employees rose from 16 % in 1974 to 22 % in 1984.[4] There remain, however, substantial disparities between sectors. The number of small firms and the percentage of employment they account for varies substantially, both between manufacturing SICs and between manufacturing and services. In general, there are more small firms in services.

This is important, because many small firms are in low-risk sectors where neglect of health and safety standards may result in accidents, but where the overall accident incidence rate is low. The problem sectors are those where there are relatively high numbers of small firms, and relatively high incidence rates, for example metal manufacture and metal goods, and construction.

The construction industry is unique, both in having the highest incidence rates and in having peculiarly complex contractual arrangements. Nevertheless, some of our findings about the industry have more general application. Many argue that the growth of subcontracting and of temporary and part-time employment which characterises construction (and, to a more limited extent, retailing) will become more general in other sectors. We would argue that this may create safety problems, hence it is worth considering the safety implications of subcontracting.

As we have shown in previous chapters, subcontractual arrangements can be extremely complex. In construction, for example, the practice of 'sub-subcontracting' implies that main contractors on sites may know very little about the safety practices of firms and individuals operating on their sites. Nevertheless, sections 3 and 4 of the HASAWA do impose safety obligations on main contractors and subcontractors even where there may be no direct contractual link at all. Section 3(1) requires an employer to conduct his undertaking to ensure as far as is reasonably practicable that persons other than employees are not exposed to risk. Section 3(2) extends this duty to the self-employed, while section 3(3) introduces the requirement to provide information on risks to those who may be affected. Section 4 establishes a duty of care on those who have control over non-domestic premises; the controller must ensure that, as far as is reasonably practicable, both the premises and the substances provided for use on them are safe.

HASAWA thus broke new ground in extending duties on employers for the safety of those not in their employ. The force of these duties was brought home in the case of R vs. Swan Hunter and Telemeter Installations Ltd. In this case, an explosion which killed eight men occurred on a partly built ship when a welding torch was lit in an atmosphere abnormally rich in oxygen due to a leaking hose. The hose had been left in this state by Telemeter Installations Ltd, a subsubcontractor in no contractual relationship whatever to the owners of the shipyard, Swan Hunter: many of those killed were Swan Hunter employees. Both firms were found guilty of charges under sections 2 and 3 of the 1974 Act. Telemeter were responsible for the defective hose and liable under section 3, while Swan Hunter were liable under section 2: they had failed in their duty to their own employees in not fully informing Telemeter of the dangers of oxygen leaks.[5]

The contractual circumstances of the case are similar to those found on many construction sites where subcontractors work, and the Act is clearly enforceable. However, it seems reasonable to suggest that safety provision on a site or factory with several employers (possibly unrelated contractually) might fall short of that possible under stable employment relationships.

The terms of sections 3 and 4 themselves imply this. The section 3 duty includes the notion of 'reasonably practicable' action; coordination of subcontractors, some performance monitoring, 'permit to work' systems and a regular flow of on-site information would presumably go some considerable way towards discharging the duty. However, this could not be said to constitute self regulation of the form possible where long term employment contracts exist. The motivational elements described in Chapter 7 would be extremely difficult to maintain in the absence of direct control by the main contractor over hiring and supervisory practices within subcontracting firms. Workforce involvement would also suffer restrictions of the form described in Chapter 7 in the absence of functioning institutions designed to ensure safety at work. If safety representatives and committees are desirable in the pursuit of a lower accident rate, then contractual arrangements which prevent their establishment or hamper their functioning are not conducive to improved safety at work unless they possess other compensating safety enhancing qualities: in this case, these are difficult to identify.

Safety in workplaces where subcontracting is in evidence thus depends to a considerable extent upon the maintenance of good practice by the subcontractors themselves. The capacity to improve safety standards of small firms which are engaged in subcontracting depends not only upon the policies of the main contractor but also on size and recruitment policy. The willingness to improve safety depends in part upon the concern of the subcontractor to continue doing business with a particular main contractor or subcontractors and also of course on the extent to which the main contractor makes it clear that safety is an important priority. As Williamson (1975) notes, opportunistic or substandard behaviour in any aspect of contractual performance is much more likely where contracts are unique or infrequent and where the identity of the parties to contract is unimportant. Subcontractors reliant on a particular large building firm are much more likely to respond to its safety requirements than are those which seldom work with the same company twice.

Section 4 of the 1974 Act similarly includes only a limited duty. Under it, the controller of premises is not responsible for the behaviour of those on the premises, merely for the site and materials used. Where those on the premises are self-employed, or not employed by the controller, safety policy and practice may then be less well-known and less rigidly enforced. If, for example, self-employed people perform reasonably hazardous tasks on site, their behaviour is regulated by the requirements of section 3(2), but the main contractor need not supplement the subcontractor's control system by external enforcement of standards in fulfilment of section 4 duties.

Sections 3 and 4 may thus be read to imply a tolerance of lower safety standards in subcontracting operations than under permanent employment contracts. Together with the absence of safety institutions under subcontracting, this may imply a greater reliance on external enforcement than on self regulation. Indeed, economic analysis of this form of contracting implies the need for third-party enforcement of contractual terms.

The logic here again is that of Williamson. He argues that different types of exchange require different institutional contexts. Where goods are standardised and exchange frequent, market relationships are most efficient: the parties have invested little in the transactions themselves and alternative sources of supply and demand are available. At the other extreme, where highly specialised investments on both sides of the exchange occur, alternatives are not open at low cost and some other institutional form of governing the contract is necessary. One way of organising the activity in question would be to incorporate the transaction within a firm. However, exchanges which occur only sporadically for which highly specific investments are necessary are a problem: each party must invest a great deal in non-transferable investments which rely on the good will of the other, but the cost of a permanent institution for governance of occasional transactions tends to be high. For Williamson, such contracts are best regulated externally by a third party (1981: 39, 60).

This is extremely important for health and safety standards under subcontracting. Subcontractual arrangements in the building industry are both specific and occasional contracts: the work has value generally only on the site (and the costs of delay or fault for the main contractor may be high) while the site itself is an impermanent place of work. Williamson himself remarks that appeal to an independent expert such as the architect is often necessary for determination of the content of construction contracts (1981: 52). These sorts of contracts are not generally self regulating and it seems reasonable therefore to suggest that external regulation or the threat of it is the most likely for the establishment of safety standards which may form part of the contract. Whatever this may say about the level of hazards experienced, the basis of establishment of standards is not, and is unlikely to be, self regulation. The corollary of Williamson's argument is that the perceived likelihood of external detection will encourage compliance with contractual requirements, including those relating to safety. In subcontracting industries, the perceived likelihood of inspection is likely to be the strongest influence on safety provision, and in construction the perceived likelihood is low.

Much of this logic applies also to franchising in the retail sector. The construction example is, however, more serious in that apart from much greater levels of subcontracting, the hazards are greater and the likelihood of inspection lower, particularly on small sites. It seems likely from our case studies that, even on large sites in which the main contractor is a large firm committed to site safety through the provision of resources within its own organisation, contractual complexity is such that little line management accountability for safety can be relied upon. If our arguments in Chapter 7 concerning the necessity of such accountability are correct, safety standards will be lower simply by virtue of subcontracting; this logic too applies to the retailing sector. Since one might expect on other grounds that all forms of workforce involvement in subcontracting industries would be limited, much of the support for self regulation within firms disappears.

The growth of subcontracting is thus a considerable problem for the self regulatory framework of the Act. Nor is this by any means limited to the construction industry. Growth in subcontracting has occurred in the private and public sectors in waste disposal, catering and other functions. To the extent that other industries adopt subcontracting to a greater degree, a reliance on external enforcement of health and safety standards is likely to become more generally necessary, unless there is a revolution in the management practices of many subcontractors which will radically alter their capacity and willingness to act in respect of health and safety at work.

In summary then, recent changes have raised some questions about the appropriateness of the HASAW Act framework for self regulation in the current political and legal environment, and about its activities to reach and regulate parts of industry. It is not the case that, by themselves, reductions in trade union membership, or recession or subcontracting necessarily lead to lower safety standards, but where they combine, safety problems are very likely to arise. Two questions thus arise. First, to what extent can self regulation provide the logic for a universal local system of safety provision? Secondly, what changes to the current statutory framework are implied by recent trends? We shall look at each in turn.

The limits of self regulation

The core elements of local self regulation in the Robens conception were effective management, specialist advice and workforce involvement. We have shown how the first two depend to a large degree on the provision of a framework within which the willingness and capacity of employers to comply with the general duty of section 2 are enhanced. The previous sections have identified sets of specific circumstances concerned with the effects of recession, changes in the structure of industry and employment and changes in trade union organisation, in which the willingness and capacity of employers is likely to be severely compromised. We have thus already identified some of the likely limits of self regulation as far as the contribution of management organisation is concerned. Furthermore we have concluded that appropriate management organisation is the fundamental requirement of effective self regulation at local level.

Compared to the contribution of management organisation however, the issues involved in discussions of workforce involvement are more complex. This is not least because the HASAW Act was silent on the measures employers might choose to take, subject only to their compliance with the general duty. Whereas the statutory framework took no view on management organisation, it laid out the broad form workforce involvement might take. Furthermore, the issue of workforce involvement was one of the few parts of the framework to becomedthe subject of political dispute.

It will be recalled that the Robens view of the appropriate form of workforce involvement was based on the assumption of a natural identity of interest on safety matters. From this fundamentally unitary standpoint, which was nonetheless grounded in a concern with the attitudes of employees themselves to industrial hazards, Robens moved by a natural logic to the proposal that the appropriate role for employees and their representatives was to be conceived in terms of consultation with employers and assistance in the formulation and observance of safety provisions which would then be enacted through managerial structures. Bargaining over safety was not favoured. However, a certain lack of confidence in the efficacy of consultation on its own was indicated in the Robens proposal for safety representatives with statutory rights.

The SRSC Regulations came to enshrine an idea of workforce involvement of a slightly different sort, which relied on trade union representation. The appointment of safety representatives and their rights both related to their trade union recognition. However, there was no suggestion in either the HASAWA or the SRSCR that safety should be the subject of bargaining, rather that workforce involvement should develop primarily within organisations committed to collective bargaining. The coverage of the statutory framework would, it was thought, itself expand as a consequence of laws passed to encourage the extension of collective bargaining.

In fact, both the unitary Robens conception and the 'union-dependent' approach present difficulties. One can envisage at least four possible forms of workforce involvement in the area of health and safety:

(a) consultation; where management elicits workforce views for consideration in decision making;

(b) participation; where the workforce actually participates in the form and content of decisions;

(c) bargaining; where, in the 'distributive' case, the workforce threatens to exert sanctions on certain managerial decisions and in the 'integrative' case bargaining has more of a problem solving character;[6]

(d) exercise of statutory rights; where the workforce mobilises external legal resources to exert sanctions on, reverse or condition management decisions.

Logically, this set should also include individual or collective withdrawal, where a sanction occurs to condition future management behaviour or to isolate employees temporarily from the consequences of such behaviour.

Of this set, Robens chose to advocate a mix of (a) and (d). The legal framework differs only in that both are dependent on the prior existence of (c). This is effectively to prescribe a form of workforce involvement for companies which may not relate either to the form or level of involvement accepted on other issues. Some non-union companies operate purely through consultation. Others do not consult at all, although the evidence is that they are decreasing in number (Daniel and Millward 1983). Amongst unionised concerns, Purcell and Sissons distinguish 'consultors' who display a preference for wide-ranging consultation in addition to bargaining from 'pragmatists' who respond in an *ad hoc* manner to union demands, without any clear policy (1983: 114–17). One might further distinguish companies in terms of the range of items over which they bargain; some items, such as manning levels and hours of work, may be both negotiable and have direct safety implications.

Laid over this variance in commitment to workforce involvement, the statutory framework for such involvement in safety provision is almost certain to have uneven effects, as would the requirement to, for example, employ a safety officer, since it takes no account of the organisational context. Viewed from this perspective, the Robens idea of workforce involvement is a mixture of pragmatism and prejudice. The generalised concept of self regulation implies the absence of detailed statutory mechanisms to be activated within companies. Such mechanisms are restricted to the formulation of a safety policy; beyond this, organisations are left to themselves. However, given the importance of collective bargaining as the prime mechanism for workforce involvement in the UK, its exclusion from the realm of health and safety was curious and always unlikely to take effect. The apparent conception of bargaining as a zero-sum game in which health and safety issues might be traded off against other items ignored integrative possibilities entirely. Yet one could argue that, even with the form of consensus envisaged by Robens over the objectives of improved health and safety, differences over the appropriate means to secure this reduction and over the control of resources for health and safety were bound to occur. Robens could usefully have relied on a more pervasive agnosticism about the form workplace involvement should take than one which sought to preclude the most common form of such involvement.

However, there are also problems with the 'union dependent' approach. The linking of safety representation to trade union representation both limits its scope and discourages some employers from full cooperation with employees on safety matters; there is evidence to this effect in our case studies. By this definition of workforce involvement, safety becomes an industrial relations issue, even where the parties are not initially disposed to see it as such.

The limits of workforce involvement on health and safety matters are thus set, legislation notwithstanding, by the general nature and extent of workforce involvement in managerial decisions on the range of issues. These in turn reflect the relative powers of workers and managers which vary in different economic and political contexts. Where managers do not consult, safety committees are unlikely to be effective. Where managers bargain over a wide range of issues, they are likely to consult and possibly to bargain over safety. Where they seek to limit or cut back the influence of shop stewards, they are unlikely to encourage the activities of safety representatives. A system of statutory support for workforce involvement must take this into account.

Conclusions, policy issues and recommendations

The final section of this book is based on four general conclusions we have drawn from the research. The first is that a system of self regulation of safety at local level can be effective, but only if adequately resourced, if related to nationally established standards and if supported by the knowledge that failures of self regulation will lead to enforcement. The second is that effective local self regulation of health and safety will not be developed and maintained 'naturally' out of the operation of deregulated market forces; elements of government regulation are an essential prerequisite for systems of self regulation at national, industrial and local levels. The third general conclusion is that the overall performance of the system of local self regulation has deteriorated since 1981 as indicated by published statistics. Fourthly, we have suggested that this deterioration is marked in specific sectors characterised by small firms, subcontracting, low pay, weak trade unionism and productivity improvements.

One central theme underlies these four conclusions. Whilst no one actually wants accidents to happen or ill health to develop, the basic requirements for local self regulation (identified in Chapter 7) of knowledge, capacity and willingness to act will only be generated and maintained if those involved are held seriously to account for their performance in health and safety. This applies to all industrial and commercial workplaces in both the public and the private sectors. There seems little evidence to support Robens' fear that too much law or 'excessive' external enforcement would make people at work think of the safety of themselves and others as someone else's responsibility. A more significant fear, it has transpired, is that without it being 'forced' on them, many people will simply not think about safety at all, until direct contact with death or serious injury temporarily reminds them of the need to take care. A number of key issues immediately arise from this conclusion. How is one to ensure that appropriate information on performance is generated and made available to those who can give sanction or approval? How are people to be made to feel accountable for their performance so that they will seek its improvement if it is unacceptable?

These considerations imply certain policy choices for the primary actors in the system of self regulation. Assuming further that all are concerned with the improvement of safety, but not exclusively so, and that safety issues are being balanced against other priorities, these policy options can be spelt out. The primary actors are employers, trade unions and government – the parties to the HSC – as well as the HSC and HSE themselves, on whom the responsibilities for enforcement fall. We look in turn at the options available to each: they do, of course, interact.

Policy options for employers

Management organisation is the single most important key to effective local self regulation. Employer action is the major determinant of safety standards. Employers must train executives and managers to install and maintain systems for the identification and control of hazards and devise mechanisms for workforce involvement in safety. This means they must be prepared to allocate resources on a continuing basis. Those who do not, risk not merely the pressures of the Inspectorate and the prospect of a small fine. Other attendant costs may be huge. Whilst there is a sort of consensus over safety – every employer wants more of it rather than less of it – the value placed on safety and the process of achieving it are often contestable.

With these considerations in mind, the current emphasis of the CBI on the cost-benefit analysis of new regulations seems misplaced; basic systems of hazard control have still not been developed in many firms. While large firms are more likely to have good safety standards, many firms – often affiliated to the CBI either directly or through employers' associations – do not. Whereas trade unions cannot do much about small or non-unionised workplaces, the CBI can seek to embrace within the system of effective self regulation those of its members who currently are not reached. The CBI and other employers' associations need to give careful consideration to the issues of how to reach more employers with guidance, support and influence in order to secure their knowledge, motivation and capacity to act so as to make their workplaces safer.

269

How then is appropriate action to be secured amongst the employers and managers who have not yet developed effective systems for self regulation, or amongst those who, having developed some systems in the 1970s, have let them fall into disrepair? In addition to more guidance and advice, the key, it will be realised, is having some person or institution 'in authority' who will both receive information about health and safety performance, and act upon its receipt so as to encourage good performance and discourage bad performance. Three suggestions will be made about how to persuade employers and managers to change their behaviour and priorities. These suggestions are limited to things the employers themselves can do: they will of course be influenced by the actions of government and unions.

First, senior executives must make a clear commitment to including safety objectives as important managerial objectives and make it clear that data on health and safety performance will be used as one criterion in management appraisals. Secondly, senior executives in both the private and the public sectors must make it clear that they will use data on health and safety performance as one criterion in awarding future contracts for subcontracted work. Thirdly, since the availability of data is one key to both of the above suggestions, employers must ensure that data in both the incidence of accidents and ill health, and on management systems, is collected, disseminated and used. Annual reports should include the presentation of relevant data (e.g. accident incidence rates, any details of enforcement action in terms of notices or prosecutions initiated by the HSE or local environmental health officers). Subcontractors should also be asked to provide this sort of data when seeking work.

Policy options for the HSC and HSE

The options outlined for employers must be backed up by action from the HSC and HSE. However favourably inclined to improving safety standards, and however much they are aware that such improvements may well be cost-beneficial in terms of savings generated by less lost time and less compensation, employers still need to know that flagrant transgressions of the law will be identified and sanctioned, otherwise the whole basis of the regulatory system is seriously undermined.

The primary policy issues for the HSE concern the need for further developments of policy and practice on three fronts. First, issues of standardisation and targetting; secondly, the balance between different types of activity, notably education, advice and enforcement; thirdly, and with considerable implications for the first two issues, the use of the

270

depleted resources available to the HSE in general and the use of a smaller number of Inspectors available for field work in particular.

The first issue of standardisation is a problem, since currently there exist good, bad and indifferent employers, in safety terms. Moreover when it comes to small firms the Inspectorate simply does not inspect with sufficient frequency to enforce standards properly. Given scarce resources, it seems inevitable that the HSE will have to develop further its approach of resourcing campaigns aimed at specific industries or hazards or at small firms, so that it can target its efforts to areas where incidence rates are increasing most rapidly.[7] Such targets need to be properly identified and campaign specific objectives developed and implemented. This in itself creates more resource demands on the HSE and its Inspectors.

The differential approach to targetting is related to the second issue of the balance of activities. Indeed differentiation may define the balance of activity, with advice and assurance schemes being considered appropriate for some sectors, with a 'blitz' of inspection and enforcement activity in other areas. Such developments are likely to increase complaints about 'uneven' treatment, at least initially. Furthermore 'advice' and 'education' are no less costly in resource terms than enforcement. It is naive to think that you can advise and educate at 'arm's length' merely through the publication of written material. Our case studies are sufficient to show that in enterprises where safety is not given high priority, written material is, at best, likely to find its way into a filing cabinet from which with luck it can be retrieved if anyone remembers it is there. More likely, however, it finds its way directly into the rubbish bin. To be effective, advice and education often need to be provided on the basis of personal contact between the Inspector and members of the workforce.

It would also be naive to ignore the fact that an employer's or manager's readiness to accept advice from an Inspector is related to the Inspector's enforcement powers. In the flurry of activity surrounding the 1974 HASAW Act there is no doubt that employers and managers were really concerned to avoid prosecution – which of course carried with it not only the threat of a fine, but of imprisonment as well. The relatively limited use of notices and prosecutions, the low level of fines, and the fact that imprisonment is virtually unheard of, with the first – suspended – custodial sentence being passed under the HASAW Act in 1985,[8] have undoubtedly contributed to a relaxation of effort on the part of some managers and employers. Sentencing is of course a matter for the independent judiciary. However, it should be asked carefully to consider sentencing policy for offences which indicate a serious neglect of safety at work.

Although we advocate a strengthening of the resolve to prosecute flagrant abuses of the law, we are aware of the difficult issues which a

271

stronger enforcement policy raises for the HSE. The tradition and culture of the Factory Inspectorate incline it towards guidance and advice except in cases of blatant or persistent disregard of statutory duties. Inspectors and many commentators consider Inspectors need to work through the cooperation of those in industry rather than their alienation. Nonetheless there is undoubtedly room – as both individual managers and Inspectors acknowledge – for a tighter definition of when the point for an enforcement notice or a prosecution for flagrant or persistent safety offenders is reached. There is also room for more frequent inspections so that flagrant breaches of statutory requirements actually come to the Inspector's attention before serious harm is caused.

Wilson (1985) has noted that one of the advantages of the UK regulatory system lies in the quality of relationships between Inspectors and inspected. One important improvement which needs to be made in the UK is the use of this relationship to generate more systematic information about hazards in employment and the experiences of particular types of firm, and to develop ways of ensuring greater compliance with the requirements of the HASAW Act as well as with more specific regulations and legislation.

In the light of this discussion there are some further specific issues the HSE might consider. First, since we know that management organisation is a major determinant of safety standards, Inspectors should be even more concerned to seek information on aspects of organisation and, where appropriate, to being their enforcement powers into play to make sure not only that a safety policy is developed but that appropriate organisation and arrangements are implemented.

Secondly, Environmental Health Officers make considerable use of 'informal notices' which are somewhere between 'a word of unwritten advice in the ear of a manager or employer' and a formal improvement or prohibition notice. Factory Inspectors sometimes write letters to employers, following their visits. This should be encouraged and the use of other informal means of emphasising the importance of certain actions should be investigated.

Thirdly, more resources should be made available to the HSE so that Inspectors can focus more directly on the problem areas of small firms and subcontracting. Those who associate the Inspectorate with burdens on taxpayers and on industry might suggest that more resources and inspections might improve safety but at the cost of increased regulatory burdens. The history and traditions of the Inspectorate belie the view that more Inspectors and inspections necessarily lead to more prosecutions although there is, as we have seen, room for some developments in this direction. In fact more resources would be likely to be devoted to basic 'preventative' inspection. This could be focused on smaller firms in order to prevent costly accidents, particularly if a Health and Safety Assurance

272

Scheme for 'licensing' the safety policies of large firms develops as suggested for discussion in the HSC's Plan of Work 1985–86. In its Report 1985–86, the HSC reported that it had set up a small firms working group to investigate how to get the health and safety message across to small firms.

We have already described the tripartite structure of the HSC. Curiously enough the fact that tripartism is anomalous within the present political climate with its bias for deregulation makes it so important a characteristic for the HSC to maintain. There are tensions and pressures within the structure; in particular its policies and approach are becoming increasingly distanced from those of individual unions and the TUC, as government pressures are felt. There are delays in making new regulations, but when they are agreed they carry the support of employers, trade unions and government. Thus we consider the HSC should retain its national structure.

The main problem with the HSC is that national developments have an uneven impact on local activities. The HSC must give more thought to how it can reach the furthest corners of its constituencies through the CBI and TUC and how it can increase its impact on groups of employees such as those employed in small firms and non-unionised enterprises, which are at present outside its representative net. The linked activities of HSC's Advisory Committees and HSE's National Industry Groups are an important basis for relating national and local levels and their coverage should be extended to include more establishments.

Policy options for government

The central issues for government turn, ultimately, on the extent to which a concern with safety is tailored to fit in with other issues, particularly concerns with industrial relations and with deregulation. For the Labour governments of the 1970s, the first of which passed HASAWA, the concern was to fit safety legislation into the general pattern of regulatory and auxiliary legislation; safety as an issue could be subsumed under the more general issues of the 'Social Contract' package. For subsequent Conservative governments, safety legislation has come to be seen as part of the 'burden' under which business, particularly small business, labours. Their preference for market regulation has been associated with proposed amendments to the legislation itself and reductions in the scope and quality of enforcement activity.

The primary policy choices for government at present can be set out as follows. First, there is a need to reform safety legislation to insulate it more fully from changes in trade union legislation. Secondly, there must be a decision as to the extent to which, in the face of a rising accident rate, market regulation can be allowed to prevail. Thirdly, there are decisions to

273

be taken about the priority to be given to the resourcing of inspection, advice and enforcement activity.

One option under the first heading might be to alter the link between union recognition and safety representation, with the introduction of some broader system for representation. Careful consideration should also be given to providing employees with individual rights to information about hazards and to refuse dangerous work. These suggestions will be discussed further below in the section on trade union options. A concern to limit the rise in accidents without abandoning the deregulatory approach naturally leads to more emphasis on resourcing industry, hazard, or size-specific campaigns, targetting the areas where incidence rates are more rapidly increasing. This would, however, pre-empt the third policy option, since such areas could only be properly isolated and dealt with by a better-resourced Inspectorate.

Other specific options have been suggested. Two will be mentioned, one on each side of the government/market regulation debate. One way to secure an increased flow of information which is a prerequisite for action, is to take up the suggestion already made to employers and to require companies to publish health and safety data in their annual reports and for companies which are not publicly quoted to provide such information on demand or lodge it with Companies House. This suggestion is by no means new since Section 79 of the HASAW Act permits regulations to be made to require such material to be included in annual company reports. On the market side of the debate, consideration should be given to ensuring that good safety records are rewarded by lower insurance premiums or by tax or national insurance concessions. Similarly an organisation's safety record should become one of the factors which are considered when awarding contracts for work in both the public and private sectors.

Overall we have found no strong arguments for the deregulation of health and safety at work. There is no evidence, either from the UK or from other countries, that market regulation can be as effective as government regulation in this context. There is little or no evidence that the operation of health and safety at work legislation is a burden on small firms or on any other sector of industry. There is, however, strong evidence that proportionately more people are being seriously injured if they work in manufacturing or construction in the mid-1980s compared with the beginning of the decade. There undoubtedly needs to be a central role for government and its agencies in seeking to regulate health and safety at work.

Policy options for trade unions

As with government, the preferred policies of trade unions are well publicised. Whereas government has sought to reduce the level of regulation, trade unions seek to enhance the powers of Inspectors and safety representatives to influence and control the activities of employers and managers. There can be little doubt that the massive training and education efforts launched by the TUC and member unions vastly increased safety awareness in the 1970s, although in the changed circumstances of the 1980s their force seems slightly spent. Our cases revealed instances where, although firms recognised trade unions, there was little activity and neither shop stewards nor safety representatives were appointed; in other cases shop stewards existed, but safety representatives did not. It is often difficult to find people to fill the positions and, once appointed, they often find it difficult to have a major impact on safety standards. Thus, even where local union organisation is good and shop stewards and safety representtatives are appointed, safety is often low down the list of priorities. Few safety specialists are, even now, employed by unions. The level of information, resources and support forthcoming from union headquarters is highly variable and in some instances could be greater. The TUC needs to give careful consideration to the feasibility of expanding its central functions with regard to policy coordination and the dissemination of health and safety information.

One issue for the unions, like government, concerns the approach to safety legislation. Some parts of industry – hazardous parts – may never be unionised. Currently, in any event, the non-union sector is expanding while the unionised sector is contracting. Unions must concern themselves primarily with members and membership growth, but the advocacy of other systems of safety representation is something which should be considered.

The law has established two standards of employee representation, one in workplaces with, and another in those without, recognised trade unions. It is not the case that all non-union workplaces are more hazardous than unionised ones, but some of them are. In these firms, employees faced by managers who lack the will or capacity to ensure safe systems of work do not have access to statutory rights to pressurise them to do so. This disparity has no basis in equity, nor does the encouragement of safety representation via the encouragement of trade unionism appear an efficient way to deal with the problem when trade union coverage itself is in decline. One proposal would therefore be to allow for the appointment of safety representatives with statutory rights in non-union workplaces where there is no union recognition. Such a proposal for employee safety representatives is relevant for two different contexts. First, there are workplaces where, although there is no recognition, there is a fair number of union members. In other workplaces there are virtually no union

275

members at all. We found examples of both cases amongst our construction sites and retain outlets. A proposal for employee safety representatives is likely to be interpreted differently in each context, although objections to the proposal may be raised in each.

One objection to the idea of employee safety representatives lies in the idea of dilution – that employee safety representatives would be ineffective without trade union support. In firms where there is a number of union members but no recognition, it is likely that individual union members would receive union support as safety representatives. Lack of support was, however, a problem which we encountered in one or two of our case studies where the crucial issue seemed to be whether or not employees have any experience of participation or consultation. Employee safety representatives in establishments where there was no tradition of consultation or participation were completely ineffective. They lacked a clear idea of what they should do; they had no direct or indirect experience of participation in discussions at work and they mostly regarded the occasional safety committee they had to attend as an unproductive ordeal. In the main they could not wait to relinquish their position. By contrast, in the firms in our study which had a commitment to (non-union) workforce involvement in a range of activities, some employee safety representatives found the position personally worthwhile and were also fairly effective, at least in managing to maintain open channels of communication and participate in inspections.

There are also problems of increasing the complexity of the system of appointment of safety representatives in workplaces where there is only partial recognition. The problem of complexity already exists in a slightly different form where multi-unionism exists; the Regulations give no guide as to the appropriate number of safety representatives in a workplace of a given size.

Other issues would also have to be resolved. It would be particularly important to give employee representatives a set of rights which would safeguard their position, afford them time and resources to undertake their responsibilities, and protect them from dismissal or harassment for undertaking their activities.

Undoubtedly there would be a number of problems if the suggestion to extend the right to safety representation was implemented, but any such problems must be considered in relation to the existing problem of many employees having no right to safety representation at all. Representatives of the workforce with statutory rights in all firms, whether individual union members or not, would be an advance on the situation where many places of work have no right to representation over safety whatsoever.

Two other suggestions have also been made to overcome the problem of

276

large areas of industry falling outside any statutory requirement for workforce involvement in safety. One is that there should be a system of regional safety representatives who could be appointed by isolated union members in relatively unorganised sectors where the employees want help and support from experienced safety representatives. These representatives would have the right of access to these workplaces. This would be an extension of the sort of arrangement which already exists with Equity and the Musicians Union, whereby under SRSCR/8(1) representatives, who need not be employees at a particular workplace, can inspect this work place on behalf of the actors' and musicians' unions. The extension of such a system to workplaces without union recognition is likely to run into at least three major problems. The first is that there is likely to be enormous opposition from employers. Secondly, we know that many union branches find it difficult enough to find sufficient people prepared to be safety representatives in their own workplaces, let alone taking on rights and functions in relation to other workplaces as well. However, if regional safety representatives were full-time, recruitment might be easier. Thirdly, existing trade unions could not be expected to resource the training and support of representatives in non-union firms. Suggestions have been made that resources should be made available through a levy on the number of employees so that companies who would be covered by regional safety representatives would pay a levy in proportion to the size of their workforce. A similar development has been started in Sweden and, together with other important activities including research and training, their Regional Safety representatives are funded out of the 'Swedish Work Environment Fund'. This is created by a 0.155% levy on the payroll of all employers.[9]

A second suggestion which addresses the issue of inadequate workforce involvement in safety is to consider providing a floor of individual rights for employees specifically in relation to health and safety at work. Two basic rights are fundamental. The first is the right to free information about hazards and how to control them. The second is the right to refuse work which the employee considers dangerous without fear of dismissal or harassment. Both are currently safeguarded in the UK to a limited degree by 'intermediate' rights associated with auxiliary legislation. In other countries, for example Canada, they exist as autonomous individual rights. Our argument is both that individual employees need enhanced statutory rights, and that these rights must be universal in coverage. We are thus suggesting sets of rights which empower individual employees to use their assessment of hazards as a basis for action.

Such rights would need to be differentiated from the current set of rights for individuals in employment, enforced through the tribunal system. Our

277

analysis shows that it would be inappropriate to restrict such rights by a qualifying period, or to employees working above a given number of hours: such restrictions would avoid the areas of employment where such rights are most desperately needed. The tribunal system, whose functions are primarily compensatory rather than preventative, would also be an inappropriate enforcement agency: the new rights would need to be safeguarded by the Inspectorate, which would thus need to widen its audience from employers and representatives to workpeople as a whole. Its educative and informative role would thus be enhanced. This suggestion strengthens the recommendation that the Inspectorate be more fully resourced. It also has some resonance with proposals to return more to market regulation of health and safety issues, by seeking to empower individual employees to use their assessment of what is hazardous as a basis for action.

A further issue concerning workforce involvement is the fact that safety committees currently have no legal powers and duties. Consideration should be given to establishing their power and duties, which might include developing safety policies, monitoring safety performance and ensuring some control over safety budgets.

There exists, then, a range of policy options facing the parties at national level. Wider political preferences may define the approach any of them take; the lessons of the past are that safety issues are not immune from wider social, economic and political matters. However, the question of safety at work is not purely a political one: considering the period from 1980 to 1985 the UK has a worsening safety record, and something needs to be done about it. Our research suggests several options, not so much to reform the system at national level as to enhance its effectiveness locally.

It was always an optimistic view not only that those in industry would agree on safety issues, but that they would give them sufficient priority. We have argued throughout that effective safety management within firms requires continued effort and resource provision. In a similar way, the effectiveness of self regulation as a philosophy guiding safety legislation as a whole requires the continued devotion of resources to improving attitudes towards safety at work. Our policy proposals stem first from the proposition that the current system of local self regulation does not extend across the entire spectrum of industry. Certain types of firm and of employee in practice escape the ambit of an ostensibly all-embracing legislative framework. They are also concerned to discover ways of stopping the erosion of systems of self regulation which have been established in larger firms in the past but are now under considerable pressure to change so they become less effective. Both sets of problems have generated deteriorating safety performance in the past: unchecked, they will continue to do so in future.

Recommendations

1 One senior executive in every public and private organisation should be deputed to establish and oversee a system of management accountability for health and safety performance.

2 One senior executive in every public and private organisation should be deputed to establish and oversee a system for vetting health and safety performance of 'would-be' subcontractors before contracts are placed.

3 One senior executive in every public and private organisation should be deputed to establish and oversee a system for monitoring the health and safety performance of subcontractors once contracts have been placed.

4 The annual reports of publicly quoted companies should be required to include health and safety data including serious and fatal accident incidence rates and any formal dealings with the courts or inspectors for health and safety at work.

5 Non-publicly quoted companies should lodge annually their health and safety data with their other company data at Companies' House. This data should also be available on request from the owners of the company.

6 Consideration should be given to ways of rewarding good health and safety performance for companies through adjusted insurance premiums, tax and national insurance concessions and through considerations of their safety record as one factor in the award of contracts for work to another organisation.

7 The HSE should further develop their policy of targetting particular types of workplace, in terms of the provision of specific advice and increased frequency of visits. The findings from these specific campaigns should be fed through the HSC and its Advisory Committees with a view to preparing appropriate regulations, guidance notes and codes of practice.

8 Every means should be taken to increase the visibility and strength of the HSE Inspectors in their relations with industry. This does not have to be at the expense of their commitment to work primarily through advice and education. Consideration should be given to
 – more frequent visits, particularly for some categories of workplace,
 – more use of clear informal letters and written advice which will be followed up,

    — more systematic application of notices and serving of prosecutions in cases where there is a flagrant breach of the law.

9 Far greater resources should be put into the field inspection and enforcement activites of the HSE and local authorities both to expand the availability of education and advice and to take account of recommendation 8.

10 Inspectors of health and safety at work should be further encouraged regularly to seek information from workplace visits on management organisation and arrangements and workforce involvement in order to establish how, if at all, health and safety policy is made, implemented and monitored. Inspectors should be encouraged to take informal and formal measures to ensure an adequate level of management and organisation for health and safety in all the workplaces they visit.

11 The courts should be encouraged to increase the 'normal' level of fines and to consider imprisonment for very serious crimes relating to inadequate safety provisions.

12 Every effort should be made to retain and strengthen the tripartite basis of the Health and Safety Commission and its Advisory Committees. A strong commitment from employers, trade unions and government to seek to improve standards of health and safety is an essential basis for national policy making.

13 Every means should be taken to seek ways to increase contact between the main participants in the HSC and its Advisory Committees, i.e. employers of large companies, national representatives of employers' associations and trade unions, and their counterparts in more peripheral, smaller and non-union enterprises.

14 Employers' associations and the CBI should give consideration to expanding their central information and policy activities for safety at work and in particular seeking to reach those employers who are currently ignorant about the subject or unwilling to act to improve safety.

15 Trade unions and the TUC should put more effort into the recruitment, training and subsequent support of safety representatives in all establishments where there are recognised trade unions. They should also give consideration to expanding central information, research and policy activities for safety at work.

16 Consideration should be given to ways of improving the scope of workforce involvement in health and safety. In particular the following suggestions warrant extensive discussion:

    — developing systems of trade union regional safety representatives with rights to inspect and advise in weakly organised workplaces,

    — instituting mechanisms for the election of employee safety

representatives where there is no recognised trade union and providing them with appropriate rights,
- establishing a floor of individual rights, including the right to information about hazards and their containment and the right to refuse hazardous work with protection against dismissal or harassment,
- reviewing the role of safety committees with a view to specifying their powers and duties.

Appendix: Industrial variations in accident rates

This appendix looks at the change in incidence rates between 1981 and 1984 at Minimum List Heading (MLH) level in relation to the impact of recession, changes in output per head, the size distribution of industrial activity and the inter-industry earnings pattern. It looks at some of Nichols' arguments about 'structures of vulnerability' and business cycle effects. He suggests that there will be a recession effect on incidence rates, but that it might be complex. We have simply tried to see if there is a linear relationship between changes in employment, productivity and output and the fatal and major incidence rate. Nichols also suggests severe problems in low-pay industries, where trade union organisation is weak, and where firms are small. We have looked also at these relationships (Nichols 1986).

There are several problems with the data.

1 HSE returns are classified according to 1968 SIC (see our Table 2.5). Employment, output and firm size data are available according to 1968 SIC from DE and CSO up until 1981 or 1982, depending on the series, but not up to 1984. The HSE kindly provided statistics for the manufacturing MLHs in Table 2.5, broken down by 1980 SIC.

2 It was not always possible to use rate-of-change variables. The relevant employment and output data were available. For productivity at MLH level we use changes in gross value added per capita. However, for earnings and firm size, we used 1984 data, because
  (i) the New Earnings Survey does not change over to 1980 SIC until 1983. Earnings data for full-time manual males are available at MLH level.
  (ii) The Business Statistics Office, which collects data on firm size, *excludes* firms of fewer than 20 until 1983. Thereafter, it includes them. The two series are thus incomparable.

3 There are no data post-1979 on union membership by MLH. Those for 1979 are, naturally, on the 1968 SIC, and are incomplete. DE figures only go to one-digit SIC level.

283

Appendix

4 There are no data on safety committee or safety representative coverage, or on number of inspections by 1980 SIC. Even data classified according to 1968 SIC are not comprehensive and do not cover the whole period.

5 The analysis is restricted to the 21 manufacturing MLHs and construction, for which data on the independent variables were available.

The variables thus are

ΔFM; percentage change in the fatal and major incidence rate within manufacturing and construction MLHs between 1981 and 1984
Source: HSE communication

ΔEMP; percentage change in employment within each MLH, December 1981 to January 1985
Source: DE

ΔOUT; percentage change in gross output within each MLH, 1981 to 1984
Source: Annual Abstract of Statistics, Table 8.1; Housing and Construction Statistics, 1975–85

ΔGVA; percentage change in gross value added per capita, 1981–84, within each MLH
Source: as ΔOUT

SIZE; percentage of employees employed by firms of less than 50 in 1984
Source: PA 1003, PA 500

PAY: percentage of full-time manual males earning less than £150 per week in 1984
Source: New Earnings Survey, 1984, Table 6.6.

The predictive equation is thus

$$FM = CONST + B\,\Delta EMP + C\,\Delta OUT + D\,\Delta GVA + E\,SIZE + F\,PAY$$

The straightforward linear least squares fit is

$$FM = -83.89 + (-0.743)\,\Delta EMP + 0.007\,\Delta OUT + 0.708\,\Delta GVA$$
$$+ 0.557\,SIZE + 1.339\,PAY$$

$R^2\,[\text{adj}] = 0.329$

ST.ERROR $= 25.102$

Durbin Watson statistic $= 3.058$

Of the individual variables, only GVA and PAY are significant beyond 0.05. The Durbin Watson and the residuals indicate negative serial correlation. The correlation matrix indicates some multi-collinearity. A stepwise model rejects additional variables after GVA and PAY. The

284

forward run model is

$$FM = -80.06 + 1.679\,PAY + 0.675\,GVA$$

$R^2\,[adj] = 0.381$

$ST.ERROR = 24.12$

Durbin Watson statistic $= 2.97$

The implication is thus that the accident incidence rate increased over the period most markedly in industrial sectors where pay was low in 1984 and where the rate of productivity increase between 1981 and 1984 was high. The effects of industrial structure (proxied by size), and of changes both in output and employment, are weak.

Notes

1. The development of health and safety legislation

1 The structure and policies of the Inspectorates are the subject of Chapter 9.

2 Section 2 of the Wages Act 1986 repeals the 1979 Wages Councils Act. Subsequent to the 1986 Act, councils set only single basic hourly and overtime rates, do not set rates for employees under 21, and must consider the impact on jobs when setting such rates.

3 Section 6 was amended by the Consumer Protection Act 1987.

4 'Reasonably practical' certainly involves economic criteria but this is not exactly the same as cost benefit analysis. There was an exhaustive discussion of the relation between the two at the Sizewell Enquiry. See evidence on day 159, pages 99–106; evidence on day 278, pages 93–6; documents NII/P/1/ADD/7 and 8. The HSC/HSE view is that the solvency of individual companies is irrelevant. Computation of 'reasonably practicable' is made on the basis of the plant, process and risk (HSE personal communication 1986).

5 The HSC issued guidance in HSC Newsletter No 2, October 1978 to all enforcing authorities on the enforcement of the SRSCR. In June 1979 it was supplemented by guidance on the provision of information to safety representatives. The HSC advises that Inspectors should not normally need to enquire into the carrying out of employers obligations, unless trade unions or safety representatives ask them to do so. HSE records show that, since 1978, only one improvement notice has been issued citing these regulations (Communication from HSE, June 1987). We understand that the HSE are in 1987 conducting a survey into the operation of the SRSCR with a view to considering whether any changes are required.

6 Tribunals have in general supported the safety representative's right to paid time off under EP (C)A S27. See Little v London Borough of Haringay (COIT 1355/194). They have also endorsed the right to go on trade union courses where the employer's own course is deemed inadequate; White v Pressed Steel Fisher (1980 IRLR 176).

7 BAC v Austin (1978 IRLR 332) and Hewitt v Newman Pugh Aerosols (COIT 1337/216).

8 Frizzel v Flanders (COIT 847/232); Martin v Yorkshire Imperial Metals (COIT 709/147).

9 Taylor v Alidair (1978 ICR 445); McKenna v G.Leslie (EAT 320/81).
10 Smiths Industries (COIT 553/2), and Smith v Palmer's Scaffolding (COIT 1280/227).
11 Fryer v Wilkins (COIT 682/238); Wightman v Grant Die Castings (COIT 928/222).
12 Smedley v S.P.Roadways (COIT 1015/54).

2. Assessing the impact: official statistics on accident rates

1 Interview with HSE staff, 1983.
2 Employment in construction (SIC XX) fell from 1244.6 thousand in January 1971 to 1173 thousand in December 1980. Employment in mining and quarrying (SIC II) fell from 405.1 thousand to 338 thousand over the same period (DE Gazette).
3 These figures are compiled on the basis of 1968 SIC. We deal more fully with the problems of changeover to the 1980 SIC on page 283.

3. Assessing the impact: safety institutions

1 There is a proposal to raise the threshold for the safety policy requirement from 5 to 20 employees: see 'Building Businesses . . . Not Barriers' (Cmnd 9794, HMSO 1987).
2 These figures do not include courses provided by constituent unions, but there does not seem to be any simple compensatory change in training provision by TUC affiliates.

4. Safety in chemicals

1 Conducted by S. Dawson, P. Poynter and D. Stevens.
2 Union density in chemicals is given by Bain and Price (1983) as 58.8% in 1979 in chemicals as compared with 36.7% in construction and 14.9% in distribution.
3 The Flixborough disaster occurred on June 1st 1974 when a massive explosion in a chemical plant making caprolactum killed 28 employees, injured 36 employees and 53 people beyond the plant boundary and destroyed the plant. The official report on the explosion was published by *The Department of Employment, HMSO 1975*, on the basis of a Court of Inquiry, chaired by Roger J. Parker.
4 In 1984 there was a release of poison gas from a Union Carbide plant in Bhopal, India, which killed 2000 people and injured 200 000.
5 This section draws on Poynter (1982).
6 'Permit to Work' systems operate through formal procedures which identify and authorise individuals to work in particular places or with particular substances.
7 This analysis consisted of a Discriminant Function Analysis which was conducted by David Stevens.
8 'Threshold limit value' refers to an estimated concentration of exposure at which most healthy people suffer no illness.

9 In fact, this is a more general policy: see Chapter 9.

10 In a different context this point was clearly demonstrated in the Report of the Investigation into the ferry *Herald of Free Enterprise* disaster, 1987. (*Dept of Transport*, Merchant Shipping Act 1894: Formal Investigation nv Herald of Free Enterprise: Report of Court No. 8074.)

5. Safety in construction

1 See, for example, the pack of educational and promotional material produced by the HSE for the 1983 Site Safe campaign. It included an analysis of accidents in the industry, advice on safe working methods and statutory requirements as well as posters, mugs, car stickers, etc. A regular broadsheet, 'Site Safe News', was also produced by the HSE. See also the article in *Building*, 11 February 1983, p. 29.

2 Inspectors will normally visit all sites where fatal or serious injuries have occurred.

3 Data are available under both the 1968 and 1980 SICs for construction. The 1968 SIC classified construction as order XX and MLH 500, but broke down figures into the general categories of building, civil engineering and specialist trades. The 1980 SIC revision puts construction in order 5 and MLHs 501–4. The data presented for the industry is largely on the basis of PA500 census returns and refers to the 1980 classification except where specified.

4 See 'Housing and Construction Statistics 1975–1985; Great Britain', HMSO 1986, Tables 3.3, 3.4.

5 This is commonly referred to as 'the lump' but stricty speaking, the term refers only to informal employment.

6 See 'Where have all the workers gone?' by E. Leopold in *Building*, 22 October 1982, p. 30.

7 See for example, 'Reorganised labour' by E. Leopold and S. Leonard in *Building*, 11 June, 1982, p. 55; 'Management options' by Professor J. Bennett and Dr R. Flanagan in *Building*, 8 April 1983, pp. 32–3.

8 A certain confusion exists as to the exact terminology: but see 'Management options' and 'Behind the fee system' by B. Heaphy in *Building*, 13 May 1983, pp. 30–1. This paragraph does not discuss the entire range of contractual types.

9 In HSE, *Manufacturing and Services Report*, 1981, pp. v–vi (HSE/4, 1983).

10 Provisions made in Local Government (Direct Labour Organisations) (Competition) (Amendment) Regulations 1982 (SI 1982 No. 325). See also *Building*, 17 December 1982.

11 The actual changes in membership of those unions primarily organising in construction are given as:

1979–80	− 10.5%
1980–81	− 11.4%
1981–82	− 5%
1982–83	− 0.6%
1983–84	− 3.8%

Figures are according to 1968 SIC until 1981–82 and 1980 SIC thereafter: see DE Gazette, various years.

12 See also M. Fleming, 'Accidents in construction', *National Builder*, vol. 59, no. 5, pp. 202–8; V. Jordan in *Safety*, October 1978, pp. 8–9; J. F. Eden, 'A review of accidents in the construction industry', *Building*, September 1975, pp. 99–102; and 'Fighting for life', *Building*, 11 February 1983, p. 30.

13 'Site Safe' Package, HSE 1983 (see note 1 to this chapter).

14 HSE, *Construction Health and Safety*, 1981/2, p. 5, para. 16, HSE/7.

15 *HSE Manufacturing and Services Report 1981:* vi–vii.

16 There is a proposal in a government white paper to raise the threshold to less than 20 employees, 'Building Business ... Not Barriers' (Cmnd 9794, 1987).

17 Evidence from an internal survey by the TGWU of building sites in London indicated that very few of the subcontractors contacted had a safety policy.

18 'Safely appointed' in *Employment Gazette*, February 1981, pp. 55–8.

19 For example, the comment made by Sir Peter Trench: 'I have always wondered why ... the trades union has not used more of its muscle ... when it comes to enforcing safety legislation. The employer has been very lucky here, for, combined with the HSE the unions could be quite a burr under the saddle.' In 'Safety campaign and those little silver balls' in *Building*, December 23/30, 1983, pp. 24–5. See also the Report in *Hazards Bulletin*, no. 14, December 1978, on an attempt to limit the activities of safety representatives.

20 *Site Safe News*, Summer 1987. Details of the first initiative in Sheffield and Humberside were given in the Annual Report of the Chief Inspector of Factories, 1986–87, p. 22. Coincidentally with the publication of this report a similar initiative was launched in London which resulted in work on more than one fifth of London building sites being totally or partially halted. In the first two days of the campaign 195 building sites were visited and 42 prohibition notices issued (*Financial Times*, 14 October 1987).

21 *Site Safe News*, Summer 1987.

22 See *New Statesman*, 18 October 1985, p. 7, for an account of the HSE experiment with the construction firm: Costain.

23 *NJCBI Working Rule 12*; see also 'Heads you lose', *Building*, 21 May 1982, pp. 28–31; 'If the hat fits', *Building*, 24 June 1983, p. 51.

7. Effective local self regulation: the capacity and willingness to act

1 Ferguson v John Dawson and Partners (Contracts) Ltd (1976) 1 WLR 1213.

8. Tripartism and the Health and Safety Commission

1 Personal communication from David Gee (National Health and Safety Officer, GMBATU), June 1987.

2 This was put forward as a proposal for discussion. A pilot scheme in the spirit of this proposal was established during 1984 and 1985 with the large construction company Costain. An account of the scheme, given in *New Statesman*, 18 October 1985, p. 7, suggests that it was not totally successful in terms of maintaining, let alone improving, standards of safety within this company.

3 On 1 July 1987 the Chancellor of the Exchequer, Nigel Lawson, announced to the NEDC that henceforth it would meet quarterly rather than monthly and that there would be a significant reduction in the individual industrial working groups known as 'little Neddies'. This announcement to scale down the operations of NEDC coincided with plans to reduce the influence of the Manpower Services Commission (MSC). The NEDC and MSC are, apart from the HSC, the main tripartite institutions in operation in 1987. (*The Independent*, Thursday, 2 July 1987, pages 1 and 2.)

9. Inspectors and enforcers: regulation and compliance

1 For example, Sections 22, 23 and 27(2) of the Factories Act 1961.

2 Detailed in SI 747/1977 and 1744/1980, HASAW Act 1974.

3 'Aspects of the work of the Local Authority Unit at HSE', HSE, mimeo January 1984.

4 HASAWA S24 provides the Appeal procedure. The tribunal's jurisdiction has its own set of regulations in the 'Industrial Tribunals; Improvement and Prohibition Notice Appeals; Regulations, 1974 S1 1974/1925'.

5 See Parliamentary Debates (Commons) written answers, Columns 268–9, 4 July 1985; also Clinton and Bamford, 1985.

6 Personal communication from HSE, August 1987.

7 See Chapter 8, Note 2.

8 See Chapter 2.

9 EHOs also serve notices concerned with public health, and with hygiene and environmental issues.

10 Personal communication from HSE, 1986.

11 89% of firms maintained compliance over a four year period (HSE/5, 1985:28).

12 House of Commons Proceedings, 3 February 1984, column 58.

13 See for example, *Health and Safety at Work*, August 1986, p. 9 and September 1986, p. 15.

14 This phraseology is taken from copies of correspondence from the HSE to David Gee, Health and Safety Officer, GMBATU, September 1979.

15 Health, welfare and safety in non-industrial employment, hours of employment of juveniles. Committee of Inquiry. Chairman: Sir Ernest Gowers.

16 Guidance Note (GM/A/3/1).

17 This argument is developed in Hawkins (1984).

10. Conclusion: the future of self regulation

1 *Health and Safety Monitor*, vol. 10, issue no. 8, April 1987, p. 8.

2 TUC Congress, *Report* 1986, Composite Motion 6.

3 *Health and Safety Monitor*, vol. 10, issue no. 8, April 1987, p. 9. Quoting Dr Cedric Thomas, the Health and Safety Commissioner, who chairs the HSC small firms working group. See also GMBATU documents: 'Freedom to Kill, a response of deregulation in the Workplace' (1986) and 'Hazards at Work' (1987).

4 PA 1002, various years.
5 Swan Hunter Case (1981) IRLR403.
6 The terms 'distributive' and 'integrative' bargaining are used by Walton and McKersie (1965) to differentiate between bargaining on a zero-sum basis over divergent objectives (distributive) and bargaining where the parties have common goals (integrative).
7 Some special campaigns have already been mounted. The 'Site Safe' campaign in construction is one such example. The Chief Inspector of Factories Report 1985 refer to another campaign in clothing 'sweatshops' (HSE/6: 7).
8 *Health and Safety at Work*, November 1985, p. 8, reported that Colin Sullivan, a property developer, was given what was believed to be the first custodial sentence under the Health and Safety at Work Act. He was given a one-month prison sentence, suspended for two years, for contravening a prohibition order, concerning work he was undertaking to remove asbestos.
9 More details on the Swedish Work Fund can be obtained from GMBATU, Esher, Surrey.

Bibliography

HSC AND HSE PUBLICATIONS MENTIONED IN THE TEXT

(Reference numbers given in the list below are used in the text for identifying the publication.)

Health and Safety Commission publications

Regular reports

HSC/1 Health and Safety Commission Report 1974–76 (pub. 1978) HMSO, London.

HSC/2 Health and Safety Commission report 1981–82 (pub. 1982) HMSO, London.

HSC/3 Health and Safety Commission Report 1982–83 (pub. 1983) HMSO, London.

HSC/4 Health and Safety Commission Report 1984–85 (pub. 1985) HMSO, London.

   * Health and Safety Commission Report 1986–87 (pub. 1987) HMSO, London.

Guidance notes and codes of practice

HSC/5 *Safety committees – guidance to the employers when employees are not members of recognised trade unions*, London, Health and Safety Commission, 1976.

HSC/6 *Safety representatives and safety committees regulations: guidance on enforcement*, London, 1978.

HSC/7 *Time off for the training of safety representatives: code of practice approved under regulations 4(2) (b) of the regulations on safety representations and safety committees*, London, 1978.

Other Health and Safety Commission publications

HSC/8 *Plan of Work 1985–1986 and Onwards*, Health and Safety Commission, HMSO, London, 1985.

Bibliography

HSC/9 *An Advisory Committee Structure*, internal document and subsequent consultative paper, May, 1975.

Health and Safety Executive publications

Regular publications
HSE/1 Manufacturing and Service Industries 1978 (pub. 1980).

HSE/2 Manufacturing and Service Industries, Health and Safety 1979 (pub. 1981), HMSO, London.

HSE/3 Manufacturing and Service Industries: Health and Safety 1980 (pub. 1982), HMSO, London.

HSE/4 Manufacturing and Service Industries: Health and Safety 1981 (pub. 1983), HMSO, London.

HSE/5 Manufacturing and Service Industries: Health and Safety 1984 (pub. 1985), HMSO, London.

HSE/6 Report by HM Chief Inspector of Factories 1985 (Pub. 1986), HMSO, London.

  * Report by HM Chief Inspector of Factories 1986–87 (pub. 1987), HMSO, London.

HSE/7 Construction: Health and Safety 1981–82 (pub. 1983), HMSO, London.

HSE/8 Statistics: Health and Safety 1981–82 (pub. 1984), HMSO, London.

HSE/9 Statistics: Health and Safety 1983 (pub. 1986), HMSO, London.

Other publications
HSE/10 *Accidents in Factories: the pattern of causation and the scope for prevention*, Health and Safety Executive, London, HMSO 1974.

HSE/11 *Safety Officers: Sample Survey of their role and functions, discussion document*, Health and Safety Executive, London, HMSO, 1975.

HSE/12 *Success and Failure in Accident Prevention*, Health and Safety Executive, London: HMSO, 1976.

HSE/13 *Health and Safety at Work – Representatives and Safety Committees*, Health and Safety Executive, London, HMSO, 1977.

HSE/14 *Effective policies for health and safety*, Accident Prevention Advisory Unit, Health and Safety Executive, London, HMSO, 1980.

HSE/15 *Managing Safety*, Health and Safety Executive, London: HMSO, 1981.

HSE/16 *100 Fatal Accidents in Construction 1978*, Health and Safety Executive, London: HMSO, 1981.

HSE/17 *Her Majesty's inspectors of factories, 1833–1983: essays to commemorate 150 years of health and safety inspection*, Health and Safety Executive, London: HMSO, 1983.

HSE/18 *Measuring the Effectiveness of HSE's Field Activities*, HSE Occasional Paper Series, OP11, 1985, London: HMSO.

* These reports were published after the manuscript for this book was dispatched for publication. Some reference to their contents was subsequently inserted into the text, but these references are unnumbered.

HSE/19 *The Scrutiny Programme: Problems of assessing the costs and benefits of health and safety requirements and the techniques available*, Health and Safety Executive, London: HMSO, 1985.

HSE/20 *Monitoring Safety: an outline report on occupational safety and health by the APAU*, Health and Safety Executive, London: HMSO, 1985.

OTHER REFERENCES

Ashford N A (1976) *Crisis in the Workplace: Occupational Disease and Injury*, MIT Press, Cambridge, Massachusetts

Alexander D (1970) *Retailing in Britain in the Industrial Revolution*, Athlone Press, London

Atherley G R (1975) 'Strategies in health and safety at work', *Production Engineer*

Atherley G R (1978) *Occupational Health and Safety*, London, Applied Science Publishers

Atherley G R, Booth R T and Kelly M U (1975) 'Workers involvement in occupational health and safety in Britain', *International Labour Review* 2, 469–82

Atiyah P S (1980) *Accidents, Compensation and the Law*, London, Weidenfeld and Nicolson

Bacow L S (1981) *Bargaining for Job Safety and Health*, London, MIT Press

Bain G S and Elsheikh F (1976) *Union Growth and the Business Cycle*, Oxford, Blackwell

Bain G S and Elsheikh F (1980) 'Unionisation in Britain; an inter-establishment analysis based on survey data', *British Journal of Industrial Relations*, **18**, 169–79

Bain G S and Price R (1980) *Profiles of Union Growth*, Oxford, Blackwell

Barrell A C and Thomas D C (1982) 'Assessing management in major hazard operations', *I Chem E Jubilee Symposium*, Imperial College, B9–B17

Barrett B (1977) 'Safety representatives, industrial relations and hard times', *Industrial Law Journal*, September, **6**(3), 165–78

Barrett B and James P (1981) 'How real is worker involvement in health and safety?', *Employee Relations*, **3**(4), 4–7

Barrett B, Brown H and Janes T W (1980) *Management Responsibilities under the Health and Safety at Work Act 1974*, final report, mimeo, Middlesex Polytechnic

Barth P S and Hunt H A (1980) *Workers' Compensation and Work-Related Illnesses and Diseases*, MIT Press, London

Bartrip P W J (1979) *Safety at Work: The Factory Inspectorate and the Fencing Controversy, 1833–1857*, Centre for Socio-Legal Studies, Wolfson College, Oxford, unpublished

Bartrip P W J (1985) 'Success or failure? The prosecution of the early Factory Acts', *Economic History Review*, 2nd series, **37**, 423–7

Bartrip P W J and Fenn P T (1980) 'The administration of safety: the enforcement policy of the early Factory Inspectorate 1844–1864', *Public Administration*, **58**, Spring, 87–102.

Bibliography

Bartrip P W J and Fenn P T (1983) 'The evolution of regulatory style in the nineteenth century British Factory Inspectorate', *Journal of Law and Society*, **10**, 201–22

Batstone E, Boraston I and Frenkel S (1977) *Shop Stewards in Action*, Blackwell, Oxford

Batstone E, Gourlay S, Levine H and Moore R (1986) *Unions, Employment and Innovation*, Blackwell, Oxford

Beaumont P B (1979) 'Research note: the relationship between industrial accidents and absenteeism', *Industrial Relations Journal*, **10**(3), 54–6

Beaumont P B (1980) 'The safety representative function: consultation or negotiation?', *Personnel Review*, **9**, no. 2, Spring

Beaumont P B (1981a) 'The nature of the relationship between safety representatives and their workforce constituencies', *Industrial Relations Journal*, **12**(2), 53–60

Beaumont P B (1981b) 'Explaining variation in the enterprise response to industrial relations legislation: the case of the safety representative regulations', *Personnel Review*, **10**(1), 1, 11–15

Beaumont P B (1983) *Safety at Work and the Unions*, London, Croom Helm

Beaumont P B, Coyle J R and Leopold J W (1982a) 'The recession bites: how the current economic climate has affected safety in industry', *Occupational Safety and Health (Birmingham)*, 1982, **12**(1), 39–40

Beaumont P B, Coyle J R, Leopold J W and Schuller T E (1982b) *The Determinants of Effective Joint Health and Safety Committees*, Centre for Research in Industrial Democracy and Participation, University of Glasgow, 1982, unpublished

Beaumont P B and Deaton D R (1981) 'The enterprise response to industrial relations law: the case of joint health and safety committees', *Industrial Relations Journal*, **12**(5), Sept–Oct

Beaumont P B, Leopold J W and Coyle J R (1982) 'The safety officer: an emerging management role', *Personnel Review*, **11**, 2

Beaumont P B and Leopold J W (1984) 'The motivation, activities and turnover of union safety representatives: some evidence from Britain', *Work and People*, **10**(2), 25–9

Benedictus R (1980) *Safety Representatives*, Sweet and Maxwell, London

Berman D M (1978) *Death on the Job: Occupational Health and Safety Struggles in the United States*, Monthly Review Press, New York

Bernstein M (1955) *Regulating Business by Independent Commission*, Oxford, Blackwell

Black D J (1976) *The Behaviour of Law*, New York, Academic Press

Bolton Committee (1971) *Report of the Committee of Inquiry on Small Firms*, London, HMSO.

Booth R T (1987) 'The safety practitioner – role and educational needs', *Towards the Millenium* (ed) St. J. Holt, IOSH, Leicester

Bowman D R (1983) *The Employer/Enforcer Role of Local Authorities in Relation to the Health and Safety at Work Act*, Institute of Environmental Health Officers, unpublished

Bibliography

Breyer S (1982) *Regulation and its Reform*, Cambridge, Massachusetts, Harvard University Press

Brown W (ed.) (1981) *The Changing Contours of British Industrial Relations*, Oxford, Blackwell

Bullock A (1967) *The Life and Times of Ernest Bevin, Volume 2: Minister of Labour 1900–1945*, London, Heinemann

Carson W G (1970a) 'White collar crime and the enforcement of factory legislation', *British Journal of Criminology*, **10**, 383–98

Carson W G (1970b) 'Some sociological aspects of strict liability and the enforcement of factory legislation', *Modern Law Review*, **33**, 396–412

Carson W G (1979) 'The conventionalism of early factory crime – a re-assessment', *International Journal of the Sociology of Law*, **7**, 175–86

Carson W G (1980) 'Early Factory Inspectors and the viable class society – a rejoinder', *International Journal of the Sociology of Law*, **8**, 187–91

Carson W G (1982) *The Other Price of Britain's Oil: Safety and Control in the North Sea*, Oxford, Martin Robertson

Castle D A (1978) 'Safety representatives and safety committees – power without responsibility?', *New Law Journal*, September, 944–6

Clark J and Wedderburn K W (1983) 'Modern labour law: problems, functions and policies', in Wedderburn, Lewis and Clark (eds.) *Labour Law and Industrial Relations*, Oxford University Press

Clifton R and Tatton-Brown C (1979) 'Impact of employment legislation on small firms', *DE Research Paper*, **6**, London, HMSO

Clinton A and Bamford M (1985) *Health and Safety at Work in the Greater London Area 1981–85*, Greater London Council, unpublished

Codrington C and Henley J S (1981) 'The industrial relations of injury and death: safety representatives in the construction industry', *British Journal of Industrial Relations*, **19**(3), 297–315

Cohen A (1977) 'Factors in successful occupational safety programs', *Journal of Safety Research*, **9**, 168–78

Cohen A, Smith M, Kent J and Anger W (1979) 'Self protective measures against workplace hazards', *Journal of Safety Research*, **11**, 121–31

Cook D (1980) *A Pilot Study to Investigate the Effect of the TUC Safety Representative Training Course on the Safety Representatives' Perception of Their Role*, MSc thesis, Department of Occupational Health and Safety, University of Aston, Birmingham, unpublished

Coye M J (1979) 'Crisis in the workplace: occupational disease and injury', *International Journal of Health Services*, **9**(1), 169–83

Cranston R (1979) *Regulation Business: Law and Consumer Agencies*, London, Macmillan

Crutchfield C D (1981) 'Managing occupational safety and health programs – an overview', *American Industrial Hygiene Association Journal*, **42**(3), 226–9

Cunningham M (1978) 'Safety representatives: shopfloor organisation for health and safety', *Studies for Trade Unionists*, **4**(13), Workers Educational Association, London

Bibliography

Daniel W W and Stilgoe E (1978) 'The impact of employment protection laws', *Policy Studies*, **44**(5), 77, June

Daniel W and Millward N (1983) *Workplace Industrial Relations*, London, Heinemann

Davies and Freedland (1983) see Kahn Freund (1972)

Davis D (1966) *A History of Shopping*, Routledge, London

Dawson S (1986) 'What is a safety officer and how should you train him?', *Occupational Safety and Health*, **16**(12), 14–17

Dawson S (1987) 'Professional safety practitioners and their relationship to line management', *ROSPA International Safety Seminar*, Birmingham, May 1987

Dawson S, Poynter P and Stevens D (1982a) 'Strategies for controlling hazards at work', *Journal of Safety Research*, **13**(3)

Dawson S, Poynter P and Stevens D (1982b) 'Activities and outcomes: monitoring safety performance', *Chemistry and Industry*, 16 October

Dawson S, Poynter P and Stevens D (1983a) 'How to secure an effective health and safety programme at work', *OMEGA*, **11**(5), September

Dawson S, Poynter P and Stevens D (1983b) *What Role for Safety Committees?*, Working Paper, Department of Social and Economic Studies, Imperial College, unpublished

Dawson S, Poynter P and Stevens D (1984a) 'Resolving the health and safety conflict', *Management Today*, April, 33–6

Dawson S, Poynter P and Stevens D (1984b) 'Is your safety policy adequate?', *Health and Safety at Work*, August, 51–4

Dawson S, Poynter P and Stevens D (1984c) 'Safety specialists in industry: roles, constraints and opportunities', *Journal of Occupational Behaviour*, **5**(4), 253–69

Dawson S, Clinton A, Bamford M and Willman P (1985) 'Safety in construction. Self regulation, industrial structure and workforce involvement', *Journal of General Management*, **10**(4)

Department of Employment (1981) 'HSE survey into the impact of legislation on safety committees', *Employment Gazette*, February, 55–8

Dickens L, Jones M, Weeks B and Hart M (1985) *Dismissed: A Study of Unfair Dismissal and The Industrial Tribunal System*, Oxford, Blackwell

Djang T K (1942) *Factory Inspection in Great Britain*, London, George Allen and Unwin

Doyle B (1980) 'The operation of S16 of the Employment Protection Act', *Industrial Law Journal*, **9**, 154–66

Drake C D and Wright F B (1983) *Law of Health and Safety at Work: The New Approach*, London, Sweet and Maxwell

Edwards P K (1984) *The Management of Productivity*, Warwick University, IRRU, mimeo

Edwards P K and Scullion H (1982) *Industrial Accidents and Industrial Conflict*, Warwick University, IRRU, mimeo

Eva D and Oswald R (1981) *Health and Safety at Work*, Pan Books, London

Fitzgerald P J and Hadden T (1970) *Strict Liability and the Enforcement of the Factories Act 1961*, Law Commission Working Paper, no. 30

Ford J (1982) 'The response of small businesses to external regulation', *Industrial Relations Journal*, **8**(3), 40–9

Fox A J and Adelstein A M (1978) 'Occupational mortality: work a way of life?', *Journal of Epidemiology and Community Health*, **32**, 73–8

Freeman R and Medoff J (1984) *What Do Unions Do?*, New York, Basic Books

GMBATU (1986) *Freedom to Kill: A Response to Deregulation in the Workplace*, available from GMBATU, Esher, Surrey

Gee D (1980a) 'Notes on the October Revolution: health and safety in the GMWU', *Trade Union Studies Journal*, **2**, Autumn

Gee D (1980b) 'Trade union action on health and safety', paper to the Society of Chemical Industry

Gee D (1980b) 'Trade union action on health and safety', paper to the Society of Chemical Industry

Glendon A I (1977) 'The role and training of safety representatives', *Occupational Safety and Health*, **7**(11), 35–6, and **7**(12), 37–9

Glendon A I (1982) 'Is safety motivation possible and worth attempting?', *Safety Surveyor*, **10**(2), 4–9

Glendon A I and Booth R T (1982) 'Worker participation in occupational health and safety in Britain', *International Labour Review*, **121**(4), 399–416

Glendon A I and Hale A R (1984) 'Taking stock of Site Safe '83', *Health and Safety at Work*, **6**(8), 19–21

Goffee R and Scase R (1985) 'Proprietorial control in family firms; some problems of quasi-organic management systems', *Journal of Management Studies*, **22**(1), 53–68

Gospel H and Willman P (1981) 'Disclosure of information, the CAC approach', *Industrial Law Journal*, **10**(1), 10–22

Graham D (1982) 'The safety officer today – professional or amateur?', *Occupational Safety and Health*, June

Grunberg L (1983) 'The effects of the social relations of production on productivity and workers safety: an ignored set of relationships', *International Journal of Health Studies*, **13**(4), 621–34

Hale A R (1978) *The Role of HM Inspectors of Factories with Special Reference to Their Training*, PhD thesis, University of Aston, unpublished

Hale A R (1982a) 'Safety training: not more, but better', *Occupational Health*, **34**(4), 189–91

Hale A R (1982b) 'Safety training 3: are you getting what you paid for?', *Occupational Health*, **34**(5), 233–5

Hale A R (1983) 'Is safety training worthwhile?', *Proceedings of the International Seminar on Occupational Accident Research*, Stockholm

Haraszti M (1977) *A Worker in a Worker's State; Piece Rates in Hungary*, Harmondsworth, Penguin

Harris D, Maclean M, Genn H, Lloyd-Bostock S, Fenn P, Corfield P and Brittan Y (1984) *Compensation and Support for Illness and Injury*, Clarendon Press, Oxford

Hawes W R and Smith G (1981) *Patterns of Representation of the Parties in Unfair*

Dismissal Cases; A Review of the Evidence, Research Paper no. 22, Department of Employment

Hawkins K (1984) *Environment and Enforcement: Regulation and the Social Definition of Pollution*, Clarendon Press, Oxford

Heinrich H W (1959) *Industrial Accident Prevention*, 4th edition, New York, McGraw-Hill

Henderson Sir Vivian (1929) *Report of the Departmental Committee on the Factory Inspectorate*, HMSO

Hepple R (1983) 'Individual labour law', in G Bain (ed.), *Industrial Relations in Great Britain*, Oxford, Blackwell, pp. 393–419

Her Majesty's Inspectors of Factories (1983) *1833–1983*, HMSO

Heywood J (1985) 'Economics of Health and Safety', *DE Gazette*, January, 21–30

House of Commons (1982) *Sixth Report from the Employment Committee: The Working of the Health and Safety Commission. Achievements since the Robens Report*, London, HMSO

Howells L (1974) 'Worker participation in safety: the development of legal rights', *Industrial Law Journal*, 3, 87–95

Howells L and Barrett B (1982) *The Health and Safety at Work Act, A Guide for Managers*, London, IPM

Hutter B M (1984) *The Law Enforcement Procedures of Environmental Health Officers*, DPhil thesis, Oxford University, unpublished

Hutter B M (1986) 'An Inspector calls; the importance of proactive inspection in the regulatory context', *British Journal of Criminology*, 26(2), 114–28

ILO (1982) *Report of the Tripartite Mission on the Effectiveness of Labour Inspection in the United Kingdom*, Geneva, ILO

Incomes Data Services, *Role of Safety Committees*, Study 202, London, 1979

Ives J (1985) *A Cross Cultural Study of the Regulation and Administration of Occupational Safety and Health Care Policies in the Workplace: The Chemical Industry in the United States and Great Britain*, PhD thesis, University of London, unpublished

Jeffreys J A (1954) *Retail Trading in Britain 1850–1950*, Cambridge University Press

Johnson, Reginald (1983) *A Century of Progress. The History of the Institution of Environmental Health Officers*, Institution of Environmental Health Officers

Jones R and Dawson S (1986) 'Strategies for ensuring safety with industrial robot systems', *Omega*, 14(4), 287–97

Kadish S H (1963) 'Some observations on the use of criminal sanctions in enforcing economic regulations', *University of Chicago Law Review*, 30, 423–49

Kahn-Freund O (1959) 'Labour law', in M Ginsberg (ed.), *Law and Opinion in England*, London, Stevens, pp. 215–63

Kahn-Freund O (1968) *Labour Law: Old Traditions and New Developments*, Toronto, Clark Irwin

Kahn-Freund O (1972) *Labour and the Law*, London, Stevens; also 3rd edition (ed) Davies and Freedland (1983)

Kelman S (1981) *Regulating America, Regulating Sweden: A Comparative Study of Occupational Safety and Health Policy*, MIT Press, Cambridge

299

Bibliography

Kinnersley P (1973) *The Hazards of Work*, London, Pluto Press

Kletz T A (1971) 'Hazard analysis – a quantitiative approach to safety', *Major Loss Prevention in the Process Industries*, The Institution of Chemical Engineers Symposium Series no. 34, 75–81

Kletz T A (1981) 'Safety audits and surveys', *Health and Safety at Work*, **4**

Kletz T A (1982) 'The safety adviser in the high technology industries – training and role', *Institute of Chemical Engineering Symposium* Seminar, B1–B8, Imperial College, England

Kochan T A, Dyer L and Lipsky D B (1977) *The effectiveness of union management safety and health committees*, W. E. Upjohn, Institute for Employment Research, Kalamazoo, Michigan

Lane R E (1954) *The Regulation of Businessmen: Social conditions of Government economic control*, New Haven, Yale University Press

Law Commission (1970) *Strict Liability and the Enforcement of the Factories Act 1961*, Working Paper no. 30, London, Law Commission

Lees S P (1980) *Loss Prevention in the Process Industries: Hazard Identification, Assessment and Control*, Butterworth

Leighton P (1983) *Contractual Arrangements in Selected Industries*, Department of Employment Research Paper no. 49, London, HMSO

Leopold J W (1981) 'The impact of trained safety representatives at the workplace', *Health and Safety at Work*, **4**(2), 27–8

Leopold J W and Beaumont P B (1982) 'Safety policies: how effective are they?', *Occupational Safety and Health*, **12**(10), 24–6

Leopold J W and Beaumont P B (1984) 'The turnover and continuity of safety representatives', *Industrial Relations Journal*, **15**(4), 74–82

Leopold J W and Coyle M J (1981) 'A healthy trend in safety committees', *Personnel Management*, **13**(s), May, 30–2

Lewis R (1976) 'The historical development of labour law', *British Journal of Industrial Relations*, **14**(1), 1–17

Lewis R (1979) 'Kahn-Freund and labour law: an outline critique', *Industrial Law Journal*, **8**, 202–21

Lewis R (1983) 'Collective labour law', in G Bain (ed.), *Industrial Relations in Britain*, pp. 361–93, Oxford, Blackwell

Lifting the Burden (1985) Cmnd 9571, London, HMSO

Livesey F (1979) *Distributive Trades*, London, Heineman

Locke J H (1981) 'The politics of health and safety', *Protection* (London), **18**(7), 8–9

Lyell K M (1890) (ed.) *Memoir of Leonard Horner, Consisting of Letters to His Family and Some of His Friends*, privately printed in London, 2 volumes

MacDonagh O (1958) 'The nineteenth-century revolution in government: a re-appraisal', *Historical Journal*, **1**

McGinty L and Atherley G (1977) 'Acceptability versus democracy', *New Scientist*, 12 May 1977

McKinnon R (1979) 'The safety professional of today', *Occupational Safety and Health Bulletin*, April

Martin A R (1978) *Environmental Health Officers and Occupational Health*, MSc dissertation, Imperial College, London University, unpublished

Martin B (1969) 'Leonard Horner: a portrait of an Inspector of Factories', *International Review of Social History*, **14**, 412–43

Millward N and Stevens M I (1986) *British Workplace Industrial Relations 1980–1984*, Aldershot, Gower Press

Morgan P and Davies N (1981) 'The costs of occupational accidents and disease in Great Britain', *Employment Gazette*, 477–81

Navarro V (1983) 'The determinants of social policy. A case study: regulating health and safety at the workplace in Sweden', *International Journal of Health Services*, **13**(4)

Nichols T (1986) 'Industrial injuries in British manufacturing in the 1980s', *Sociological Review*, **34**(2), 290–306

Nichols T and Armstrong P (1973) *Safety or Profit? Industrial Accidents and the Conventional Wisdom*, Bristol, Falling Wall Press

Olsen M (1965) *The Logic of Collective Action*, Cambridge, Harvard University Press

Page G (1975) *Environmental Health Administration: Implications of the 1974 Reorganisation*, MPhil dissertation, Brunel University, unpublished

Paulus I (1974) *The Search for Pure Food. A Sociology of Legislation in Britain*, Oxford, Martin Robertson

Peacock A E (1984) 'The successful prosecution of the Factory Acts 1833–55', *Economic History Review*, 2nd series, **37**, 197–210

Peacock A E (1985) 'Factory Act prosecutions: a hidden consensus?', *Economic History Review*, 2nd series, **38**, 431–6

Petersen D (1978) *Techniques of Safety Management*, 2nd edition, New York, McGraw-Hill

PPITB (1983) *Evaluation of Written Safety Policies in Use in Polymer Processing Companies*, Brentford, PPITB

Powell P I, Hale M, Martin J and Simon M (1971) *2000 Accidents: A Shop Floor Study of Their Causes*, National Institute of Industrial Psychology, London

Poynter P (1982) 'Workplace hazards and problems', working paper, Department of Social and Economic Studies, Imperial College, unpublished

Price R and Bain G S (1983) 'Union growth in Britain: retrospect and prospect', *British Journal of Industrial Relations*, **21**, 46–69

Purcell J and Sisson K (1983) 'Strategies and practice in the management of industrial relations', in G Bain (ed.) *Industrial Relations in Britain*, pp. 95–120, Oxford, Blackwell

Redcliffe Maud (1969) *Royal Commission on Local Government in England*, 3 vols., Cmnd 4040, London, HMSO

Renton J (1975) *An examination of the reports of HM Chief Inspector of Factories (1878–1974)* MSc dissertation, University of Aston, unpublished

Rhodes G (1981) *Inspectorates in British Government, Law Enforcement and Standards of Efficiency*, London, George Allen and Unwin

Rhodes G (1984) 'Relations between central and local government', Research Paper: Health and Safety at Work, Research Report, London, Royal Institute of Public Administration

Bibliography

Rhodes G (1986) 'Central–local relations: the experience of the Environmental Health and Trading Standards Services; Final Report', London, Royal Institute of Public Administration

Richardson G, Ogus A and Burrows P (1982) *Policing Pollution. A Study of Regulation and Enforcement*, Oxford, Clarendon Press

Rideout R (1979) *Principles of Labour Law*, London, Butterworth

Robens (1972a) *Safety and Health at Work, Report of the Committee 1970–72*, vol. 1, London, HMSO, Cmnd 5034

Robens (1972b) *Safety and Health at Work, Report of the Committee, 1970–72*, vol. 2, Selected Written Evidence, London, HMSO

Robertson J A S, Biggs J M and Goodchild A (1982) *Structure and Employment Prospects of the Service Industries*, Department of Employment Research Paper no. 30, HMSO

Robinson O and Wallace J (1976) *Pay and Employment in Retail*, Saxon House, Farnborough, Hants

Sass R and Crook G (1981) 'Accident proneness: science or non-science?', *International Journal of Health Services*, 11(2), 175–90

Scase R and Goffee R (1980) *The Real World of the Small Business Owner*, Beckenham, Croom Helm

Schmoller S and Grayson (1981) *Safety Representatives and the Factory Inspectorate*, Workers Educational Association, vol. 6, no. 24

Shover N, Clelland D and Lynxviler J (1982) *Enforcement of Negotiation. Constructing a Regulatory Bureaucracy*, State University of New York Press, Albany, New York (SUNY series on Critical Issues in Criminal Justice)

Steele G R (1974) 'Industrial accidents; an economic interpretation', *Applied Economics*, 6(2), 143–55

Stone A (1982) *Regulation and its Alternative*, Washington DC, Congressional Quarterly Press

Stone C D (1975) *Where the Law Ends: The Social Control of Corporate Behaviour*, New York, Harper and Row

Stuttard G (1979) 'Health, safety and industrial democracy', *Employee Relations*, 1(33), 23–5

Taylor A J (1972) *Laissez-Faire and State Interventions in Nineteenth-Century Britain*, London, Macmillan

Terry M (1986) 'How do we know if stewards are getting weaker?', *British Journal of Industrial Relations*, 24(2), 169–79

Thomas M W (1948) *The Early Factory Legislation*, London, Thames Books

TUC (1974) Supplementary Report B. 'Industrial democracy' in Report on the Proceedings at the 106th Annual Trade Union Congress, Brighton, 1974

Veljanovski C G (1981) *Regulating Industrial Accidents: An Economic Analysis of Market and Legal Responses*, PhD dissertation, University of York, unpublished

Veljanovski C G (1983) 'Regulating enforcement, an economic study of the British Factory Inspectorate', *Law and Policy Quarterly*, 5(1), 75–96

Wade J F and Lindsay F D (1980) 'Measuring management performance', The National Health and Safety Conference 1980

Bibliography

Walton R and McKersie (1965) *A Behavioural Theory of Labour Negotiations: An Analysis of a Social Interaction System*, New York, McGraw-Hill

Warren M A (1983) 'An inspection guide to small meatcutting bandsaws', *Environmental Health*, September

Webster D (1978) 'Paving the way for safety representatives: the fringe story', *Personnel Management*, **10**(6), 30–2

Wedderburn K W (1971) *The Worker and the Law*, Harmondsworth, Penguin

Wedderburn K W (1976) 'The Employment Protection Act, 1975: collective aspects', *Modern Law Review*, **39**, 1098–83

Wedderburn K W (1980) 'Industrial relations and the courts', *Industrial Law Journal*, **9**, 65–96

Weidenbaum M L (1981) *Business, Government and the Public*, Englewood Cliffs, New Jersey, Prentice Hall

Williams J L (1960) *Accidents and Ill-Health at Work*, London, Staples Press

Williamson O E (1975) *Markets and Hierarchies*, Glencoe, Free Press

Williamson O E (1981) 'The economics of organisation: the transaction cost approach', *American Journal of Sociology*, **87**, 548–77

Wilson G K (1984) 'Legislation on occupational safety and health: a comparison of the British and American experience', *Essex Papers in Politics and Government*, 12, University of Essex

Wilson G K (1985) *The Politics of Safety and Health: Occupational Safety and Health in the United States and Britain*, Oxford, Clarendon Press

Winstanley M J (1983) *The Shopkeepers World 1830–1914*, Manchester University Press

Woolf A D (1973) 'Robens Report – the wrong approach', *Industrial Law Journal*, **2**, 88–95

Wrench K J and Lee G (1982) 'Piecework and industrial accidents: two contemporary case studies', *Sociology*, **16**(4), 512–25

Wright C (1986) 'Routine deaths: fatal accidents in the oil industry', *Sociological Review*, **34**(2), 265–89

Name index

Index

Subject index

Index